APOCALYPSE

APOCALYPSE

On the Psychology of
Fundamentalism
in America

CHARLES B. STROZIER

BEACON PRESS

BOSTON

Beacon Press
25 Beacon Street
Boston, Massachusetts 02108-2892

Beacon Press books
are published under the auspices of the
Unitarian Universalist Association of Congregations.

99 98 97 96 95   8 7 6 5 4 3 2

Text design: Christine Taylor
Composition: Wilsted & Taylor Publishing Services

LIBRARY OF CONGRESS CATALOGING-IN-PUBLICATION DATA

Strozier, Charles B.
Apocalypse: on the psychology of fundamentalism in America /
Charles B. Strozier.
      p.   cm.
Includes bibliographical references and index.
ISBN 0-8070-1226-2 (cloth)   ISBN 0-8070-1227-0 (paper)
1. Fundamentalism.   2. End of the world—History of doctrines.
3. New York (N.Y.)—Religious life and customs.   4. Psychohistory.
I. Title.
BT82.2.S77   1994
277.47′10829—dc20   93-39540
CIP

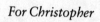

For Christopher

CONTENTS

INTRODUCTION

This is a book about the apocalyptic in contemporary life. Because we all die, everyone reflects at some point about individual and collective endings. But what might be called endism, or the location of self in some future, ultimate narrative, pushes such reflection into a profoundly different realm, wrapping the future in magical projections that isolate it from meaningful, human connection with the past. My concern in this book is with the psychology, or mind-set, of endism, especially as it expresses itself in contemporary Christian fundamentalism, as well as its history, or where it comes from, and why it is now so significant in our culture. This study has no simple answers but some rather interesting questions.

"Apocalypse" is a transliteration of the Greek word *apokalypsis* meaning "to uncover or disclose." Within the Judeo-Christian tradition it means the specific ways in which God reveals himself or herself to humans. For nonliteral Christians, such "revelation" of the ultimate can come close to what is called "insight" in psychoanalysis, or that profound understanding that connects thoughts and feelings at their deepest levels. Prophecy, in turn, is the form of our access to that apocalypse, though some scholars have distinguished the prophetic from the apocalyptic traditions. In prophetism, it is argued, we are called to a change of heart, to repentance in the present, to a new way of living. It is a call to efficacy and a challenge to change so that we can avoid catastrophe. In the apocalyptic, or the already-determined future, hope is deferred, which is why it is so often associated with the poor, the broken-hearted, the oppressed.[1]

The apocalyptic energizes contemporary fundamentalism, which in its many garbs has become a familiar global happening. It is not at all clear how one should properly define "fundamentalism," but all students of the subject, from Selma to Tehran, have noted that fundamentalism has a decidedly apocalyptic character. In its Christian form, fundamentalists believe that God will remake the world in a huge firestorm of destruction, that he will send Jesus back to rule for a thousand years, and that in the end the faithful will conquer death and live forever. The unsaved die once, and then are resurrected to face God at the final judgment, after which they are cast into the lake of fire for all time. It is a remarkable myth of violence, revenge, and renewal.

The apocalyptic is not new to human culture, and certainly not to the religious imagination. The apocalyptic has, however, taken on a new dimension in an age of real scientific threats to human existence. Many Christians who subscribe to fundamentalist end time theory differ on the exact sequence of events they envision as human history ends and we move into God's time. There are dogmatists, to be sure, but most fundamentalist Christians are more loosely apocalyptic and believe only that this earth will somehow be purged in the fires of God's anger, that Jesus will return, and that a new heaven and a new earth will be reborn. Many, especially African Americans, link such beliefs to a perceived human drama of oppression and look toward the Apocalypse with a unique sense of rebirth. Even more loosely, in the culture at large, endism of one kind or another, from New Ageism to nuclearism, is remarkably widespread. While my focus is on the Christian side of things—largely because of the distilled clarity of its apocalyptic vision—it would be parochial to isolate considerations of endism from its wider cultural context.

Apocalyptic myths are necessarily rooted in private dramas of great significance and pain. In various ways death and its equivalents, along with constant efforts to hold off fragmentation, play a central role in the self experiences of fundamentalists. Their passionate religious commitments are an authentic expression of Christianity, one that grips the imagination of many millions of Americans (though not my own). I am in no position to judge the truth claims of fundamentalists, their position on biblical interpretation, or their certainty of the return of Jesus. Nor is that my purpose. I do feel that there is generally something unsteady about fundamentalists and there are some worrisome aspects of the apocalyptic within fundamentalism. But my larger purpose in this book is to argue that we are all unsteady in an age of ultimate threats to existence; fundamentalism is simply one form of response, and a more interesting one than has been appreciated, to what can only be understood as a kind of collective illness in our contemporary culture.

In this book I explore lives in detail from which to cull such themes. For five years in different settings and with varying frequency, I visited carefully selected fundamentalist church environments as a participant-observer; I also had several researchers who worked in the churches under my supervision. In these settings I became familiar with the fundamentalist experience and got to know people well enough to interview them at least two times, often more, in taped, structured yet open-ended, psychological interviews. Perhaps these Christians merely "put on their worship faces" for me as an avowedly nonbelieving outsider, but I would like to think I spent enough time with them, was sufficiently empathic, and am psychologically astute enough to cut through such deceptions. I could, of course, be wrong.

I bring several disciplinary perspectives to bear on this study. I basically see things psychohistorically. My own background is as an historian: I am a professor of history at John Jay College, CUNY. I have written about Lincoln and the Civil War, but more recently I have turned my attention to issues of ultimate human extinction. I am also a practicing psychoanalytic psychotherapist and on the faculty of a psychoanalytic institute in New York (TRISP). Within psychoanalysis I have training and a special interest in self psychology (Heinz Kohut, with whom I did a book, was once a mentor). But out of necessity in the investigation of the fundamentalist subculture I had to become something of an anthropologist as well, taking elaborate field notes, keeping a journal, and tracking my own subjective reactions to my experiences (including my own dreams). Finally, of necessity I brushed up against religion and theology. It's a rather heady mix that is either creative or a witches' brew.

In structure, this book moves quickly into a discussion that is immediate and psychological. In chapters 1 through 6, I try to understand the individuals I interviewed within the fundamentalist movement in relation to their end time beliefs and in the context of the inner dynamics of their life experiences. Each chapter in the first part opens with the story of one particularly interesting and informative respondent, which begins with an account of their apocalyptic thinking and then fits those beliefs and attitudes into their life history. The second part of my inquiry reaches out to the more conceptual, historical, and comparative dimensions of my topic. I treat the detailed questions of the cultural reach of the apocalyptic, the meanings in general of getting close to fundamentalists, and the issue of community and totalism in fundamentalism (chapter 7). From there I explore the history of the apocalyptic in America (chapter 8) and the complex ways Jews and Israel have worked their way into the minds of fundamentalists in the last century or so (chapter 9). In chapters 10 and 11, I turn to two comparative cultural expressions of the apocalyptic in America: the Hopi Indians and New Age. Both show the broad influence of the Christian end time myth but also reveal alternate possibilities of imagining the ultimate within American culture. Finally, in a brief conclusion I try to end a book on the end by looking toward the future.

Christian fundamentalism in America at the end of the millennium is a mass movement that broadly describes the religious orientation of roughly a quarter of the population. In general, Christianity is, as

Frank Kermode has shrewdly noted, the "most anxious" of all the major religions of the world and the one "which has laid the most emphasis on the terror of death."[2] Christian fundamentalists, in turn, have a particular orientation toward biblical literalism ("inerrancy," or the idea that every word of the Bible is the authoritative voice of God); the experience of being reborn in faith as described in John 3 (especially verse 3: "Verily, verily, I say unto thee, Except a man be born again, he cannot see the kingdom of God"); evangelicalism (or the obligation to convert others); and apocalypticism in its specifically end time form. The polling data on American beliefs are startling. The historian Paul Boyer wisely cautions against too much reliance on polls, which have no way of probing the extent to which expressed attitudes about belief impinge vitally on daily life.[3] But even with that caution, the survey data suggest that some 40 percent of the American public believes in the Bible as the "actual word of God and is to be taken literally, word for word." That would approach 100 million people. Approximately 84 percent of Americans believe that Jesus is the son of God, and 80 percent said they were convinced they will appear before God on judgment day. The same percentage believes God works miracles, and half the population believes in angels. Nearly a third of all Americans firmly believe in the rapture. As Garry Wills puts it: "It seems careless for scholars to keep misplacing such a large body of people."[4]

There are, however, differing fundamentalist styles. Most studies of fundamentalism deal with its white, rural, Baptist, puritanical, southern face. But the way we look shapes what we see. I want to shift the ground of the debate about fundamentalism out of the South to its northern, urban, racially and ethnically mixed environment where the whole notion of one's response to modernism is profoundly ambivalent and developed not in fantasy from remote areas of the country but up close, in an often stagnating immersion in the city. When you live in Sodom you have no easy retreat from it into idealized rural passions. What seems to drive people instead is an apocalyptic yearning for renewal within the degradation and chaos of the city they know so well. New York City is a good place to test that idea, and that is where my interviews took place.

The most inclusive fundamentalist style is the evangelical, an umbrella term used to describe a broad spectrum of beliefs, churches, and organizations, not all of which could be considered fundamentalist. In much of Europe and the Middle East, the term "evangelical" is used to refer to the historic churches of the Reformation and is therefore synonymous with mainstream Protestantism. In the Americas, however, "evangelical" has quite different meanings and is associated with being born again, reading the Bible literally, personal evangelism, and apocalypticism. There are different wings within the evangelical movement, including the nonfundamentalist progressives (about 20 percent), represented by groups like "Sojourners" or, more interestingly, Bill Clinton, a firmly believing Southern Baptist who once regularly attended Pentecostal summer revivals. In order to keep my sights clear, the term "evangelical" in this book should carry with it the descriptor "conservative."[5] At its ideological center conservative evangelicals are those born-again Christians associated with Billy Graham, the National Association of Evangelicals, and Campus Crusade; with schools like Moody Bible Institute, Fuller Seminary, and Wheaton College; with publishing firms like Zondervan; and with magazines like *Christianity Today*, *Eternity*, and *Moody Monthly*.[6]

In my work, I encountered conservative Evangelicals in a richly endowed center for Bible study and outreach to business executives that I call Grady House (in naming the churches and church settings where I carried out my research, as with all the respondents whom I interviewed, I use pseudonyms). I spent nearly two years attending Bible study and the various programs at Grady House, which was located in a prestigious section of Manhattan. The people at Grady preferred not to call themselves "fundamentalist" and were at pains to stress that they were "neither a cult nor a club" (a line used by one of the staff leaders during a Bible study session); instead they described themselves as "historic Christians," which in my two years of active field work seemed a distinction without a difference, and reflected mainly their wish not to be associated with what they felt to be low-class fundamentalists. The orienting rituals of Grady House included Bible study and other on-site programs; direct evangelical outreach by the staff of missionaries to executives in the city; and free dinners for as many as seven hundred guests that included business leaders and members of the Social Register. The dinners were personally hosted by Mrs. Grady and were always held at special New York spots like the Plaza Hotel or the restaurant adjacent to the ice rink in Rockefeller Plaza.[7]

Pentecostals, whom religion scholar Martin Marty once said are difficult to get "in focus,"[8] define a second fundamentalist style. Pentecostals overlap with the Evangelicals in often confusing ways but also need to be considered as a separate fundamentalist style. The most important Pentecostal denomination is the Assemblies of God, though there are many independent white, black, Hispanic, and Korean Pentecostal churches. Their liturgical enthusiasms make Pentecostals most easily identifiable. They wave their arms in supplication and regularly speak in tongues. Their services run on for hours with responsive prayers and heartfelt singing. Partly due to their enthusiasms, Pentecostal leaders like Jimmy Swaggart or Jim Bakker have taken great falls with dramatic public confessions. Bakker's sprawling Heritage USA in North Carolina, including a giant water slide, was built on financial fraud, and he was drawn to liaisons with many women and even some men.[9] Swaggart, it turned out, had a passion for prostitutes, which was the basis for his fall. Most such leaders return in time to the church, or some church, even if chastened. It is not that sin is allowed but forgiveness is assumed. As people believe about faith healing, the instrument of God's power can be flawed and yet the action efficacious.

I spent a good deal of time with the Pentecostals, some of whom I encountered outside of a church. For the most part, however, my work with Pentecostals took place in two churches. The church I call Abiding Light, in midtown Manhattan, had a multicultural mix of whites, African Americans, and Hispanics, though historically it was a white congregation and the leaders remain white now. Abiding Light, which was declining in membership, sustained itself financially partly by renting out the church on Sunday mornings to a huge group of fundamentalist Koreans (who even hosted a full orchestra for their services). The Abiding Light congregation itself met in small Bible study groups early on Sunday afternoon and then gathered for a mid-afternoon service and some kind of evening dinner and prayer session. During the week there were other activities as well, including a prayer meeting on Tuesday evenings, choir practice on Wednesday, special events on Fridays (like occasional all-night prayer sessions), and outreach programs for poor adolescents on Saturday led by the assistant pastor.

Abiding Light led me, indirectly, to Calvary, an independent African American Pentecostal church in Harlem that was self-styled as "an end time church with an end time message."[10] In the early 1900s Calvary had begun as a "church planting" of Abiding Light, but the racist policies of the mother church in not allowing blacks to join the church council led Calvary to split off and become independent. Calvary remained small for many decades, indeed a storefront, until its current charismatic minister, the Reverend Charles, took over in the 1970s. They then grew dramatically in size (to about one thousand) and used their collective purchasing power to buy a large, old building. Members of the congregation personally rehabilitated the building, and it came to function as a thriving church and something of a community center for its surrounding dilapidated neighborhood. The three-hour Sunday service—which was the most important event in a week crammed with other meetings, prayer services, and activities—was quite a lively happening. Many brought their own tambourines. They stood and talked in prayer as the spirit moved them. They swayed to the music and sang lustily. There was much clapping and ritualized saying of "Amens." Anyone praying from the podium was answered from the congregation in a continuous and spontaneous dialogue. The singing was exquisite, and the piano and electric organ, placed at opposite sides of the podium, played along with a multi-piece drum set and several trombones.

The dominant fundamentalist style, however, that anyone would agree to designate as "fundamentalist," consists of those now largely southern and white Americans who most directly inherit the fundamentalist traditions forged in the nineteenth and early twentieth centuries. Such believers are most visibly Baptists, but they may also find their home within any Protestant denomination. These fundamentalists are the actual literalists, as Erik Erikson might say,[11] those whose certainty about faith borders on absolutism. They are ambivalent about the somewhat looser standards of belief of the conservative evangelicals and mock "holy-rolling Pentecostals." Such fundamentalists believe in and talk about "inerrancy" and spend many hours of Bible study on the end time theory of "premillennial dispensationalism." In this theory God is revealed to humans through a series of dispensations, or stages, each with its own narrative sequence that ends in violent disruptions in the transition to the next dispensation (the expulsion from the garden, the flood, and so on). Inevitably in such a theory, we are at the end of the last dispensation before the violent end of human history and the opening up of the millennium. Furthermore, the "premillennial" part of the theory holds that Jesus returns to rule at the point of the transition as human history ends, or before the millennium itself, an idea that is also linked to the rapture of the faithful away from the violence of the end times. Any theory that brings the end closer at hand and puts its violence in focus lends end time chronicles a certain urgency. At the ideological core among fundamentalists, in other words, a new theory of ultimate death energizes the apocalyptic as it ripples through the mass movement of fundamentalism.

My direct experience with this fundamentalist style was in St. Paul's, an independent Baptist church in the northern reaches of Manhattan. St. Paul's was a thoroughly mixed congregation of whites, African Americans, and Hispanics with a white minister. They ran a variety of programs, including a soup kitchen, and aspired someday to build a new church building. St. Paul's kept close to its ideological commitments in its Bible study program and nurtured their version of the truth in the young they taught in the school. More than any of the churches I attended, St. Paul's was totalistic in the kinds of commitments it expected of its members and in the involvement of the congregation of all ages. The interviews with people in this church, furthermore, showed an unusual degree of ideological certainty, together with a marked suspiciousness of outsiders.

In my view, then, the fundamentalist movement in America includes three distinct, if overlapping, styles. Largely because the styles are so close and yet distinct, the movement is rife with what Freud called the narcissism of small differences.[12] Strict fundamentalists find the liturgical enthusiasms of the Pentecostals repugnant, who in turn speak with disdain of the rigidities of their brethren (many of my Pentecostal respondents talked of their "full gospel" beliefs as a "step forward" from the Baptists and one young African American woman, raised an Episcopalian, said the mainstream church needed to "get off this . . . social programs–type stuff"). The privileged members of Grady House dissociate themselves from vulgar street evangelizing. The members of Calvary still bristle at the insults they endured from the founders of Abiding Light four score years ago. And at the fringe the battle over end time ideas can be especially intense. Whole groups are formed around whether they believe Jesus will return to rapture the faithful before, during, or immediately after the seven-year period of tribulation that marks the transition out of human history, a distinction that might well seem both arcane and meaningless to outsiders, unless one appreciates its psychological significance. The survivalist groups in Idaho, for example, many of whom are Neo-Nazi or Aryan, tend to believe Jesus will rapture them into the clouds only in the middle or at the end of tribulation, because they first want to experience the violence directly and fight it out with the beast.[13] The distinctive characteristic of Jehovah's Witnesses is their reading of Revelation 7:4–8 and its mention of the 144,000 who are "sealed," an idea that also obsesses other ideologues in relation to the ingathering of the Jews, which some mainstream Evangelicals dismiss out of hand.

The noise of difference, however, should not obscure the underlying unities within the fundamentalist movement. All within it would agree with the inclusiveness of what a middle-aged man, Otto, told me ("My definition of a Christian is someone who has a personal commitment to Jesus Christ"), and the location of the outer boundaries of the movement as defined by another man, Isaac, who scorned the "easy believism" of "nominal Christians." The strict "fundamentalists" may be the chief carriers of the idea of inerrancy, but it is a term frequently used in Pentecostal churches, in Bible studies, and by individuals when talking about scripture. It is in the discourse, one might say. Furthermore, what defines the movement psychologically is its unique Christian commitment to the apocalyptic. The ideologues place the greatest emphasis on premillennial dispensationalism, but I found that virtually all my respondents carried often large, if somewhat undigested, parts of the theory with them.

Images of the rapture, tribulation, Antichrist, the beast, and Armageddon are quite universal, if by no means always the same, in the minds of fundamentalists. Calvary, remarkably enough for an African American Pentecostal church, required of new members in the congregation that they study premillennial dispensationalism in special classes. The apocalyptic is more than subtext. It is the ground of fundamentalist being.

I do not presume to pretend that I was a fly on the wall in this study, removed from the intense religious experiences into which I rather unwittingly threw myself. My formal psychoanalytic training and involvement in clinical work perhaps justify such avowed subjectivity, though any observer of fundamentalism needs to account to the reader for his or her special connection to the subject. That this almost never happens is a commentary on the false positivism that prevails in much of the academy. Throughout this book I use my own reactions as a vital source of data, while studiously trying to avoid the luxury of self-indulgence. I wrote extensive field notes after every service, Bible study, interview, or encounter I had in the churches over some five years. In these notes I tried to capture the externals of the setting and the mood, the songs and prayers and general happenings, as well as what was happening to me inside in response to these events. My reactions are woven into the text, but I will begin with a specific word on my own religious origins, which I realize now were an important, if only partly conscious, influence on my decision to undertake this study, as well as my curious first encounter with fundamentalism.

I was raised as an Episcopalian on the South Side of Chicago, near the University where my father was a professor of French literature and a dean. He had been born and raised in Georgia, where I was also born. My paternal grandmother, an ardent Methodist, practiced her form of Protestantism in a simple, whitewashed church directly across the street from their house in a small Georgia town. After her husband's death at the turn of the century, she was left in near-poverty with six children to raise. Her faith helped keep her strong. A rich aunt sent my father through school, though when she died all the money went to the Methodist Church. In his thirties, studying at the University of Chicago, my father married up. My mother was a doctor's daughter from Colorado who had had servants as a child and had spent a year in a finishing school before college. At thirteen she had become an Episcopalian. That became our family church as well, reflecting in part the social aspirations of my father, though he also used to joke that he sometimes missed singing "Beulah Land" from the pews of our incense-drenched church.

We attended church every Sunday and on all important holidays, like Good Friday, as well as some of the lesser holy days. Before dinner we always held hands and said a lengthy prayer. We sang Christmas songs together in our living room after dinner, and I have fond memories of nestling close to my father on an old brown felt couch as we sang from a worn songbook. Everyone in the family gave up something for Lent (chocolate, desserts, whatever); I would worry about what I was going to give up for weeks each year before Ash Wednesday and feel a large dose of guilt if I ever broke my vow. All these rituals that bound our family to the church gave us a sense of togetherness. We never actually talked of God per se and certainly never read the Bible or made reference to heaven, hell, or even, really, to Jesus.

None of this was artificially imposed on me. I was an active partner in our relationship to the Church of the Redeemer that was at the end of our block. For one thing, I was an earnest and, at least for my mother, an angelic choirboy singing soprano solos in our traditional (and paid) men and boys choir from about the age of seven until my adolescence. That involved two long practices after school on Tuesdays and Thursdays and before the Sunday service, monthly performances for shut-ins, concerts that required extensive preparation, and long hours of services during Christmas and Holy Week. Besides regular Sunday School, I was also an altar boy through these years. I would thus serve at the first Sunday service, attend a class on some innocuous topic, grab a roll at the coffee hour in the basement, go to choir practice, and then sing at the larger 11:00 A.M. service. I also got up on Wednesday mornings at 6:00 A.M. to attend the minister in a service in the chapel. I even confessed my sins, such as they were, three times a year, kneeling alone beside the minister in the small chapel.

I guess I was marked for some future role in the church, for I was also recruited early into a number of special activities and programs. For several summers I attended a church camp, which I remember as distinctly unpleasant and quite removed from anything to do with religion. I also had a special relationship with our minister (who later became a bishop). He seemed to want me as his acolyte at both the Sunday services and at the Wednesday morning chapel. He also decided to put me on the fast track for confirmation. At all of eight years old I was therefore enrolled in the training program to be confirmed four years ahead of schedule. I dutifully learned the rules and expectations of a true Christian, which were in any event hardly burdensome and lightly shared, and worked hard to memorize the Lord's Prayer and the Nicene Creed. These I had to recite before Father Moorehouse, alone, in his office. I was terrified. I did okay with the Lord's Prayer, but the Nicene Creed got mixed up with some phrases rattling about in my brain from my Cub Scout activities: "And I believe," I said, "in the Father, the Son, and the Holy Ghost, and the Republic for which it stands." I was confirmed, but Father Moorehouse also had a good laugh about my examination with my father over a stiff glass of bourbon.

Religion was serious but not oppressive. Family and ritual mattered much more than Jesus and God. The Bible was hardly opened. Sunday School dealt with issues of ethics and life, not spirituality or religion. I never owned a Bible as a child, never took one to church, and was never expected by anyone in my world to know anything about biblical stories. We sang to the glory of God and filled our church with incense but never once mentioned anything about what happens to infidels, let alone something as coarse as hell. The sermons were intelligent and witty. They were not particularly profound, but they were blessedly short. I was never inspired but also never offended. Besides, my main concern in any service was my role in singing or carrying the communion materials to and fro.

At thirteen I left the church with a sudden realization that life inside Christianity could be insidious, if not evil. It was 1957 and we had moved to the very old South in north Florida, where my father became president of Florida State University. Although I had been born in Georgia, I really knew little of southern ways until then.

Naturally, we started attending an Episcopal church. One Sunday, not long after our move, I sat astonished through a sermon that argued for "negro" racial inferiority based on biblical passages. I decided something was seriously amiss with this church and probably church in general. Besides, I cared then about football and girls, and worried about pimples.

For the next twenty-five years I hardly went to church, except for an occasional Christmas Eve service and a few weddings and funerals. After my father died when I was sixteen I went through a spiritual crisis and decided to read the Bible straight through. It had some meaning for me but also got frankly boring somewhere in the middle of the Old Testament and after the Gospels in the New Testament. I lost that Bible at the end of my summer's reading. The closest I came to continuing my childhood involvement in religion was when I attended conservative Jewish services at Harvard with my devout roommate. I liked the singing, the mystery of the Hebrew, and the friendly ecumenical spirit in which none of the Jewish students objected to the presence of a tall, blue-eyed, blond WASP in their midst.

I raised my first pack of three children without any church in their lives. I was living on an old farm in central Illinois, trying to make it in my first teaching job at the nearby university, Sangamon State. I was in analysis and doing my psychoanalytic training in Chicago, as well as writing my first book. My marriage was troubled, there was never enough money, and my horses kept breaking through my makeshift fences and eating my neighbor's corn. Church seemed an unnecessary luxury, something I might get to in another decade of my life, but certainly not vital. Besides, I considered myself an agnostic of major proportions and it seemed hypocritical to raise children in a faith in which I did not believe. A part of me remained nostalgic about the church, especially its sense of mystery and ritual, and the way it had worked in our family to build cohesion. As my marriage crumbled, that image gained some renewed vitality, especially through several years of single parenthood with my three boys.

In the mid-1980s I came to New York with a new wife in a newly reconstituted family to take a new job at the City University. Perhaps it was the change and the opportunities it offered for remaking myself (or maybe it was having just turned forty), but I decided to search out a church. Powerful Christian images that contributed to my social and political passions had clearly never left me during my years away from the church. My new wife and growing boys were only mildly interested in my project, so I decided to find a church first, then try to lure them into it. While jogging I spotted an Episcopalian church not far from where I lived in Brooklyn and noted the time of the Sunday service. I wondered whether I could really go home again, but I certainly was not prepared for what had happened to Christianity since my departure at thirteen.

It looked familiar at first, as the robed minister at the altar busied with the chalice and stacks of wafers for communion and other tasks preparing for the beginning of the service. I felt a warm glow looking at the stained glass windows. Maybe the church could in fact reinvigorate the moral principles that my Christian upbringing had instilled. There was nothing pretentious about the church and the large number of people filling the pews suggested an active and vital congregation. I was also pleased to see that the congregants were thoroughly integrated. The church reflected the social and ethnic diversity of the community.

My first sign of change came when a man sat next to me and asked if I would like a "prayer partner." It was clear he expected to "help" me through the service. I wanted to explain that I could manage quite well, thank you, but sensed something peremptory about his demeanor that made him someone who was not going to be deterred from sitting at my side as my "prayer partner." I realized I would just have to go with the flow that morning and see what this church would bring. The man suggested I might want to keep a pencil and paper ready at hand, along with my Bible, when the priest spoke, for "He really roams quickly through scripture." I explained that I had none of those items with me. The man looked surprised but quickly produced paper and pencil and moved close to share his Bible.

Everything from that moment on was completely outside of my experience. The service was interminable and at least twice the length of anything I had ever attended as a child. The congregation belted out hymns more like "Beulah Land" than Bach, reading from a screen in front of the altar on which the words were projected.

Most parishioners raised their hands with palms open, presumably to let in the Holy Spirit, a gesture I had only once seen in a TV broadcast of some Billy Graham revival. The sermon mentioned innumerable biblical passages (as my prayer partner quickly flipped through his Bible to locate each reference and share them with me) and talked about them with a literalism I found strange.

But the most disorienting experience of the morning was the communion. I never questioned that I would participate; I was, after all, confirmed in the church. I had always thought of taking communion as a way of celebrating membership in a congregation and perhaps opening oneself up to a spiritual process the end of which was murky indeed. Taking communion had something to do with faith, to be sure, but one could be a long way from certainty about belief and still be eminently qualified to participate. Not so in this church. As I walked to the railing to take communion, I saw a number of those assisting the minister look alarmed and whisper among themselves. As I knelt three people surrounded me. One asked if I was confirmed but seemed not to believe me when I replied in the affirmative. They then encircled me, touching my shoulder and arms, praying intensely for (and they thought, with) me. When they felt I was ready, to my great relief they moved on and the minister brought me the bread and grape juice (as a child we always used real wine).

After communion I felt inclined to just walk down the aisle and out the door. This was not a form of Christianity with which I was familiar. It was literal, exclusive, intense, and, for me, quite alien. Part of me wanted to flee and never return. Perhaps I should have. But for better or worse the anthropologist in me took over. I stayed that day, and though I only returned once to that particular church, which in any event only bears a "family resemblance" to fundamentalism,[14] I went to many like it over the next five years.

That stunning first encounter with fundamentalism in the Brooklyn church connected with a conversation I was then (1987) beginning with my colleague Robert Jay Lifton about how ordinary people imagine ultimate threats. In time, with MacArthur Foundation funding, our common interests led to an elaborate interview study of which fundamentalism was a part. From these shared beginnings,

I took off in my own idiosyncratic directions to complete the research for this book.

I limited my work on fundamentalists to New York City, because it was a domain in which they had not previously been studied and was available for my personal involvement. Fundamentalism as I understood it as shaped in three styles determined the types of fundamentalist communities I wanted to locate: conservative Evangelicals, Pentecostals, and more doctrinaire fundamentalists who would probably be Baptists. Within those styles I also felt it was important to include representation of the racial and ethnic diversity of New York fundamentalism, to the extent possible given language constraints. Consultation with authorities familiar with the New York church scene generated some five or six possible communities for each of the styles. I then visited churches (and Grady House) to find the best ones for my purposes. I sought churches in which I was made to feel welcome; in which the minister seemed accessible; in which the number of parishioners was neither too small to be suffocating nor too large to feel lost; in which the diversity of the city was reflected and one African American church because of its special importance for understanding the subject; and in which there existed an active program throughout the week into which I could fit myself.

The selection of respondents for interviews was a rigorous and exhausting process. Sometimes the pastors helped identify members of their congregation whom they felt would be interested in the work and good to interview. But in general I found respondents on my own within the churches as the logical extension of my active participation in services, Bible study, prayer meetings, and other activities. Respondents were people who had to feel sufficiently comfortable with me to be willing (and sufficiently articulate) to talk. I had to begin the dance, or courtship, and it could take anywhere from several weeks to as many months to convince a respondent to agree to formal interviews, which then might take another month or so to conduct.

In my work I sought to be empathic with my respondents and their world and yet never lose sight of my research purposes. On the one hand, I had little trouble entering into most fundamentalist rituals. I sing well and thoroughly enjoy a spirited service, though I never took communion again after my experience in that Brooklyn church and was never able to raise my arms in supplication with the Pentecostals. I came to tolerate the innumerable Bible study sessions I attended, which I more or less accepted (or rationalized) as filling a gap in my education. I found a certain spiritual nourishment in all my church-going and Bible reading that touched my early experience and deepened my ethical commitments. On the other hand, I never lost sight of my identity as a researcher nor my sense of personal discomfort with the religious attitudes of most fundamentalists. I tried not to be false to myself or to my respondents. I never pretended to be reborn, or even Christian for that matter. I readily shared my doubts about faith but always focused on my quite genuine interest in understanding what other people believe. I know outstanding scholars of fundamentalism who were raised as fundamentalists and move delicately at the edges of the experience; others like myself who had a religious background in mainstream churches feel a deeper ambivalence about the potential totalism of contemporary fundamentalism; still others have conducted good, though usually antagonistic, work from the outside. Each stance has its merits. What does matter is honesty in understanding oneself in relation to the experience itself.

My self-presentation, however, had some important consequences in the very ambiguity it presented fundamentalists. They feel acutely the scriptural commandment to evangelize. "God has no grandchildren" is the phrase I often heard, meaning that each generation has to be converted, each person born *again*. Otto was quite clear about the evangelistic purpose of fundamentalism. Nonbelievers must be reached, because "We're mandated by scripture to take the gospel to every creature." Now, of course, "We're losing the battle," but we must struggle on. God wills it. Everyone must have an "opportunity" to know God, whatever they then do with that knowledge. If they refuse the word, they die, not once but twice. "If you believe the Bible, you have to believe that." In fact, however, except for such deeply committed individuals (besides Otto I might also mention Monroe, Sam, Mary, Frank, and Reverend Charles in my study), and certain marginal fundamentalist groups like the Jehovah's Witnesses within which all individuals fiercely spread the word, most fundamentalists do little actual work converting people.[15] But they believe they should evangelize, and my unusual presence offered special opportunities. I was the perfect target. I came to services, Bible studies, and talked with them over coffee. They had repeated chances to work on me. I was a self-confessed nonbeliever but knew a lot about their beliefs and deepest commitments and was both sympathetic and genuinely interested in them and their world. A kind of nonverbalized contract came to cover my work: I was granted interviews in exchange for making myself available for conversion. This contract was not without its psychological stress, though it also had its moments of humor and absurdity. And for my part it was not a devil's bargain. The offering of myself for conversion was genuine. Otherwise I would have felt dishonest in the dialogue. I listened carefully to their pitch, and made every effort to let it enter my own spiritual imagination. Besides, how could I know for sure how the repeated evangelical onslaught to which I subjected myself would turn out? At some level I had to keep open the option that they would succeed.

In the churches themselves, which are hierarchic institutions, I could never expect to interview without the tacit approval of the pastor. The procedure therefore was first to attend Sunday services for a while to get known and somewhat legitimized. But before too long one had to talk with the pastor and explain the purposes of the work. The responses varied, but it is a mark of the relative openness of most fundamentalist churches that tentative approval from the pastor in no way assured contacts and certainly not interviews with individuals in the churches; it simply removed the veto at the top. For the rest, I was on my own, meeting people and generally immersing myself in their lives. But it was never easy getting close. I courted Otto at Abiding Light, for example, for months. We both attended Ian's Bible study, and I took every opportunity to talk with him, ask questions, and generally make myself a familiar part of the surroundings. I sensed in him a valuable respondent for my study but also a vague distance that would make it difficult to set up a formal interview. Even after I finally asked him for an interview it took several frustrating weeks to find a time and place to conduct it. He always returned to New Jersey immediately after the 2:30 P.M. Sunday service and arrived for the 1:00 P.M. Bible study just as it began. But it turned out that on one Sunday he was staying through the evening for a 7:30 P.M. Christian movie at Abiding Light and agreed to an interview between the end of the service and the movie.

It was hard at first to find a place to set up. The sanctuary would have been inappropriate and I was not close enough to the minister to ask to use his office. That left some corner of the basement, which was bustling with activity. After some indecision, during which I could feel Otto's suspiciousness mounting, I at last found two chairs in a corner of one room with a third between us on which I could place the tape recorder. It was clear he could not understand the need for such privacy, and I had not anticipated the fear that filled Otto's eyes as he saw me handling the tape recorder. He visibly pulled back, and asked again what my study was all about. I said I was studying what people believe, especially about end time things. He paused but then suspiciously agreed to go ahead. Quickly, however, he warmed to the subject, and was even enjoying himself by the end. He was surprised an hour and a half had passed, said, "Time flies when you're having fun," and warmly invited me to visit his church in Jersey and agreed to a second interview. I think he felt listened to, even though it had taken months of fieldwork to get him to talk.

Another researcher, Laura Simich, working in Abiding Light, attempted to interview a white woman named Nan who was in her early seventies. Caustic, chronically depressed, and in pain from arthritis, Nan played very hard to get. She had only converted in her early sixties after a lifetime of loneliness and various treatments for her depression (including some electroshock therapy). Since then, however, the church had become the mainstay of her existence. She spent most days in bed mobilizing herself to come to the church for something in the evening. Laura even took on the task for several weeks of escorting Nan to church from her apartment, riding with her on the bus. Nan told some of her history in informal chats and made abundant references to end time concerns. But when it finally came time for Laura to ask her if she could interview her more formally with a tape recorder, Nan suddenly grew highly suspicious. She withdrew for a few days and resisted any contact. When she next saw Laura she said the Lord had told her not to talk into a tape recorder. This honest answer, as far as one could tell, showed a typical aspect of fundamentalist thinking: the shift in agency. She was a passive agent in divine hands. God willed that she not give the interview. His instructions freed her from responsibility for the refusal, or for facing in herself why she was afraid to grant an interview. Whatever dangers Laura represented were kept at bay.

For most of the first six to eight months, in church rituals and in interviews my ambiguous status sustained my work. Interviews proceeded well, which deepened my relationships with at least some members of the congregations. But the commitments of fundamentalists eventually led them to see me as a highly suspect presence. One man who actually agreed tentatively to an interview pretended, the next time I asked him about it, not to hear me. When I repeated my question, he waited nearly five minutes (during which time I thought it would not be wise to ask again) before turning to me with a nervous smile and said, "We'll see." One time Nan, at Abiding Light, referred to me as "that tall, blond fellow" who is "not impressed with us" because he is not converted.[16] Why was I not converting despite their most earnest efforts? How could I know so much about the Bible and not believe it as they did? Perhaps I was a fraud, a spy, or worse, an agent of the devil sent to undermine their own faith? Now I should stress that I never encountered anyone who was openly hostile and was never asked to leave any church. On the other hand, you are never left alone by fundamentalists, who check regularly on the status of your beliefs. After about half a year, and certainly by nine to ten months, whatever benefit there was in my continued presence was more than offset by the ambiguity of my persistent nonbelief. The antagonism I began to feel was subtle. Heads turned, no one granted interviews, and I felt shunned.

There were some exceptions. I had long since passed the ten-month mark and was in fact into my second year of Bible study at Grady House. I had not completed my interviewing and so, despite the discomfort, needed to continue attending Bible study. I returned to a meeting after a month's absence, which had reflected my own ambivalence. At first, I had to endure a number of critical comments about my absence, especially by Monroe, Luke, Larry, and Sam, all of whom I had interviewed at least once by then and I suspected felt somewhat betrayed that I would leave after I had them on tape. But with that backdrop, we finally got into the Bible study. At this meeting, somewhat unusually, we were asked a series of set questions from a pamphlet that asked you to relate belief to your personal life. Everyone in our small group had to give some kind of answer to each question. I managed nervously to stay with generalities in answering questions like "Who is Jesus Christ to you?" (a religious leader of great significance who redefined human ethics, I mumbled) but knew there was no escape from the last question, "What does it mean to you now to have Jesus living within you?" I happened to be the last person to answer and thus followed seven sincere statements of belief. I said I respected those answers but that it was difficult if not impossible for me to answer the question. I had been raised a Christian but had never made a decision to accept Jesus into my heart, which would make it inauthentic to describe the ways in which my life had been changed by having him within me. There was an extended moment of silence in the group, after which, to my surprise, I immediately became the object of devoted attention. Luke commented on his own struggles with accepting Jesus, and others assured me it was normal to have doubts (I did not think it was necessary to respond that doubt understated my stance regarding my faith). Then, during the final prayer, Sam said: "If I may be so presumptuous, I would ask your prayers for Chuck in his ongoing search for Jesus, and may he continue his search and end up finding you, Lord, in his heart." When we broke up the meeting, several people gathered around me and were solicitous of me and talked in an overly friendly and earnest way.

I had a number of complicated feelings in response to this sequence of events. Initially, I felt that my need to be honest made me a pariah among the faithful. My immediate thought when members of the group drew toward me was that now I had my perfect opportunity to secure some additional interviews I needed (and in fact the experience in the Bible study gave me the opportunity to get my second interview with Luke and my fourth and final one with Monroe). On the other hand, and at a different level, the scene left me feeling invaded and exposed. I felt swallowed up by the oppressive goodness and decidedly uncomfortable when Sam prayed for me. It all made me think of the "love bombing" of the Moonies. At the same time, I was left with a sense of emptiness and a longing for the security they all talked about finding with Jesus. I wished quite genuinely I could have their beliefs. It was as though two parts of myself were carrying on a dialogue. One part said I should accept Jesus and take comfort in him as my friends advised, while the other said how ridiculous such feelings were. The very fact of my split feelings gave me insight into the incredible power of using the human need for love and acceptance within a group as a tool for conversion. I was clearly the outsider to this group, and they were reaching toward me to pull me into their magic circle.

I based my interview style largely on Lifton's approach that modifies the psychoanalytic model. The interview data consist of fifty-four different interviews with twenty-five respondents divided between the four churches or church settings in which I worked. Some of the interviews were conducted by talented researchers working closely under my supervision; all were taped and later transcribed. Structured yet open-ended interviews are perhaps the only way to uncover the deepest understandings of the self. Such psychological conversations aim to identify relevant images and themes that can emerge in this narrative form. It is a search for meanings in a life history, in a whole self whose story is still unfolding. The conversation is process oriented and, though carefully structured by means of a protocol, moves with the respondent in terms of thoughts, fantasies, feelings, even dreams.[17]

In this kind of qualitative and psychological research, one nagging question that always arises is whether the respondents were "typical." In one sense, no one is typical. Any life explored in depth is unique, even extraordinary, and if told at all well anyone's story is unusual. But were the people I chose to interview colorful in other ways and so far out of the ordinary as to distort my findings? Were these bizarre people who gave voice to their endism in ways that cannot be said to be "representative" of the larger movement of fundamentalism? I believe not. For one thing, the psychohistorical themes and images of significance for my work appeared with regularity in most of my respondents, who were otherwise remarkably different people and members of completely separate congregations. The churches in which I decided to work were also in no way out of the ordinary (to the extent that there is something ordinary about fundamentalism). Except for the ministers, all the respondents were typical members of the various churches or communities in which I worked. Some figures were immediately striking in visiting a church, but on the whole the people I talked with were quite like the other members of their churches. None of their peers, and certainly not I, saw them as odd or disturbed. In fact, in the few cases when an initial encounter produced visible stress in a respondent he or she was immediately left alone and the research taken elsewhere. That is part of one's ethical obligation in this kind of work.

But interviews, however central to my work, were only part of my data. Singing hymns and joining in Bible study with fundamentalists was an equally significant part of my research, as was the systematic exploration of my own feelings about what was happening to me in the churches or during the interview process. I also only began to comprehend endism in a larger sense as I deepened my historical and comparative study of the subject. Abraham Lincoln and the Hopi, who enter significantly into this book, were not incidental parts of my work but central to my emerging understanding. Such a blend of psychological and historical perspectives that led to this book is what I at least mean by the psychohistorical method.

ONE

THE
PSYCHOLOGY OF
FUNDAMENTALISM

1

THE
BROKEN
NARRATIVE

ARLENE. The first time Arlene revealed her end time self to me came after she had told me her story up to the point of her most recent arrest and incarceration. She was talking about her feelings of being a prostitute, particularly her guilt, and the way it connected to her relationships with men. In the course of her description of the period just before going to jail, I asked her what she felt about her continued work then as a prostitute. "I didn't want to do it anymore," she said, "but it was the only way to survive." That statement, however, was somewhat disingenuous, for Arlene needed easy money at odd intervals only because she was then drinking heavily and into crack. At some level Arlene was aware of her own contradiction, for she next shifted time quite dramatically in her associations. She asserted: "I didn't like it. I, in fact, I rebelled, I resisted, that's where the battery came in, I didn't want to do it."

I was confused. She had been talking about the period just prior to her arrest but had suddenly reverted to the previous year with her abusive lover, "dirty dog" James. She seemed to be listening now to an inner voice that had entered our dialogue for the first time. Any open-ended interview has a certain looseness to it, but up to this point in my discussion with Arlene I had been impressed with the coherence of her self-presentation, despite the horrors of the experiences in her life. Suddenly I felt far less connected to her. Something had intruded and broken our bond. That new voice seemed to me to be coming from deep within her.

Arlene began to elaborate on how James had wanted her to work as a prostitute and bring money home. When she refused he beat her up. "I just wouldn't do it." The issue, she explained, was money and self-respect. "I'm this kind of person that I have to see something for my money. . . . I wasn't seeing anything for the money." She said the main objection she had to James was his drug dealing, though in another context she had made quite clear that the real issue was his other girlfriend. "I never ever worked [as a prostitute] and said I'm going to give it to a drug dealer, no. That's a no-no. I'm not supporting any drug dealer." She wanted to see her money buy something visible like a car or a home. For that "I'll pound the pavement twenty-four hours a day." Then Arlene mentioned her sister who works a regular office job, and has to struggle for such a long time to acquire something like a down payment for a house. Arlene got that kind of money in six months. The thought of houses and her sister brought Arlene back again into the present. "See what I'm saying?" she asked me. "I wanted to re-establish, and once again, that basis I didn't have, I went and I got myself a house in six months. I went and got myself a car," both of which were quite true. "That's why you hustle," she added with less conviction but obvious pride at her success. She was now almost sad at her train of thought, which trailed off into illogic. "Otherwise, you wait for the five years of the down payment. And those are the only reasons why I do, you know, it now."

At that point a whole new self took over, one that sharply condemned her work in prostitution, and flooded her with guilt. "Being a believer, of course . . . it's against my beliefs, and, and, when God has a plan . . ." Now I felt on familiar ground. "What do you think God has as his plan for you?" I asked. "Good things," she replied warmly. "You know, there are certain, um, biblical promises, and if we live by God's laws and principles, I find that he's just and he's faithful to, to these things . . . and he's fulfilled all his promises [to me]. Any of the promises that I stand on, he fulfills them." She found in her faith that she was learning more about herself and growing daily in knowledge. Her faith in God even had a metaphoric shape to it. "I can actually feel it," Arlene said. Since her conversion, she had become sensitized to things in her life, more receptive to her own thought processes, more receptive, finally, to divine intervention. "Your spiritual eye becomes clearer," as she evocatively put it.

But the world is a sad and terrible place. People are mean and stupid. Everything seemed without rules, both within herself ("I really don't have any boundaries") and in the world. Chaos reigned supreme. We need a ruler, Arlene said, another Martin Luther King, maybe even Jesse Jackson ("if he just got his eye off that presidency"). "It's time for a revolution," Arlene asserted, with a note of political awareness and a sense of efficacy. She was too much in and of this world, too committed to change within herself to give up altogether on trying to radically alter for the better the course of human affairs. "Let's start a revolution against the drug dealers," she said angrily. They are destroying our children, and our sisters are being ruined by thirteen or fourteen. "Nobody is taking care of the children." There are no rules, she says repeatedly. "It's hari kari."

Such political reflections and healthy assertiveness proved fleeting. "It's all part of the end time and the approaching Armageddon," she said without apparent reference to the world but clearly speaking in the context of her inner text. What we've seen is bad, but there is much more to come. There are the signs, such as AIDS. "That's a plague. It's a plague. *Literally*. And there's *no* cure for it." Even syphilis is back on the rise and running rampant. It's another plague. Another is illiteracy. It's terrible. Then there is the greenhouse effect. "It's God trying to get our attention." We are marching toward the Apocalypse, she said with certainty. History will end and we will be healed, and "with history ending, all those things, it won't matter. Nothing will matter." Right now, Arlene believed, earth is under the rule of Satan and *his* angels. "He is loosed, he is loosed," she said, "he's having a field day" (evoking Revelation 20:2–3: "And he laid hold on the dragon, that old serpent, which is the Devil, and Satan, and bound him a thousand years, / And cast him into the bottomless pit, and shut him up, and set a seal upon him, that he should deceive the nations no more, till the thousand years should be fulfilled: and after that he must be loosed a little season"). Even though Arlene tried not to slip into too much demonology—the chaplain advised against it, she confided—she felt the presence of the devil against whom she has to valiantly struggle. Sometimes, at least, she was successful, as with her intravenous drug use. In overcoming that habit, Arlene felt she won one specific victory over the devil.

Arlene was aware that some people have always said the end is at hand and feel that what they are experiencing is the worst in history. But what's happening now, she believed, was unlike anything else that has ever occurred before. It is much worse. She was convinced that Jesus will return soon—in her lifetime—and rapture her and the believers before retaking the earth for his millennial rule. "When the rapture comes, there'll be no doubt in our minds that God is involved, okay? That'll separate the believers from the unbelievers." It's like with the Jews in the old days, Arlene said. They were very disobedient and had to go through much suffering. But in the end God heard their prayers. "We're praying [now] for his kingdom to literally come so this can be over with."

Within her largely conventional fundamentalist schema, Arlene inserted some creative and idiosyncratic variations. She had, for example, an image of God as an old black woman. Black women, she said, are the "nurturers of this earth," the caregivers and helpers. They keep things together, even to the second and third generation. Her endism also had a refreshing note of ambiguity to it. "I don't know what's in store," she said about the future. "But I *do* have a tomorrow. I'll always have a tomorrow." Nor will human error or folly be the instrument of human destruction. "I don't see the nuclear bomb or misuse of that as being our end." She did not preclude the possibility of nuclear war, or even of New York being wiped out in some kind of nuclear exchange. But that won't be part of the end of the world. That would be too much in our control, too "attributed" to humans, as she put it. The end of human history, in other words, will be beyond human comprehension. We will be responsible for it, but we can't make it happen. God may use us, but we cannot control his plan. The end is absolutely at hand (certainly in her lifetime) and yet she hoped for tomorrow and lived partly committed to a human future. It was inconsistent, and fully human.

The way Arlene worked out such contradictions was to carry within her at least two opposing ideas about ultimate violence, in particular the explanation for the transition into the millennium. One such image was a magical vision of destructiveness at the end that was both grand and grim, a violent and total cleansing that will purge the earth of sin and suffering. In this vision, Arlene evoked Sodom and Gomorrah, as well as the flood of Genesis, to explain her thinking. She noted once, for example, in a rather menacing way: "Like whenever there's an act of God, you're going to know this is an act of God." In this frame of mind the devil was a real and terrible thing (*He* is not, she said, a "beautiful angel of light" but epitomizes evil and "looks like black lungs filled with cancer," a horrible monster, rather "like the AIDS virus under a microscope").

On the other hand—and at different points in our discussions—Arlene stressed that between now and the end things will get worse but that the actual transition into the millennium will be peaceful. "We don't have to wipe out this earth to get a new one, we don't have to." God will simply "transform the earth," and make it over into something resembling her childhood in Jamaica. That will be "our New Jerusalem." Everything will grow abundantly and no one will have to toil on the land. It will be beautiful. We'll all walk around like Adam and Eve. There won't be black or white; we'll all just commune with each other. There will be no diseases, or robbery, or greed. All that will be gone. The weather will be perfect, and when it rains the sun will keep shining. We won't even need houses. There will be "flora and fauna" everywhere, and when you need fruit all you'll have to do is reach out and take some. "The name of the Lord is a tower where the righteous can run and be safe," Arlene said. We must hope for that. "I know where to go to get peace, and I have joy in this, as a believer." She can get peace with God, more peace than anything else. "Peace of mind, peace of my spirit, even my body." But without hope life is terrible. You'll commit suicide. One must hope for tomorrow, for deliverance. "It suits my personality just perfect," Arlene said. "It gives me order, it gives me discipline." When you've known tragedy, "you can learn from it," it can make you strong.

I met Arlene on Rikers Island, the huge New York City jail located just northwest of La Guardia Airport. In each of the four long interviews I conducted with her over a two-and-a-half-month period, we talked in the small but private office of the Catholic chaplain. The bedlam of prisoners moving about outside, laughing, talking, smoking, sometimes fighting was cut off from our little world of temporary peace. When Arlene first walked in, I was not at all sure that she was an inmate. She moved quickly and had an air of confidence as she set down a stack of papers on the desk and turned to greet me. As an (as yet) unsentenced inmate, she wore civilian clothes and seemed so much in charge of her environment that I thought maybe she was a staff member coming to get something in the office.

Arlene was a thirty-one-year-old woman at the time of the interviews. The beatings at the hands of her most recent boyfriend (including a deep scar on her arm from a knife wound and a somewhat distorted left jaw where it had been severely broken) and the effects of overeating had left their imprint. She was highly intelligent and articulate, able to express complex feelings in clear, evocative terms. She had an excellent vocabulary that far exceeded the bounds of her limited formal education. She was also self-reflective. She had had some therapy both in and out of prison that had clearly nourished her natural introspection, and made her receptive to the interview process.

Arlene was born in Jamaica. When she was very young her mother left her father and moved to New York. Arlene came to stay with her mother when the mother sent for four of the eight children. She spent a year in America, but was then sent back to Jamaica until she was eleven. At that point Arlene left Jamaica for good and came to live with her mother in Brooklyn. Arlene's father was a construction worker in Jamaica who once made pretty good money. "I had a father," she said remotely, "[who] was an alcoholic and he slept around and wasn't there, and was just difficult." He was "abusive" to Arlene's mother, who came to America to get away from him. But Arlene adored her father. "I thought he was the greatest." "He was this magical guy," she said. "Those are the most impressionable years," she said of the time before she came to America, "things I can remember . . . all these outings to the beach, and my father as a swell guy, all my happy moments, the happiest time of my life, I associate with my father."

Arlene hated her mother as a child, especially after coming to America. "I hated her," Arlene said, "because I didn't like America." The mother was distant, rigid, moralistic, and demanding. She also seemed to be unhappy, especially at the treatment she had received from her husband. The mother clearly sought allies in her various struggles and spent a good deal of time trying to turn Arlene against her father. The result, however, was only to create bitter resentment on Arlene's part toward her mother and deepen her yearnings for her father in faraway and somewhat mythical Jamaica.

Meanwhile, Arlene's stepfather began to sexually molest her, at first hesitantly but soon with abandon, fondling and kissing her regularly. Arlene feared to tell her mother, for she believed, reasonably, that her mother would deny it and claim it was Arlene's fault. Later, in fact, when she did tell her mother about the stepfather that is exactly what happened. Arlene felt abandoned and hopeless. Her mother kept saying she was going to send her back to Jamaica, but it was a lie and she said it only to quiet Arlene. "I cried, I cried, I wouldn't eat, I cried, it was terrible," she said. Twice Arlene tried to commit suicide. Once she jumped out of a third-story window but only sprained her ankle when she landed on a rose bush. A second time she took a bottle of aspirin and spent a day vomiting but was otherwise unharmed. The mother denied both attempts. She simply ignored the aspirin sickness and rationalized the jump from the window as an accidental fall. "My mother has a knack for that," as Arlene put it. "Anything that happens, she changes it." Arlene's life was in a shambles, and no one knew or cared. Of the responsible adults in her life, one lived in a remote world of self-centered fantasy, and the other was trying to seduce her. Even potential helpers, like neighbors, compounded her troubles. The man across the street raped her when she was twelve. It was her first sexual experience. "I had little white panties with bows all around it, with blood all over it and I just threw the panties away." She never told her mother.

Arlene was running out of options. Somehow she had to get out, escape, be free. She would consider anything, even prostitution, which a friend of hers suggested to her at fourteen. It didn't take much persuading. In a matter of hours Arlene was recruited by a pimp who whisked her away. For the first time since she had come to America, Arlene felt appreciated, even at the cost of turning herself into a commodity. She was treated well and made friends. Men often picked her up and went out for the evening, did things, went to a show, had dinner. She felt wanted. She had a number of regular dates, "nice people," she says, men she got attached to and saw every week. "I was on top of the world, I had the world at my tail," she said with enthusiasm (and without irony). And the money was important. It was a "representation of just how good you were, so you tried hard and made more money."

Part of the pleasure Arlene took in her work as a prostitute was the knowledge that it would drive her mother crazy to know what she was doing. It seems the whole family spent a good deal of time looking for Arlene that first year she worked as a prostitute. All her brothers roamed the streets trying to find her. "I used to see them looking for me," she said, curiously, since she was some distance from Brooklyn. It seems, however—and Arlene was vague about the sequence of events here—that she returned fairly often to Brooklyn "for bookings," and used the opportunity to visit her old haunts, walk the familiar streets, and observe her family and mother from a distance. Eventually, her mother hired a detective who located Arlene and insisted that she return. She was just sixteen. It was a moment of decision for her. To go back would have meant a renunciation of self at many levels, a return to an impossibly childish role for someone who was now highly experienced in the world, and an admission of guilt that would have established her mother as morally superior. Arlene instead chose to marry Alex, whom she had met on one of her Brooklyn bookings.

Alex was a pimp. He wanted Arlene to stop having so many outside dates and instead work a house in Bed-Sty. It was supposed to be the best in town, where the "mayor's friends" visited. Alex, however, seemed largely motivated by a complex blend of love, jealousy, and a need to control. He wanted Arlene safe and free to work her trade, but he also sought to insure that she would not have fun at it and most of all not develop relationships with her clients. As she said: "It was unfortunate he met me in that profession. He just never trusted me [*laugh*]. And I wasn't doing anything wrong." Arlene made a valiant effort to make her marriage work. Her earnestness was a central part of her personality, as was her deep and abiding desire to be accepted, recognized, and honored. After a year or so she quit prostituting and went back to high school, which she finished in record time. Together Arlene and Alex opened a small business. She also got pregnant and decided to have the baby, even though her first response was to have an abortion. Some things were finally working out for Arlene.

But Alex never lost his suspicions. He became obsessed with Arlene, jealous of her every move, fearful she was out whoring. He "wouldn't leave me alone," she said with irritation, especially since she was dutifully playing the role of the loyal housewife. Arlene was then eighteen. She decided she had to get out of her marriage. It could only lead to continued heartache. Besides, she felt she could never raise a child in the grubby world of pimping and prostitution. She secretly got an apartment and fixed it up for herself and the baby to escape to after the birth.

Part of Arlene's character, as she realized with a vengeance, was that she could not live without a man, and that she had only been able to change her life at crucial times by changing men. At this point in her life, feeling stifled in her first marriage, Arlene's solution to her dilemma was to set out to find a new husband. This time, however, she was more cunning than the first time around and determined to find someone who would open up new financial and social opportunities for her. After the birth of her baby, whom she basically turned over to her mother to raise, Arlene did in fact leave Alex to live in the apartment. Then she set out to find someone white, secure, older, and rich. She was very calculating about it, and did exactly what Alex most feared: She worked her "wiles," as she put it, on Long Island, in a house that she somehow found out about. It didn't take long for Arlene to find what she was after. When she first saw Ben she knew he was just right. He was fifty, widowed, Jewish, and had lots of money.

Arlene soon moved in with Ben, who seemed decent and in love with her. Within two years they were married and settled down to live in an upscale community on Long Island. "He was a very, very good husband, and he loved me because I was a good wife." But it was not a happy time. Suddenly this young woman with experience only in Caribbean American, working-class culture was the lover, then wife, of a rich and respected Jew in a New York suburb. Class, race, culture, and a thirty-year age difference opened up a vast chasm between them. Ben remained absolutely devoted to Arlene throughout these trials and tribulations of their relationship. The only tension came when she got pregnant early on when they were dating. He insisted she have an abortion, which she undertook reluctantly. But he did everything else he could to make her happy. He doted on her, bought her clothes, took her out, and insisted she not work. He also fiercely defended her blackness and broke with many of his white friends who objected to the relationship. But Arlene never adjusted. She was deeply troubled by all the rejection of her, including, to her surprise, rejection from many of her black friends. In her culture—by which she meant Jamaican—she said it is not uncommon or frowned upon for a black woman to find someone white to marry. Besides being rich, she wanted someone kind and gentle, which for her meant someone white. "I'm not a rough person," she stressed, as she sought to explain her feelings to me. "I didn't like being black," she said, "so I considered myself . . . Jamaican." American blacks, she thought then, were a "disgrace" (her mother's favorite word). They didn't work, lived off welfare, and the men were all in jail. Arlene's empathy was later considerably expanded. "I'm learning I have to consider the plight of black Americans because it affects me." And she concluded mournfully in terms of our own black-white interaction: "You don't see that I'm Jamaican, you don't see that I'm different."

Arlene had found her white man in Ben, but she had also come up against the full force of American racism, not to mention her mother's continued chagrin over her life. She began to get into drugs seriously for the first time in her life. She would drive to Harlem to buy cocaine with her black girlfriends, sneaking away from Ben. She felt numb about everything in her life. It all seemed pointless. She also experienced fresh trauma: her two closest brothers were killed in a robbery. She had grown up with these two brothers in Jamaica. One was slighter older, one younger. The breakup of the family had thrown them on each other for support. Arlene adored them both. The older one was a master craftsman who could fix anything; the younger one was to be an engineer and had just received notice of a full scholarship to college. The death of Arlene's brothers was utterly senseless and brutal. It also simply faded into the tapestry of violence in East New York: the police never came up with a suspect, in fact hardly investigated the crime.

The renewed loss, the closing down of options, and the rejection by family and neighbors made Arlene feel life was worthless. Once again she tried suicide, this time very seriously indeed. She took an overdose of valium, cut her wrists, and climbed into the shower, where Ben found her. She woke up in the hospital, tied to the bed, her wrists bandaged and wires and tubes everywhere. Recovery came slowly, and the scars remained. As a gesture, Ben bought a huge house for Arlene's mother and extended family in New Jersey. He also nursed Arlene back to health. But problems remained. Ben continued to be caught up in his own problems losing friends and dealing with the censure of neighbors; he also had an angry break with his daughter over Arlene that led him to take his daughter out of his will. Arlene meanwhile struggled to make sense of feeling a kind of misplaced responsibility for all these problems. She had always felt she should make everyone happy; now she blamed herself for Ben's loss of friends, her own loneliness, even the despair in the world. She took everything onto her own shoulders.

Among her other problems, she was also bored. Though Ben did not want her to work, he eventually relented and helped her set up a small women's clothing business that she ran part-time. Arlene tried school, but that didn't fill her needs. Sometimes she cavorted with her friends. Ben saw that things were hard for her in their suburban community, so he tried as much as possible to take her away. He was in semiretirement anyway, for his business was pretty much in the hands of his stiff and distant son. Ben and Arlene traveled all over

Europe, to the Caribbean islands, indeed all over the world. It was all she had dreamed of; it was also empty. She started drinking with a vengeance. Arlene had drunk before when working as a prostitute but only occasionally to excess and never on a regular basis. But she and Ben soon worked themselves into an alcoholic pattern: two large drinks at home at cocktail hour, another one or two at the restaurant before dinner, a bottle of wine, perhaps also some champagne, with dinner, an after-dinner drink, and a nightcap. "That's a lot of alcohol on a daily basis," Arlene said.

And then a strange thing happened. Someone robbed their home and Arlene was accused of masterminding the heist. It took me some time in our talk to get the facts of this robbery straight, for Arlene obviously felt guilty about it. But after much hemming and hawing she finally explained what had occurred. Her partner in her clothing business was in deep financial difficulty and conceived of robbing Ben's house with Arlene's permission and knowledge. Arlene claimed her friend was only supposed to take a few items, but "it went awry" and the friend cleaned out the house when they were away. She then shamelessly implicated Arlene. Three times the district attorney tried Arlene in an effort to convict her of masterminding the robbery; finally he succeeded, and she got eight and one-third to twenty-five years.

Not surprisingly, the case drew tremendous publicity as well as racist approval from the community. But Ben never abandoned Arlene. He stood by her, paid her huge legal fees, and did everything humanly possible to keep her out of prison. But something had broken between them. As she admitted to me, Arlene had in fact helped her friend rob her own husband of his possessions, even though she never expected to be cleaned out or that she would be punished if the robbery was discovered. It was a betrayal of Ben at many levels, and she knew it. Arlene seemed to need to find some way out of a stifling relationship that was complicated by issues of race and class and the determined adoration that Ben lavished on her. "I was always trying to find myself, and he was always keeping me," she said. "I didn't want a relationship with this old white man anymore." Though Ben visited her regularly in prison, after a couple of years she asked for a divorce. She regretted it, however. "I numbed it while it was happening, I numbed it out afterwards. I refused to think about it, you know."

Prison life, as Arlene soon discovered, can have some decided advantages. "It's easy to survive on the inside," she said. She got all kinds of "positive input from everywhere." Group therapy and a "lot of stuff" helped her orient herself and get her life together. Jail gave her back a sense of future, and stirred hope. "When I was [upstate in prison] you know . . . I had five-year plans and year plans and everything else." "It is so structured," she said with enthusiasm. She didn't have to pay rent and got her own private room. Outside, she was dependent on a man to support her. Inside the jail "I have *my* room," and three hot meals a day. On the other hand, Arlene was too smart not to know that free food and a room were not the real issue. For one thing, when she was in prison she was full of guilt and shame at what had happened to her. "Those of us in jail," she told me, "are the lowest spectrum." What she welcomed were the controls, the limits, the clear boundaries. "Sometimes you do need that healing, you just, you do need to stop running and just be still. Especially when you've done a lot of running when you're out there, you're actually glad for the rest." The jail for Arlene was a holding environment in which the chaos of her inner self could be stilled.

Prison also brought new experiences in love and sex with other women, something not without its complications for Arlene. Against much resistance, she confided that she had actually had a series of affairs in prison. She never considered herself "gay." True lesbians, in her view, "have an identity crisis." She was just "having a little fun." The problem for her was that she saw homosexuality, even masturbation, as a sin. "Sin is sin," she told me with the confidence of her current fundamentalist view of these past matters. "I don't believe there's a first-degree and a second-degree sin with God. Sin is sin." Arlene's ethical dilemma with her relationships grew out of the fact that she went through a conversion experience in prison and was born again. She saw her acceptance of Jesus as a turning point in her life. She had been something of a Christian as a child, but in prison she embraced faith more earnestly, symbolized by a full immersion baptism. Her trauma in her life, however, was only beginning to move toward healing.

Once out of prison, Arlene jumped parole. She went south on the run with her new lover, James, "no-good, low-down scoundrel, I mean, dirty dog. Lower than a dog." In an attempt to hold onto her faith, she joined a church in Georgia and renewed her commitment by a second full immersion baptism. But she was unable to do any serious work, because she feared that by signing W-2s and other paperwork she would be traced via her social security number. She therefore fell into menial and unsatisfying jobs that left her hard up for money. She began to commit various petty robberies to stay afloat, and entered into the "subculture" of crime and drugs that took her further "outside of the norm." Not surprisingly, she got arrested while in Georgia for prostitution and some kind of assault charge. The authorities sentenced her to two years, but they never figured out she was on the run from New York State authorities. They told her they would not put her in prison if she would leave Georgia.

She came back to New York angry and depressed. "I had a death wish," she said. "I had no hope . . . I didn't want to go on." In no time she was drinking and had fallen into crack use, about which she was quite analytic. "Crack changes you," she said. "I mean, you can tell the personality of a crack addict. You're brash, you're very, very aggressive. You turn into this crazy person . . . a literal monster." Her "drug of choice," however, was alcohol. "I've been alcoholic all these years, and finding more and more about alcoholism and myself, I realize that with alcohol not in my body, I'm a rational human being that you're talking to. But that drinking, I'm off and running."

New York City, as Arlene knew, is not a good place to wander alone through the night, especially as a woman. Somehow she never got hurt. She moved in with a man named Henry but seldom spent much time with him, even though they were engaged in theory. There was a fierceness to her, a mean streak of pure violence that often found expression in attacks on people who irritated or threatened her in any way. She told me, for example, of attacking one man with a baseball bat and seeing his head "busting all over the place." Nor was that her only experience with violence that year. Another time she hit someone with an axe. She also stabbed someone. "I just kept stabbing and stabbing till I got him twice in his arm, his forearm." She understands all this violence as partly a response to the crack, which made her crazy, and as a way of working out the ferocious anger she felt after all the battering she had received at James's hands (James, for example, cut her on her arms just the way she attacked the man with the knife). But she could make little sense of her uncharacteristic anger and cynicism that year. Normally, she wanted to "do the right thing."

Arlene got so bad that her girlfriends insisted she get away. They packed her, barely conscious, onto a bus with a one-way ticket to South Carolina. Once there, Arlene temporarily came to her senses and got one job waiting tables and a second managing a small store near where she found an apartment. She was not in treatment but for the next six months managed to stay off crack. She enjoyed the hard work, the regularity of her life, the new people. But perhaps inevitably she could not make it alone so far from what she knew as home. That fall she returned to Brooklyn and moved back in with Henry, who seemed eager to help her. He was a born-again Christian who attended a well-known fundamentalist church on Flatbush Avenue in Brooklyn (which had a charismatic white minister and a huge African American and Hispanic congregation). Henry prayed constantly for her, which she believed was what made the difference. He was also long-suffering in his determination to help. She cut his face a number of times and once broke his foot. He had no use for drugs himself, but told her that he was so devoted that he would be willing to sell crack himself to support her habit if that would keep her home. He repeatedly searched through an endless series of crack houses to find her and bring her back. He insisted she was a good person; he even wanted to bring her home to live with his mother. The only real anger he ever showed her was when she once insulted his mother and he slapped her. She grabbed a knife and stabbed him twice. Many other times he let her beat him up ("You see he can't beat me, he has never beaten me. As a matter of fact I have abused *him*").

In the end it was raw jealousy that pushed him over the line rather than crack. Arlene and Henry had fought early in the evening. She stabbed him and he bled all over the room, on the drapes, on both sides of the window, everywhere. "Do you know that all this is my blood," he kept telling her, trying to get through to her feelings. But she was numb. All she knew was that she wanted to get high but wasn't comfortable doing it around him. He just sat there and wept. She started drinking and got some sushi, then returned to sit on the street corner. Suddenly, he insisted on knowing whether she had slept with one of her drug contacts. She denied it but he kept "picking and picking."

They moved the fight inside the room where they circled warily for a time. Arlene felt Henry was fed up with her for the first time. Perhaps it was the jealousy, perhaps he had just lost hope in his crusade to save her. She in turn felt an awesome sense of death in the room. She told him to stop moving about, to be still, but he refused. As though in a movie she could see that one of them was going to die that night and it could be her, "because he was tired of being defeated in these battles." He kept telling her she held nothing sacred. "Baby, baby, don't sleep with my friend." She told him to go outside and cool off, walk down to the pub at the corner and have a beer, but he was afraid she would sneak off and get high. He wouldn't leave. She got enraged and picked up a lamp and threw it at him, then a jar of pickles, then a hammer. To her surprise he threw the hammer back at her. She went berserk, both in fear and anger at this sudden turn of events. The all-suffering, ever-loyal Henry seemed so full of righteous indignity at her supposed infidelity that he could well kill her. With a sudden move—"I can be fast"—she picked up a can of kerosene and poured it all over him. She pondered whether to light him.

At that crucial moment, reason prevailed. She called the police and asked for help. She said she was turning into a monster and desperately needed treatment. That got her into jail, for the police noticed that she was wanted for breaking her parole. I saw her first a few months later after a renewal of her faith through daily work with a devoted chaplain.

THE DIVIDED SELF

The most general psychological observation about fundamentalists one can make is that they demonstrate inner divisions that find expression in their beliefs. *All* fundamentalists I met described their personal narratives as broken in some basic way. Before rebirth in Christ they described their lives as unfulfilled, unhappy, and usually evil. Their stories were discontinuous and full of trauma; faith healed them. That moment of finding a "personal relationship with the Lord," as they put it, was the great divide in their lives. It would be wrong to say that fundamentalists *only* thought about their pre-Christian selves as bad because the dogma of conversion demands a self-transformation (John 3:3: "Except a man be born again, he cannot see the kingdom of God"). A biblical passage cannot impose trauma on the self. But it is fair to say that fundamentalists experience trauma and then find a way to talk about it in the rhetoric of literal Christian belief. That rhetoric, in turn, builds on divisions. Satan opposes God; only a remnant of the faithful survive the end times; violence pours out on the ungodly; ordinary church life moves toward totalism; and our bad, discarded, pre-Christian selves are washed away in the apocalyptic transformation of the rapture.

Not all fundamentalists, however, experience the revelation of Jesus as a blinding moment of truth that transforms their lives. Very broadly speaking, I found two categories of fundamentalists: those who are raised in the church and those who come to it later in life, usually in their late adolescence or early adulthood (almost never old age). For those who come to fundamentalism later, there is the enormously significant moment of being saved, which can take many forms but is always a transformative personal experience. For those raised in the church, being saved usually has rather different meanings, for it occurs so early as to be without much conscious or symbolic significance. Sometimes, as with Mary (a thirty-year-old Pentecostal from Abiding Light) or Nigel (a twenty-eight-year-old Wall Street broker from Grady House), an early salvation was followed by an adolescent period of "falling away from God" (Mary) that ended in a rather dramatic return to the faith. For others the continuities were more evident. Harriet, widowed and in her early sixties, never seemed to drift from the church; her total identity was fused with it. Her grandparents joined Abiding Light when it opened. For the next several decades it was a thriving congregation, and Harriet was raised within it, saved there as a child, regularly attended the church's summer camp with its tents and sawdust floor revivals, raised her children in it, and buried her husband there. She has spent her life quietly working in the church, preparing for the "soon coming" of Jesus. "As a result," she said, "I never was out in the world." Another member of Abiding Light congregation, middle-aged Otto, also never experienced a dramatic break with conversion. He stressed that, of course, he wasn't an "angel" as a child. "I used to get sent down to the principal's office, you know, but that's not the worst of it." He even had trouble defining what it meant to be reborn or saved. He ended up distinguishing between the two in a very idiosyncratic way. He said he was born again at five or six, as best he could remember, but only saved at thirteen. In this way Otto reserved for himself at thirteen the choice he never experienced at five or six.

But no matter how conversion is experienced, an overlay of human evil from deep within Christian tradition always permeates the fundamentalist sense of their stories. Humans are born bad, in this view, and even the saved remain open to the workings of the devil. It is a constant struggle. Even if you are saved at five, you were born an evil person. Most of mainstream Christianity has found ways to soften this harsh, Manichaean view of human nature, but contemporary fundamentalists keep the notion very much alive. Reverend Matthew, patting his Bible, said (quoting Jeremiah 17:9 almost verbatim from memory), "The heart of man is deceitful above all things, and desperately wicked." This theological claim to evil works together with whatever happens psychologically in fundamentalist individuals *and* with the forms of badness and violence in the world. Fundamentalists fight to hold on to their God-given virtues. They know Satan was once within and could return; certainly he is about in the world. Life is dangerous, scary, and fragile.

Such divisions in the self, however, are relative. We all have them to a degree. Some difficult thoughts and ideas are truly repressed, as Freud argued, but for the most part the self functions under stress by splitting off aspects of troubling feelings and experiences that then become dissociated memories. We know of them but not completely. They are disavowed, as Michael Franz Basch has put it.[1] It is quite rare that memory is really blank. If encouraged, most people can recall aspects of even traumatic experiences, though they may well filter out much of what happened at first in the process of remembering and certainly separate out the feelings from the memories to mute the suffering. In more extreme cases of trauma, however (say of long histories of sexual abuse), dissociation serves to protect the self against fragmentation. Most victims of such violation report the sensation during the abuse itself of leaving their bodies and watching the unfolding encounter happen from some safe, unfeeling distance.[2] Repeated trauma then requires repeated dissociation, and the patterns of separateness in the self take on a structure, with its own memories and feelings (or history, one might say).

The challenge in talking with fundamentalists is to locate the appropriate meanings of whatever divisions exist, without ever describing their lives as pathological. I am not arguing in this book that fundamentalists are crazy; at least they are no more so than anyone else in our culture (including myself). Categories of pathology, in the first place, are meaningless in trying to figure out the psychology of a mass movement.[3] As William James knew well, there is also something ethically obtuse in using reports of religious transformation against the committed. What is valuable (and what James demonstrated as well as anyone) is that one can learn a great deal about the phenomenology of religion from the direct reports of the faithful about their experiences.

Fundamentalists' broken narratives profoundly distort time, a break that is rooted in experience. The past is separated off, to be remembered only as an object lesson. You recall to forget. Except for the testimonial, so important in converting others, the past might not be remembered at all. The present, in turn, is profoundly degraded and full of evil. God is furious, and about to end it all. The handful of the faithful must keep struggling, but they are persecuted and doomed to failure. Things can be delayed but not solved. There is no redemption in human purpose. Culture is rotten. The only hope lies in the mythical transformation of the future, in the remaking of the world during the millennium and the ultimate salvation in heaven after the final judgment. Such a profound reconfiguration of historical time and a dramatic move into the magical as the means of salvation reflect the extent of trauma in the lives of fundamentalists.

If all that seems a bit arcane, perhaps a parable will help, one told to me by a theological friend, Karen McCarthy Brown of Drew University.[4] Most of us, if we made a movie of our lives, would have it circle back on itself after death and show the ways in which we leave pieces of ourselves in our children and family and work and communities. We remain embedded in the past. Our imagined future is part of our experienced past. With fundamentalists, however, the movie camera would stay with the individual after death and move into the misty heavens.

DEATH

The sources of the kind of trauma I've just described in the pre-Christian selves of fundamentalists I encountered, while as varied as human experience, centered on themes of real or symbolic death. These fundamentalists divided their lives into a period of psychological deadness, or virtual nonexistence, and a revival through faith into life, vitality, and hope. The religious dogma of rebirth requires such notions of death, or at least of non-self, in pre-Christian existence. You are *saved* from death, according to the theory, and salvation in the kingdom of God brings eternal life. All badness is overcome. Deborah, a forty-five-year-old single woman from Abiding Light, literalized the idea of being "born again" in her image of a "spiritual birth canal." Hearing fundamentalists' born-again testimonials surely fills one's own story of a spiritual journey with borrowed elements and evocative descriptive phrases. But the pain of death and deadness that creates trauma in the lives of fundamentalists is not fictive. Death and rebirth operate on a collective level among fundamentalists, and individual stories reveal such larger "shared themes," as Lifton calls them.[5] In the fundamentalist world these themes then get organized according to conventional religious rules.

Life before Jesus for fundamentalists is remembered as death-imbued, empty, lonely, depressed, and often meaningless. Sam, the executive director of Grady House, presented himself to the world as a secure member of the upper class he spiritually tended. He dressed in tailored and expensive suits with subdued ties and wore shoes with little tassels. The handkerchief in the outside pocket of his suit coat was carefully folded. Sam and his wife lived in the rent-free, elegant apartment on the top two floors of the Grady mansion; they also owned a house that his wife had inherited in a posh resort on Long Island. Since he both lived and worked in the mansion, Sam moved comfortably through its rooms with an air of ownership. I conducted my interview with him in one of the second-floor meeting rooms that was once a parlor. The walls were covered in a beautiful wallpaper. An ornate mantel along one wall held vases containing dry flowers. Along the wall to my right were two windows covered with fine, soft, embroidered drapes. In front of the couch was a glass coffee table with six Bibles on it, a small plastic glass of pencils, and three copies of a pamphlet, "The Christian and the Abundant Life."

On the surface Sam had led a happy, middle-class life into his early forties. He was successful in his advertising business and his children were moving through school without apparent distress. He lived in an expensive home in a good section of an eastern city. He was always under pressure in his business but seemed to be making the necessary moves upward at the right times. But in ways that this tense man ("I've always been a worrier," he said several times) only suggested, there was great distress underneath. His work itself was flat and without any ultimate purpose; working every waking moment to sell pet food was Sam's image of all that was wrong with his life before Christ. But as he talked it became clear that his sense of the fatuousness of advertising was only part of a much deeper life crisis in which he found himself. For one thing, he missed a crucial promotion at his agency, and the suggestion was made that he might well stagnate as an account executive and never become a partner. He also went through a personal tragedy: his depressed wife committed suicide. It was almost more than he could bear (and in fact he only mentioned it in passing, with pain on his face).

In the middle of this crisis, Sam attended an evangelical dinner for businessmen. Sam had always gone to church but never with much enthusiasm or committed belief. At the dinner he heard the testimony of a prominent lawyer from California who talked about the new sense of "peace and direction" he had found in his life after "establishing a relationship with Christ." Sam was impressed, but in his typically cautious way (that is perhaps also appropriate to his class position) he never experienced a moment of blinding truth when the scales fell from his eyes. He simply got closer to Jesus and an inner truth the longer he stayed with it. He started attending Bible study sessions and learned about a new approach to Christianity. "I always thought, you know, that you got [to heaven] through being a good person and keeping your nose clean and giving turkey to the poor at Thanksgiving. I don't mean that it's not important [to do those things], but that's not biblically how you get in a relationship with the Lord." He kept reading and talking to people, seeking guidance for his troubled soul. One night his new commitments came together: He prayed to Jesus alone in his bed, asking him into his life. Even then he hedged, for he added something like "So, let's see how this works out."

After that, however, things began to change more rapidly for Sam. His potential leadership was recognized, as well as, perhaps, his availability for a fundamental change in his life course. He began working with the national organization with which Grady House was affiliated and was soon selected to begin some evangelical work with businessmen. He found that he was good at talking with well-to-do business leaders whose spiritual quest paralleled his own. For nearly four years Sam continued in this middle level of commitment, reading, learning, and changing. He also found a wife whose beliefs were as deeply felt as his own and who warmly supported his changing life course. When asked to head up Grady House, Sam was ready to make the leap. He quit advertising to serve the Lord full-time, though he was refreshingly frank about the irony of living as such a privileged missionary.

Sam's dying self found perhaps the most graphic kind of expression in the actual death by suicide of his depressed wife. More conventional forms of Christianity, which Sam knew well, for he had been raised as an Episcopalian, seemed not to offer the kind of radical transformation he sought. To be born again, however, and get locked into the absolute security of biblical literalism, was more attractive. "I feel that the major question in life which is what happens at the end, has been answered for me," he said. And the answer came not through being good but just by believing. That was God's great gift to him. With the knowledge of eternal life, Sam could then live his life in a "triumphant way." He was secure on many levels. His daily life and work gained meaning. He became well known for his intelligent, witty, and compassionate lectures on the New Testament. His own empowerment made the staff at Grady House more confident. I would be hard pressed to name a person I encountered in my work who seemed to derive more personal rewards from his faith. Only the occasional haunted look in his eyes revealed the torment that still lingered in his soul.

The middle-aged Sam had his counterpart in the adolescent past of the Reverend Dean of Abiding Light. Reverend Dean had experienced a personal crisis that led him to leave the church in his early adolescence. The first topic Reverend Dean brought up about himself was how "rebellious" he had been, his use of drugs, and the difficulty he had then of accepting Jesus. He described a scene of going to the altar at twelve to accept Christ, but "rather than being led in any sort of a sinner's prayer or any sort of form of repentance, or encouraged to trust to Christ for salvation," he was simply signed up for a water baptism. He felt he should have been "better handled, instructed" by the adults in his congregation. He seems to have felt abandoned, ignored, as though the baptism he did in fact go through with was merely conventional and without meaning. Not long after his baptism, he stopped going to church, he said, though he later added a qualification that he attended fitfully for a couple of years before stopping altogether.

Reverend Dean recognized that his personal crisis occurred in the broad context of the cultural revolution of the late 1960s and early 1970s: "Maybe everybody feels this way about their high school years or their childhood but it doesn't seem to me that there has ever been a period of time quite like that one." His first experience with fundamentalism was when, just after graduation from high school, a born-again friend invited him to attend an Assemblies of God service. He was very moved. He found it "free flowing" with "a lot of love" and "expressive" in its forms of worship. The people were happy and sincere and "had a joy on their face that I had never seen anywhere." He felt none of the "blank stare" of the "cultish thing" but only a "genuine warmth that was very appealing." After he had left the church, he had been at odds with himself, adrift, psychologically fragmented. Drugs were probably an attempt to mask the pain of fragmentation but seemed only to worsen his feelings. When he found Jesus, on the other hand, he felt reintegrated.

The kind of inner deadness that Sam and Reverend Dean felt prior to conversion can have physical correlates in the sense of bodily deterioration. Arlene was raped at twelve, an alcoholic before she was twenty, and a crack addict less than a decade later. Isaac, an actor in his thirties from St. Paul's, was locked in a ferocious struggle with cocaine that left him always fearful of backsliding into his deadened life before being born again. For others this process of decay was more symbolic and its dread purely psychological. Monroe, a missionary to executives in his forties from Grady House, worried about being overweight and spent an extraordinary amount of time in my interviews with him musing about what he will look like during the millennium. According to the theory, the faithful are eternal by the time of the millennium, but there is no dogmatic position about what one will actually look like, or feel. It is left largely to individual fantasy to conjure up one's appearance after death is conquered. That conundrum provided Monroe with all kinds of opportunity to give indirect voice to his underlying fear of disintegration back into his pre-Christian self.

Family crises (sometimes hints of sexual abuse) also stirred a pervasive sense of guilt and despair in the imagination of fundamentalists. Deborah reported a happy childhood but in a dreamy-eyed tone that seemed based more in denial than fact. She described how her "compassion for others" came from her training and her "secure" position as the youngest child who was always pampered. She talked of all her siblings and how close she was to them as an adult, and how that more than made up for the loneliness she sometimes felt in being single. But there was something deeply sad about Deborah and she had a too-eager need to portray the difficulties in her life as not significant. The only clue to some of the deeper sources of trauma she may have suffered emerged in the second interview when, presumably feeling greater trust in the process, she revealed that her father had been an alcoholic. She immediately added that he wasn't "mean," but noted how painful it was when he started drinking again when she was eighteen (he had stopped when she was five).

The sense of deadness in the lives of fundamentalists before conversion seemed usually to be symbolic but could become directly suicidal. Larry was raised in a large working-class Catholic family in a midwestern city. He was always outgoing and articulate, hammed things up, and found that he was the actor in the family. Besides three other siblings, Larry had an identical twin brother with whom he had an almost mystical unity.[6] That brother also ended up in New York and seemed to have had the same spiritual strivings as Larry. The ethnic Polish community in which Larry grew up was surrounded by the worst of urban decay. "It was crumbling all around us," Larry said, "going black," while his neighborhood got increasingly narrow and constricted geographically; the image of constriction perhaps described his inner life as well. As a child Larry always attended church, but "mainly because it was something I had to do. There was really no true understanding," he said. In the parochial high school he attended, Larry was always at the top of his class and won a merit scholarship to a local college, as well as a starring position on the football team. He was in fact still fit and athletic looking when I knew him. The college he first attended, however, proved unsatisfactory. He was majoring in theater, and he found the program limited and unimaginative. Besides, he dreamed of bigger worlds.

He came to New York at twenty to make it as an actor. He felt it was then or never. He was an experimenter, a player of roles, yearning for cohesion. At first he found the New York acting scene quite enjoyable, including the "side benefits of booze, sex, and drugs." But he soon realized that he was not going to make it in New York as an actor. "There might have been some potential," he said of himself, "but I was just so tied up in knots of tension. Why, I was just scared, just so scared, no confidence." He felt the pressure of people expecting him to make it, and the unusual experience of failure for the first time in his life. In one of his first attempts to speak some lines before a small group of twenty people, "I couldn't stand up and speak a word without getting [nervous], it coming out so miserably." And he never really could relax. He could barely talk. "My voice would shake so miserably," he said in a way that made me feel the pain he must have been going through.

Things began to close in on Larry. He withdrew from the acting school he was attending and separated himself from the world of the theater. He was regularly drinking a six-pack of beer and then Scotch on a daily basis and fighting his erupting anger. His relationship with Ellen, whom he had known as a child and who was also acting in New York, was on the rocks because he was unfaithful to her. He felt trapped. He had no friends and no one to talk to about his problems. Even at his day job at a local retail clothing store he ended up in the stock room all by himself. He started planning his suicide. He intended to jump off the Queensboro Bridge. It has a walkway he had scouted out and knew was high enough to knock him out on impact with the water, after which he would surely drown. He planned his note for loved ones that would have explained how "I just didn't like the person I was becoming."

As his crisis intensified, Larry began to attend a fundamentalist Baptist church in Manhattan that was easily accessible from his work. He was not yet born again, but he found the service congenial. The church's abundantly varied programs gave him a lot of choices. He began to talk with people, hesitantly but genuinely. One Sunday afternoon, hanging around the church after the morning service, he watched a famous Christian movie about the end times, "A Thief in the Night," by Mark IV Productions (the New Testament has six references to Christ returning unawares as a thief; the one most frequently quoted by fundamentalists is 1 Thessalonians 5:2: "For yourselves know perfectly that the day of the Lord so cometh as a thief in the night"). After the interview, I rented the movie and watched it myself. It is set in the early 1970s, and portrays the agony and terror of those not raptured. Its dramatic appeal turns on not sleeping through the Lord's alarm. "A Thief in the Night" has proven the most durable of Christian videos over the years and has become a kind of underground Christian classic known to most fundamentalists.

Larry was transfixed by the film. He was instantly filled with the Spirit and accepted Jesus into his heart at that very moment. He has never strayed since. He got out of acting and into accounting, returned to school, and eventually married Ellen. He kept his faith cohesive by regular attendance at a church he and Ellen found but more importantly by their intense work at Grady House. He could not believe his luck. He kept waiting for the day when he would wake up to find things had changed for the worse. It was all too good to be true. Somewhat curiously, however, given the role of "A Thief in the Night" in his conversion experience, Larry had trouble talking about and was distinctly uninterested in issues of the end times. "I'm not future oriented," he said. He even claimed to have no fear at all of death, individual or collective. With a self-satisfied grin on his face, one that contradicted his words, he even said he had never feared death as a child. Once his grandmother died but it was "no big deal" for him. He said he "just doesn't care about such issues" as death, the return of Jesus, or tribulation. He immediately added, playing student to me as professor, that he wanted to learn more about these issues and planned to take a Bible course on Revelation before too long. But that was an afterthought. In fact, the end times did not play in Larry's head. It seemed he was too young, now too full of his own promise in business, too happy with the relief at being saved from the icy waters of the East River and saved again by his faith in Jesus.

Death of the self for fundamentalists, however, is more than a personal experience. The world is also dying. The personal and collective become mirrors of mutual despair. It is a profoundly painful existential dilemma. Cynthia, a Baptist in her late thirties from St. Paul's, grew up in a Christian home with parents she idealized. She accepted Jesus at eleven. She said that actually she was aware of her need for the four or five years before that. Every night the family prayed together and the parents read Bible stories to the kids. She thought constantly of God. "And so when I lay in my bed at night there would be times that I would be really fearful and I know now that it was the Spirit of God that was convicting me and showing me my need." Cynthia's dread of death, of "not knowing my destiny," had, as well, a connection to fears of ultimate human endings. She felt drawn to Jesus as a way out of these fears, of finding meaning. She had a fear of being "eternally lost" and of "eternal death, a sense of dying never ending." "It's torment," she said directly.

What was existential for Cynthia was more explicitly communal for Reverend Dean. For the most part this appealing minister based his motivation for conversion in personal issues of vitality and rebirth. But in a subtle way Reverend Dean felt deeply ultimate issues of human survival. A month before his conversion he chanced on a magazine with articles by leading end time commentators like Hal Lindsey. The message at first terrified him—he "had some thoughts about suicide" which could have been in part a reaction to his mother's unspecified sickness that year—but it also opened him up for conversion. Lindsey links the symbolic end time rhetoric in the book of Revelation with the more immediate political world of the early 1970s, the cold war, and the threat of nuclear annihilation. His work makes the metaphorical concrete. The end could be imagined. Those images of collective death, working together in the various dimensions of his personal crisis, finally brought Reverend Dean to his knees. It was an existential crisis. He was then ready for the full impact of the Pentecostal community into which he happened to be thrown a month later. He was saved and got his life together and has served in the church ever since.

Nigel, in turn, stressed that the actual experience of death was something he, like any sane person, feared. But death itself will be transcended in his mind through the return of Jesus, he said. And that could happen tomorrow, or anytime, he added, "through the advent of my death," a phrasing that suggests a linking of himself with God. Since the return of Jesus marks the end of human history, its image freed Nigel from death in quite concrete ways. "That was really the motivation behind my getting serious with God," he noted. Not only because he felt a "deep sense of emptiness" in his life, "but knowing that, you know, Christ is coming back at some point and I don't want to stand before him and say, you know, I'm sorry about this and I'm sorry about that, you know. I wanna stand before him having, at least to the best of my ability, lived the life that he would want me to have lived." Conversion united the separate strands of Nigel's self into a meaningful cohesive whole.

The broken narrative is the defining characteristic, spiritually and emotionally, for fundamentalists. The past is bad and worthless, even tainted with death. One yearns for transformation. The individual believer struggles with personal sin, a struggle expressed collectively as a cosmic battle between the forces of good and evil. The converted claim to find salvation from their suffering in the born-again experience. But radical divisions in the self are grounded in trauma, which can operate in personal and idiosyncratic ways but can also be based in collective experience. The born-again experience, which is an attempt to heal the broken narrative, is also a direct religious response to our common traumas.

2

ULTIMATE
THREATS

████████████

MARY. Mary was a thirty-two-year-old white woman who had lived in New York City for a little over a decade at the time of my interviews with her. She had a beautiful singing voice and was the lead singer in the tiny Abiding Light choir. Mary stood erect on the podium as she lifted her hands in supplication and lustily praised Jesus in song. She often threw back her tousled blonde hair when she was carried away by the Spirit. Sometimes her dress also got thrown in disarray from her vigorous movements both in song and prayer. No one sang louder or prayed harder than Mary.

Mary seemed frantic to straighten out the narrative sequence of end time things, to clarify the meaning and inner logic of human history. The thought of Jesus' return, for example, reminded her of the signs of his second coming, which in turn means the end of human folly, sin, pain, and death itself. If you can read scripture with the

Holy Spirit in you, she said, you would see not just the famines, the wars and rumors of wars, and the earthquakes—those specific "signs" mentioned in Matthew 24:6–7—but also the "change in human nature that's occurring." As she said in a (somewhat confused) torrent of thoughts: "Human nature in the twentieth century has taken on a distinctly more with existentialism on downwards, there's been a plunge . . . you know, and also, it seems, that man, as an animal, has more to his plus than ever before, but his decided minus, his atrocities, man-to-man, are blossoming." And she continued: "Men will be lovers of themselves, boasters, they will be high minded, they will be traitorous, the love of many will grow cold, they will be disobedient to parents."

"In this world," Mary lamented, "you will have tribulation," a thought that led her to identify another sign, namely that people are so full of despair and fear that they are flocking into psychiatry and psychology. "If this country gets invaded, we'd lose because all the man force is lying on a couch somewhere being counseled." We have lost our resolve. We are all "into ourselves." If we had to call up recruits they would all be "wimps." Maybe there's a "fighting tiger" hidden deep inside the American soul, but she doubted it. The sins of modern culture abounded in Mary's mind as further signs. "In America we are just fat cats." It's just like in ancient Greece and Rome, where they had pedophilia, homosexuality, an advanced state of art and culture, and "vomitoriums." Her idiosyncratic sequence of horrors reflected her own concerns, for she added: "I have a weight problem, I know." Man is not magnificent, she said. Just go take the subway at 42nd Street and watch people claw each other getting onto the train. "That's really a good sign. You go and examine people at rush hour." They're even eating children in California, she said in an extraordinary associative leap. "Sacrifices . . . we look forward to the end."

These end times will be excruciatingly violent in Mary's scheme of things; she never lost sight of the central role of the violence that will be necessary to overthrow human history and move into God's redemptive time. On all issues Mary spoke with authority, for knowledge of scripture and prophecy gave her more than a hint of divine intention. She was at one with God's knowledge and grand plan. Yet her very psychological closeness to God created a dilemma for Mary: she tended to shape God in her own uncertain image. Mary thus seemed to doubt whether God actually knew what he was up to. He was anxious about the onrush of events, unhappy with human evil and the course of history, but somewhat confused about what to do and when to do it. Even his knowledge of the future was not much greater than Mary's. He knew "the end of things from the beginning" and had "foreknowledge," and yet, though he would have peace, he seemed unable to prevent imminent nuclear destruction.

Nuclear threat worked in Mary's imagination in complicated ways. Her Christian fundamentalist ideology served to absorb and contain the terrors of ultimate destruction that she had so actively let into her thinking. A clue to this arcane connection lay in the way she contradicted her end time story as her feelings about nuclear threat changed in different interviews. That threat first emerged early on in my first conversation with her. She then seemed quite clear about the certainty of nuclear war. As one of the "signs" of the approaching end times, Mary mentioned "war materials" that now make it possible for us to "annihilate" ourselves. I asked her about her choice of verbs, and she said spontaneously that she expected World War III and a nuclear holocaust. "I definitely believe it," she said. "I believe it with all my heart." For one thing, a depression greater than that of the 1930s is threatened (which had some kind of special meaning for her), and "I see a lot of baby boys born, Chuck, I see baby boys being plopped out all over the place."

Astounded, I put the logic of her thought into more general terms: "You think," in other words, that "the Lord is bringing more boys [into the world] because there's going to be a war?" She said, "Absolutely," and continued, "There's going to be a great fight." Humans are not going to push the button and blow up the world, but we will come close to it. "I believe there will be contained nuclear warfare." "There are going to be a number of nuclear wars," she said, though the "big one" at Armageddon is not necessarily going to be nuclear. It will be when Jesus will finally "triumph over evil," and it will be violent in ways we cannot even conceive. As reborn Christians we are "aliens in the scripture," said Mary in her expressive way. We are not of this world, only in it. We are born "from above" in the "Spirit of God." Our bodies will either "rot in the ground" or "get blown up." But we also have spirits. And these are eternal, even there now, "seated in heavenly places." We already have "conversations that are in heaven."

Mary's apocalyptic language was generally laced with nuclear allusions. She referred once, for example, to Ezekiel's prophecies of "flesh coming off bone, eye sockets—eyes dissolving in the eye socket, and this sort of thing—and you look at a nuclear poisoning victim, someone who has been through a—even Chernobyl—you know if you were standing nearby, see what you get in a nuclear warfare." This vivid description of the effects of nuclear poisoning in a text several thousand years old evoked for Mary the return of Jesus in prophecy. "You see the Lord's return as it is prophesied," she said. "He will return to Mount Olive [in present-day Israel]," which will also be the site of the "great and mighty" battle against Antichrist. And the "primary catalyst" for all these developments, she continued, leaning forward earnestly, is oil. It complicates everything in relation to Israel and centers world tensions on the Middle East. Russia has a "keen clear eye on this whole Persian Gulf area." It is a "hotbed of dissension and unrest" and has been that way for centuries. The battle is for water, for land, and for oil. All the forces are going to "converge" there, because we are depleting, "you know, we just deplete."

One could say Mary's end time rhetoric was in a nuclear key. In one tumult of associations about the end times, she noted, evoking Ezekiel 22:20–22 and 2 Peter 3:10, that the Lord will "destroy this world and heaven by fire, melt it down, and there will arise a new city, the new Jerusalem." At another time she noted that there have been endings of civilizations but not yet an "ultimate, final end." On the other hand, she added astutely, "there has never been an atomic age." We live in a hard time when "little winds of war start whispering" (her own version of Matthew 24:6) and small conflicts become big ones and we risk blowing up the whole world. In general, Mary's mind turned on "huge battles" and "nuclear holocaust that's going to blast off everybody." Such thoughts vividly occupied her imagination. Her prophetic and redemptive vision was nuclearized. There is going to be "suffering," she said typically, "suffering, and many calamities."

There was, however, no simple way that nuclear violence intersected with Mary's sense of the future revelation of God's purpose. Without doubt she had fully taken in the violence of nuclear threat and given it a place in her end time story. In her first pass at these issues, Mary argued that some kind of nuclear conflict is inevitable and will mark the process of transition out of human history and into God's time. That battle at Armageddon will, however, be a "showdown in the OK Corral in Israel," violent in ways that we cannot even comprehend. Nuclear war, in other words, begins the process of God's final revelation but cannot conclude it. Mary made it clear that God needs to preserve the earth for Jesus to rule over during the millennium; he cannot allow a complete holocaust. She was clearly relieved when she sorted all this out, connecting Antichrist and the end of human history with limited nuclear war, and preserving the final battle for God's mysterious ways. Things seemed in order, and she was calm.

And yet during her second interview, Mary contradicted her earlier account of the certainty of nuclear war. In discussing Antichrist then, for example, she noted that part of his deception of the world in his self-presentation as a man of peace will be that he will purposely avert World War III and a nuclear holocaust. She even easily changed her mind about God's destructive attitude toward humanity at one point. She described God's fury at the way man (or subtextually, the Jews) broke his promises and allowed Jesus to endure "untold sufferings." Then why not just wipe out humanity? she asked herself. It is because "God restrains himself." He is willing to wait for a faithful people who will worship him. He has always been seeking that, "from the time he taught Adam to worship in the Garden."

Psychologically, this contradiction and conflict are part of the same inner thought process. For Mary, the image of nuclear destruction both demands a central place in her end time story as a way of taming it, and yet is so terrifying that it cannot stay put. Nuclear images, which "fit" the destructive images of the book of Revelation so accurately, feed apocalyptic musings. But the anxiety caused by these death-related imaginings can easily force a reworking of the end time story to calm fears. Mary's future vision, which is full of nuclear imagery, thus alternated between normalizing nuclear threat (a limited nuclear war will occur but God's violence at Armageddon will be greater and will not destroy the earth for Jesus) and reworking her idea of Antichrist to take out nuclear war altogether from her end time story. In her decidedly human contradiction lay the deepest level of a psychological attempt to bring together apocalyptic faith and an awareness of nuclear threat.

I asked if she was afraid of all the horrible things that are to happen in the end times. She said she feared only for all those who will suffer and die. For herself she feared nothing. She would be delighted at being a martyr and having her hands sawed off. ("You know, the gift of martyrdom" to which she was drawn: "Peter, you know, he blundered, he made dreadful mistakes, he put his foot in his mouth all the time, but after the baptism in the Holy Spirit he was able to get up and preach and then go and get crucified upside downwards for the Lord and [not] deny him then.") Mary's faith made her confident that she would reign supreme with Jesus. She felt she had been persecuted some for her faith and therefore knew what it was all about, even though she had not shed any blood. But she stood prepared: "In the end times there are going to be many persecuted for his name."

Mary was raised in Georgia as a Baptist. Her mother was the apparent source of strength in the family, and Mary's own religiosity seemed to connect her to her mother in special ways. As a strictly observant Baptist, the mother never washed clothes, worked, or allowed Mary to play in any way on Sundays. Mary expressed some ambivalence about the fact that she was never taken to the beach or the movies on Sundays but then immediately praised the way the sabbath was observed in her family.

Mary's father was an alcoholic. It clearly pained Mary to talk about this fact of her family life, and it only emerged in the context of relating how he was not saved and required her constant prayers. Immediately after saying it, however, she rattled off his positive aspects ("He's the most intelligent man I ever met"; "He's the funniest man I know"; and "He says some shrewd things"). It seemed Mary did not want to acknowledge her anger or disappointment in him, though these found reluctant expression. After she said he was not a Christian, I asked her if that bothered her. She said no, but a minute or so later, in another context, indicated that "he doesn't believe like I do." Her father was not even a "nominal Christian" but a complete heathen. But she had hope for him. She was convinced he would be reached, "as difficult and downtrodden as he is." We can be certain of that, she said, an idea that switched on her believing self. "He [God] knows us by name. He knows the hairs on our head," she said, alluding to Matthew 10:30. "He knows. He's intimately acquainted with the way, your fabric, your emotional framework, and he will reach that."

Mary's early life seemed full of terrors. Her feelings about her father and her ambivalent identification with her mother filled her life with stress. From an early age she was full of apocalyptic dread that of course drew energy from her southern Baptist environment and which she connected with events in the world. She related, for example, feeling certain the world would end during the Cuban missile crisis and recalled hiding under her grandmother's dining room table at age six as protection against the bombs raining in from ninety miles off the coast of Florida. "I thought we were going to get bombed. Cuba's not far away. It's right off Florida. You know, this is it. This is the end. I was terrified."

During her adolescence, Mary fell away from the church in what she described as a period of "self-indulgence" and "fascination with herself" as she discovered her abilities as a singer. She became a "cynic." She was ambitious, self-absorbed, and a "Sunday School drop-out." In fact she had quite a remarkable mezzo-soprano voice that ranged widely and could subtly explore nuances of musical expression. She performed often in local theater and became well known regionally. She aspired to an opera career; it is indeed easy to imagine her as a blonde diva, wrapped in purple robes, singing her swansong as she lay dying in some nineteenth-century Italian opera. From her perspective now, however, the discovery of her voice brought a large degree of narcissistic absorption that took her away from God. The classic definition of sin for believing Christians is just such a separation. Mary felt it keenly, as she drew away from religion and the oppressive closeness of her parents, even though she never entirely (and certainly never formally) left the church. But in such a strict Baptist world that defined boundaries so narrowly Mary pushed up against the limits of what was possible. Mary's mother fought vigorously against her daughter's move away from faith. When Mary told her mother at thirteen that she didn't believe in the Noah and the Ark story, the mother "fell on the floor and screamed and cried before Sunday dinner and said, 'I created an atheist.'"

Singing brought Mary to New York and the Juilliard School, a long way from west Georgia. Juilliard is a part of the Kennedy Center for the Performing Arts and is widely recognized as probably the best conservatory of music in the country. Singers come there to study from all over the world. It is a highly competitive and decidedly secular world, very much a part of the frantic art scene in New York. During her training things seemed to go well for Mary and she showed promise. She even got "some debuts and some works with some orchestras and things." She dreamed reasonably of getting one of the 125 or so jobs in opera in the city upon her graduation, even though she realized New York has at least five thousand good singers. She didn't make it.

Mary's failure to make it as an opera singer caused the great trauma in her life. Everything she had aspired to for over a decade was a failure. Life seemed worthless, and she was completely adrift. "God was taking me out in the desert and tumbling me and humbling me," she said. Without a career she also had no means of support, and soon fell into working as a maid. She ended up "cleaning toilets for millionaires on the Upper East Side" to survive. She wasn't singing, she had no career, she was far from home and family, she was working at humiliating tasks just to eat, and she was alone and alienated in a great big, terrifying city.

She resolved that crisis in her life when she was reborn and became a "follower of Jesus" in the October following her June graduation from Juilliard. The Holy Spirit "buckled" her by the "scruff of the neck" and brought her the "blessing" of her life. It was a blinding moment of truth for her. That was when she found Abiding Light, her sacred home from which she has not since strayed. She kept free

of what she called the "New York Christian revolving door thing."
During the week (besides the Tuesday evening prayer service at her
church) she also attended and sang in the choir of the "Jews for Jesus" ministry; participated in the "Arabs for Jesus" at times; and
was the pianist of a small church on Sunday morning.

Her dream was to become a full-time minister. She already held a
"Christian Women's Permit." She was not certain she wanted her
own congregation but was sure that she wanted to "itinerate as an
evangelist." She had already visited seven countries and she went
every year to the United Kingdom with the "Billy Graham Mission
England." She had, she said, a "deep burden on my heart for this
particular country." What drew her to England is that it has had a
"massive, culture-transforming revival" every century for eight
hundred years—except in the twentieth century. This absence
weighs "heavy" on Billy Graham's heart; he's been leading revivals
in England for some thirty years and has not seen a change. Mary
felt chosen to join in his efforts there.

There was an important continuity of self in the reborn Mary.
Singing still defined her life. She had to give up dreams of opera but
found abundant opportunity for creative self-expression and even
performance in the church and in "religious gigs" in the city, as well
as some summer stock throughout New England. Even in the millionaires' homes where she worked her new centeredness brought
her back to familiar territory: she stopped cleaning toilets and became a kind of nanny and piano teacher for the children of several
families.

Mary's subjective sense of change at her religious rebirth, on the
other hand, was quite dramatic. She contrasted her Christian status
as a "nominal adherent to a congregation" before being reborn with
becoming a "real Christian" afterward, which related to the whole
issue of being "saved." She connected what might be called her sense
of an "authentic self" with her childhood innocence. What she was
doing today, she said, was like what she did between three and five,
when she was a "very pure child" and "loved singing, playing the
piano, doing plays." It was as though, in finding Jesus, she had found
herself as she once was, a self she had lost in her ambitions to become

an opera star but one that continued to exist and, with God's help, could be expressed.

Mary's shifting from bad to good selves with her conversion and a rediscovery of something authentic in her earliest experience could not always hold off the demons. She let slip once that, since her conversion, "I'm a much worse person." She then explained that her increased awareness of the majesty of Jesus made her more conscious of her own insignificance, which seemed to express a basic self-loathing. After a lengthy discussion of the sins of modern life and the signs of the end everywhere, for example, she noted how humans are depraved. "I don't believe there is one good thing in me," she said. Then she told a story that probably has elements of fantasy in it and may have served her as an improvised parable. She was once acting in a play, she said, and, as a part of her role, she wore a cheap ring that she didn't bother to take off between performances. Evidently, her skin reacts powerfully to the chemicals in such metals. One day she was ironing and smelled something awful. Her first thought was "good grief, no deodorant today." It seemed to affect the whole apartment. She decided to go wash, and while scrubbing her hands accidentally loosened her ring. In horror (but for some reason without any pain) she saw that her flesh under where the ring had been was literally rotting away. The smell had been from her decaying body.

Mary drew a religious message from the story: "Our bodies decay while the spirit lives on." But the image that stayed with her was that her body was worthless and going to rot. "You, me, even Joan Collins, will all rot." This body is going to stink. Our righteousness is but "filthy rags." We bring nothing to our redemption (which she repeated). And yet in that salvation lay her hope for renewal and eternal life, which for her moved with apocalyptic urgency. It is "imminent, really imminent," though "we might have one hundred fifty or two hundred more [years]." Who knows or really cares, she asked rather falsely, for in fact she cared a great deal. But, like other fundamentalists I talked to, she covered her predictions of immediacy in order not to seem to be speaking for God. "He knows all generations," she said. He knows when to return. And he is "always on time." Whenever it is "right" he will return. Until then we only "oc-cupy" and do what he told us to do by going into the world to preach his word.

Still: "Not a day goes by that I don't think about it [the return of Jesus]," she said, which suggested the separateness of what might be called her end time self, a split-off part of her being that is grounded in the Christian tradition. This split-off part of herself was projected forward into her image of the millennium, which was not a place with "clouds, harps necessarily, and angels with big floppy wings." It was instead a city for those "redeemed people of God, where the whole light of the place is the light of Jesus Christ." If you receive his gift, if the Holy Spirit comes and dwells within you, then you have the promise of millennial renewal and eternal life. But if you reject that gift, she said ominously, you go where the "worm never dies."

NUCLEAR AND ENVIRONMENTAL THREATS

Many of my fundamentalist interviews were conducted in the wan-ing years of the cold war, which partly explains the emphasis in them on images of nuclear threat, something Daniel Yankelovich (using a different method) emphasized in 1984 was firmly rooted in the cul-ture.[1] With many people I talked with, however, I also uncovered a subtle shift in the late 1980s from nuclear to environmental con-cerns.[2] This shift suggests to me that fundamentalists are oriented to collective death, which they describe in terms of their theology and their specific personal concerns. Their beliefs, in part, neutralize the threat. In their groping attempt to relate their beliefs to ultimate dangers, they are at least dealing with authentic issues—unlike most of our culture, which foolishly acts as though the end of the cold war has wiped out nuclear threat, even though tens of thousands of war-heads remain in the hands of a widening circle of unsavory charac-ters and even though nuclear power (including the waste it gener-ates) continues to present the greatest of all environmental threats. To end history slowly, choking from pollution or dying early from unnatural cancers, poses threats of the same kind of absurd death as nuclear war. Thus, nuclear issues in my interviews are only seem-ingly dated; the psychological processes and spiritual beliefs that underlie Mary's nuclear vision remain as relevant now as they were six years ago. Were I to conduct interviews today, though, I believe environmental threat would probably occupy the imagination of fundamentalists with greater salience, though in fact both nuclear and environmental threats are closely related images of ultimate destruction, and in the case of nuclear power (Chernobyl) they become one and the same.

The range of imagery and the depth of fear I encountered about ultimate destruction, particularly by nuclear weapons, was quite remarkable. Mary, although unusually evocative, was hardly exceptional in this regard. For example, Reverend Dean noted that "The potential [for destruction exists] . . . *more now than ever*." The end is imminent, the "time is ripe." Reverend Lester, the mid-thirties pastor of St. Paul's, said: "It could happen anytime, everything is in place. . . . All the prophecies are fulfilled for this to happen. . . . We have nuclear weapons." And: "Satan is coming with the missiles," as he said in one sermon. The Reverend Charles of Calvary Church linked his nuclear themes to contemporary developments in the Middle East: "Now we've got a situation and it's a key thing to watch, what's happening in the Middle East. Those Palestinians are not about to stop throwing rocks and the Israelis are not about to stop shooting them down. . . . And what they say is the worst kept secret, that Israel has the bomb. . . . It could be the fuse[3] that lights the whole thing." The specter of nuclear war cast a dark shadow. Such war seemed all but inevitable. "I don't think there's any stopping it," said Isaac, from Abiding Light. "Look around you. There are women who kill babies when they think the baby is the devil. We kill young people because there are too many people on this earth." Besides, he continued, nuclear war is close at hand. It "almost happened" several times during Reagan's years, Isaac added darkly. The nuclear concerns of fundamentalists were diverse and often touched issues more central to the post–cold war era. Nigel located his imaginings primarily in terms of proliferation: "I'm sure that some third-world country is going to let one loose somewhere."

Much of the Bible, as they saw it, confirmed a sense of an imminent nuclear end. Reverend Lester, for example, in the middle of an interview, noted that "the Bible is explicit about bombs," as he reached for his well-worn book and quoted 2 Peter 3:10: "The heavens shall pass away with a great noise, and the elements shall melt with fervent heat, the earth also and the works that are therein shall be burned up." It's talking here about the "scientific word," he said. "We are talking about hydrogen bombs. We are talking about atomic bombs, nuclear warheads." Ordinary believers as well found the same confirmation of their nuclear imaginings in the Bible. Isaac specifically connected the discussion in Revelation about the "sores on a man's body" and the "skin coming off" with radiation sickness. "Even Carl Sagan," he said, "talks about the earth burning up and the ashes rising to form a shadow over the earth. That's in Revelation." Sam added that "the Bible talks about heat and fire . . . [which] clearly fits in with our capacity to blow ourselves up nuclearly." Wilma nervously declared, "I believe [nuclear weapons] are part of the end time scenario. . . . He said it won't be by water, it will be fire and I believe that's going to happen." The Bible doesn't say it's going to be a nuclear war, she added, but it's "going to burn." It "could be a bomb, because the Bible says the earth shall burn with fire. Could be a bomb."

The end time process, based as it is in apocalyptic texts, makes special sense in terms of nuclear destruction. The book of Revelation reads for many fundamentalists as a handbook of nuclear themes. The book's prophecy of doom ends in a great judgment (Chapter 20) that finally separates out good from evil and rewards believers with a secure place in heaven. The logic of the theology, therefore, makes destruction the necessary precursor to salvation. But destruction has to be justified. Here the theory turns to human sin and our evil ways. The signs are everywhere, though once again they are often nuclearized. For example, "these weapons are being advanced so fast," Deborah said, "we're more or less going down the road of destruction." Otto even suggested that "the bomb has caused an acceleration of all that's going on." Everything seems to be happening at once in his troubled mind, and the creation of the bomb lies at the center of the chaos. "All these things are just coming together and getting worse."

Fantasies about Antichrist, as well, spark thoughts about world government and nuclear destruction, an association that runs throughout popular fundamentalist texts. "The Bible speaks of one world government at the time of his [Jesus] coming back and I think the world is heading toward that," said Otto. "That may be a very important sign. We're getting to the place where people are saying, 'Well, we need just one person in control of everything.' So we eliminate the possibility of nuclear war, [have] equal food distribution, these things." The fear of nuclear war, in other words, makes "people" turn to one strong ruler who staves off nuclear conflict but also uses his power to take control of everything else, including "food distribution." Such world government, by centralizing everything, ends up creating something far worse, a monster who can then manipulate the end time events. In Otto's vision: "First you centralize the world, the technology and the government and that's what allows the Antichrist."

It is, of course, inherent human evil—aided in obscure ways by the devil working in history—that both creates nuclear weapons and threatens their use. Destruction results from our "increased wickedness," said Isaac. "Man has incredible evil in him," he continued. "We all do. And if the Christians are gone, if the people who keep telling the world about the value of man are gone, then I'm afraid to see the evil that will be unleashed [*he bangs the table*]. . . . Man will just rise up and destroy everything. For the first time in history we have the ability to destroy ourselves." Nuclear war cannot be prevented. The signs of it and of the end in general are much too pervasive. Furthermore, the corruption and moral deadness of human society works for evil and destructive purposes in the world. Frank mused, weaving nuclear weapons into the message in Revelation 21:1: "At some point there will be a new heaven and earth . . . the old heaven and earth just passing away completely. . . . Nuclear war, to a certain extent we can picture it happening. There are real possibilities." As Wilma said, in her quietly dramatic tone: "Burning will cleanse the earth."

Chernobyl, in turn, was the environmental image of nuclear power gone awry, the disastrous and unsuccessful attempt to harness the knowledge of the atom. Among fundamentalists, though important, it was less often evoked on its own terms than as part of an overall image of environmental destruction. As Isaac astutely put it: "I don't even know if God needs nuclear weapons, but we do see a period in the history right now that man can destroy himself, he can destroy a third of the earth, he can destroy." Isaac's third part of destruction was an obscure reference to the successive waves of violence that unfold in Revelation in what might be termed a "biblical genocide."[4] Otto had a haunting sense of pressing toward the Apocalypse, which he was sure will bring worldwide death and destruction. He calculated precisely the rolling waves of death in Revelation. "It [the Bible] talks about one place where He sends out judgment over one quarter of the earth to kill. That means to kill one quarter of the earth. At another place it talks about . . . killing over one third of the earth, so if you take one quarter, you have three quarters left, and if you take one third of three quarters you have half the population gone." I asked him how the idea of all those people dying made him feel. He answered calmly: "Concerned, I guess, in a way, and yet, at times, I think the way the scripture points, brings it out, is that when it happens, it will be a judgment that is just." Those who refuse to accept Jesus into their hearts, in other words, shall justly die. Nearly everyone on the earth has had an opportunity to know Christ; even in grass huts, Otto said, there are portable TVs on which they can watch Billy Graham or Jimmy Swaggart. Everyone has the chance to believe. "Then it's up to them," he said darkly, "whether they accept or not."

Otto's embrace of end time violence, as it was with most fundamentalists I met, had an oddly dissociated quality. He was personally a gentle man, yet he nourished in his mind a stirring cauldron of images of end time destruction. After my first interview with him in which he laid out the violence of the end justified by human sin and disbelief, Otto told me a touching story of the crib death of one of his children. It was just after he was out of Bible school and he had a milk route. His wife thought for once she was getting a chance to sleep in. The baby was nineteen days old. By the time she found the baby it was long since dead and was already turning blue. He said that only now, some twenty years later, can he tell the story without emotion, and for years it affected his and his wife's ability to sleep easily without constantly checking the other children. This same man can have God wipe out 2.5 billion people without blinking an eye because they are not saved.

But even Otto did not think God would let humans destroy the earth in a nuclear holocaust. "I really don't think man's going to blow this world up," he said. "Because the scriptures speak of God judging it. And I feel there has to be something for God to judge [*he laughed*], so I don't see how . . . I really don't . . . the book of Genesis talks about God judging Sodom and Gomorrah. He didn't need a nuclear bomb to pour out fire and brimstone on Sodom and Gomorrah." Mary also moved easily back and forth between nuclear and environmental imagery of destruction. No one had more nuclear themes in their end time story. But even she believed that the battle of Armageddon between the forces of good and evil at the end of the period of tribulation would be somehow *even worse* than nuclear war.

In fact, most fundamentalists show considerable equivocation about the end, mixing a very human kind of hope that the world will not self-destruct with a conviction that the end is prophetically assured. In this respect they sometimes suggested that God would prevent the end of the world. A kernel of this idea lies in Isaac's statement that "I don't even know if God needs nuclear weapons." Similarly, Nigel saw nuclear weapons as superfluous to God's plan: "If he wanted to destroy this earth, he could do it in a second. He doesn't need nuclear arms. . . . He created it all, he could certainly destroy it all." Otto commented: "He could use nuclear bombs, no question, but I don't think he needs that." Reverend Dean also cautioned against dwelling on the nuclear end time scenario: "When you emphasize to what extent nuclear activities take place, that's strictly speculation." Yet he implied that humans can do little to alter the end time course when he said: "Again God's plan is going to be perfected regardless of what weaponry man may have."

Some people expressed the hope that God would step in to prevent complete destruction. Reverend Dean stated: "Well, I don't think the planet is going to be annihilated because God, he made it, he'll take care of it." Frank suggested that "when things get to the point where it is utterly and completely hopeless, at least as far as the Bible teaches, that's when Jesus returns . . . and intervenes at what seems like the moment of utter despair for the planet." Yet, as he also admitted, "It's hard in our natural understanding to picture God coming down out of the sky, invading, and stopping the ultimate war. Some people would laugh at that, you know." Deborah echoed this idea: "He knows what our potential is to destroy ourselves and I think even with all these nuclear plants and everything else . . . you know, exposure to radiation and all that . . . he realizes . . . he sees everything, but things we don't even think about he can see the danger. . . . I think that's why he'll come back soon. . . . He wants to curtail that. . . . We're going to destroy ourselves if God doesn't escalate the time," she said.

All these equivocating images of nuclear and other related forms of violence are part of a pervasive ambivalence on the part of fundamentalists toward end time violence. It is simply not the case that they actively want nuclear war, suffering, and widespread death to bring Jesus back sooner, which one might infer from the logic of their theology. I find reports from other researchers regarding fundamentalists' violent wishes highly suspect.[5] They seem, instead, to have an anticipation of destruction, but it is a kind of half-wish from which, once expressed, they quickly back off. The closest anyone in my study came to expressing a direct (but still qualified) desire for a nuclear war to hasten the return of Jesus was Reverend Lester: "So I'm kinda looking forward to all this stuff [nuclear destruction], to the whole thing because once the rapture takes place the church is glorified." But most fundamentalists responded, when asked, as Wilma did: "No, I don't look forward to the end. I want to live, don't you? I love life. I always thank God for life."

There was, however, a good deal of confusion about the place of nuclear violence in their end time musings. "I don't think it scares people anymore, you know," said Deborah in an ambivalent tone. "Weapons are being advanced so fast it's almost like you become hardened. Like if it's going to happen, it's going to happen. What can you do about it by worrying about it? Maybe people don't think about that, but in the papers now, how can you not." And Sam replied, when asked whether he was frightened by nuclear destruction: "Not a great deal . . . uh . . . you know obviously, [I'm] going to go in twenty or thirty or forty or whatever number of years. . . . And I think that the world is going to end at some point. I would rather have it later than sooner, for my [*nervous laughter*] for the sake of my children and now one grandchild, but I don't stay awake at night or anything like that, worried and concerned about, you know, the world being blown up. It might be a lot quicker way to go than cancer, but [*and he laughs again*] . . ."

Having let in the terror, even if partial and numbed, my respondents struggled constantly with issues of efficacy. How should one live in the end times? How does one prepare? What obligations exist toward one's fellow humans? What difference does life make? For many, especially white fundamentalists, a political quietism prevailed, except on selected issues that they would designate "spiritual," like abortion, pornography, and prayer in the schools. On the whole, one does not generally associate social action with fundamentalists, though some are involved intermittently in politics (the 1992 Republican National Convention, for example). An important exception, as we will see in a later chapter, was Reverend Charles, who found a special kind of hope in these end times. For him the sense of being on the brink was enormously vitalizing. It gave life a sense of permanent urgency, and the chance of "reaping an end time harvest." He should, perhaps, have been in a state of despair and hopelessness. In fact, exactly the opposite was true. "This is the time to get *involved*," he said with enthusiasm.

But for most fundamentalists nuclear threat had a deadening effect, even if a certain excitement was also mixed with the fear. Reverend Dean believed the effects of nuclear threat have been to wipe out a sense of future. "We have a generation of young people," he said, "that for the first time feel that they don't have a future." The young don't think they will grow up to marry and have children, and "in many cases" they don't even think "they'll live through high school." It was a grim image.

Frank, from St. Paul's, likewise related the pain of living with nuclear threat. He talked of his childhood and how wrenching it had been when both his paternal grandfather and maternal grandmother died within a few weeks of each other when he was fifteen. Both had been vital in his life, almost more important than his parents. His grandfather had been a spiritual model. And his "Nana" had cared for him for many years after school because his mother worked. Oddly, though, when Frank talked of his grandparents and their almost simultaneous deaths, he seemed impatient to get on to other topics: "I don't know where this is really going in terms of the past, but that's [all there is]," he said, letting his sentence trail off. He also had a friend who had been killed, though he was just as numb to that.

The death that really haunted Frank, a man of unusually intense spiritual longings, was collective death. "What is it that so fascinates me about atomic bombs?" he asked himself. "I mean, even when I was a kid, I would go to the library and look at the pictures and read the stories about it. And it was horrible. It was horrible . . . there's something so powerful about it that it just evokes fear and awe." It seemed Frank's search in the library followed his first encounter with nuclear issues, which was some unit in fourth or fifth grade dealing with Hiroshima and Nagasaki. Somehow that touched a powerful chord in him. Even today, when he sees a clip of something nuclear on TV, it has a huge effect on him.

Yet for all the images of nuclear and environmental violence that are integral to the end time story, for all the death and destruction during the period of tribulation that marks the end of human history, fundamentalists still grapple with ways to soften the story, even to the point of contradiction, and force their narrative to yield hope for the earth where it seems most unlikely. For many it is a question of emphasis: the violence of tribulation during which the blood will run up the bridles of horses or the regenerative image of Jesus descending from the clouds to a cleansed but preserved earth over which he will rule with the faithful. The difference in emphasis corresponds in large part to the class position of respondents. Sam and Monroe, both well educated, once successful, and still financially secure men, moved relatively quickly through the violence of the end times to images of hope in the millennium and in heaven. In contrast, Otto, Mary, and others dwelt on the violence of the end, and often got stuck on it. Their lives at the bottom of the social scale were full of struggle and the forces of society and history often seemed to work against their best interests. It was interesting, however, that they, too, sought to embrace images of the earth's renewal. Mary beamed with excitement as she described the millennium, and Otto expected to be raptured within the decade.

3

THE
NEW SELF

███████████████████

MONROE. In Monroe's apocalypticism, the millennium was a kind of Christian Wall Street. The first thing he said about it was that during the thousand years of Jesus' reign the earth is going to have "super productivity." Believers who will rule with Jesus then will have bodily form as Christ did after the resurrection; they will also "do work, will perform work." The GNP during the millennium will be "astounding."

Such fantasies are not really so surprising. The concept of the millennium for fundamentalists lends itself to highly subjective constructions, since it is not literally biblical; that is, the literal form of the millennium is nowhere explicitly described in the Bible (compared, for example, with the Garden of Eden). It is necessarily left to imagination how earthly life continues with Jesus as the ruling king, whether there is money and work, and whether something like the subway system continues. Monroe was perhaps more concrete than most in the projection of his own experience into his imaginings about the millennium, but the way he extended his world into God's space in no way compromised the boundaries of fundamentalist ideology. Nor was Monroe altogether a new Christian phenomenon in this regard. Augustine, in *The City of God*, details a remarkably unequal distribution of "grades of honour and glory" in the Heavenly City. There will definitely be such distinctions, he says, "of that there can be no doubt."[1]

The explicitness of Monroe's future narrative was an integral part of the doubts he harbored about the meaning of life that had led to his conversion experience in the first place. He had to tie down the apocalyptic, because everything else closer at hand was so problematic. But the same doubts that had forced his radical midlife transformation carried over into his thinking about end time issues. As he described the rapture to me, for example, he said the "saints" will be called to meet Christ in the air (which is the conventional definition). In this way, he said, they avoid the death and suffering of the tribulation. I asked him then what happens to someone who accepts Jesus after the rapture but during the period of tribulation. He said, nervously, that some people will convert during tribulation and live into the millennium itself. These new Christians will then continue to have children, and to die, though the "resurrected saints" (who return to earth with Jesus after the tribulation) will do neither. But even as he said it he realized his answer only restated the problem, which addressed the finality of the rapture. Once history as we know it is over with, can there even be such a thing as a *new* Christian? If one can convert once the terrors of tribulation commence, can such Christians later be saved from death? If so, the whole system begins to crumble, especially the absolute necessity of conversion now, which was, of course, the whole focus of Monroe's life work. Indeed, he mused in some confusion, why would new Christians who convert after the rapture hold onto their faith without any hope of heavenly reward or an end to their separation from the "saints" who rule with Jesus as king? His effort to describe the Apocalypse in concrete detail had backfired and he quickly backed off from his speculations: "How all that works out, I'm not certain."

This confusion in end time details threw Monroe into a small state of panic. If he was wrong about converted Christians, maybe he was wrong in other ways too? Maybe death is not conquered? Maybe the theory of premillennial dispensationalism itself is mistaken? In the room where we talked, he leaned forward intensely and knitted his brow in deep thought. He tried again to go through what happens, but this time he got even more confused. For a man who was not articulate in the best of circumstances, Monroe became barely intelligible. "My understanding," he said, is that there is not going to be sickness and "those kinds of things" and "there's not going to be death." But right away he added: "It doesn't mean some people can't die." But that in turn led to a *non sequitur* that showed a latent authoritarianism: "Christ will rule [with] an iron hand. People will be punished for doing wrong." Monroe then tried again to deal with this troubling issue of Christians who die during the millennium, and in stating the issue realized there was yet another thorny issue to face: What about the children born to these mortal Christians? Can the children be saved? Who is going to convert them? All of these concerns and questions were compressed into an otherwise confused statement: "Christians, or those Christians that made it through [to] the millennium and then through birth, people are going to be not Christians in that period because they'll be born and they'll have a choice to make."

Monroe then tried to escape his confusion by returning to a much earlier question I had asked, namely how the idea of Christ's second coming and the end of human history affected his daily existence. He said vaguely how much of scripture is revealed, and how prophecy is fulfilled. "God put it [the prophecy] there by design" as a "motivational factor." That's it, he said twice, that's it. "It's a motivational factor in my life," by which he meant prophecy motivates him as a Christian. "Okay?" he asked me and himself. "The more that I believe it, the more that my life will really be committed to Him in obedience to Him." Now Monroe was on firmer ground. He had stated a basic issue of faith and gotten away from exploring the details of his end time imagery. At last he felt a measure of security. He added: "I guess that about answers it."

In general, Monroe's literalism kept his anxiety in check. He

could discuss the horrible death and destruction of the end times
with marked detachment, as long as he felt he was elaborating on
scripture and thus quoting God. He often introduced descriptions of
violence with "It [the Bible] tells about what's going on." I felt he
could almost see the passage, and I had the idea, when Monroe said
this kind of thing, that immediately after the interview he would go
back to the Bible and reaffirm himself in it.

> The thing that's so incredible to me, after going to
> school and spending all that time in the Bible, [is]
> that I had real confidence in taking God at his word
> [about] what happens when I die. . . . And when I
> looked at the supernatural things that he has done
> just in the prophecies alone in the Old Testament . . .
> just incredible. It's through faith, but also, faith is
> based on how God has operated before. I really
> believe Christ is going to return like he said. . . .
> I really think it could happen in my daughter's
> lifetime.

Monroe always sought to turn the metaphorical, the mystical, the
poetic into the concrete. His was more than an abstract belief in
"inerrancy." His belief governed how he read the Bible and taught
him how to understand life after death and how to deal with daily
life. During my fourth and last interview with him, when we knew
each other quite well, he told me how his dying father told him that
much of life is wasted on things that don't count. Monroe's response
was to launch into a literal counting of his years left, translated into
a count of the number of days left for him (9,000, he estimated), and
what he planned for himself so that he didn't waste time. To make
things count became, for Monroe, an actual counting, a way of mas-
tering death in meaningful days. It seemed to take the pain out of
death. Security thrived in the literal.

On the other hand, literalism presented Monroe (as it did Mary)
with exactly the dilemma he sought to avoid. The fear of death motivated his literalism, but the imagery of destruction in the Bible that
was so much a part of his life stimulated his worst fears. The torrent
of violent images in Revelation holds death back from conscious-

ness by abstracting it, except that the very experience of entering into it could, and often did, flood him. Then the personal joined the theological. The result was terror.

The apocalyptic cannot stay completely dissociated if it is to continue grounding the self and act, as Monroe put it, as a "motivator." But as soon as the end time images are let into the experience of the self, one is confronted with what the "end" really means in a personal sense. Monroe, it might be said, moved from easy dogmatism to pained confrontation. Ultimate violence was a well-grounded idea for him. We think of God as a God of love, he said, but he is also a "God of justice." When God sent Jesus he gave humans a certain time frame in which to act and make that revelation apparent to the world. But it's not going so well. "When he looks down at New York City, I honestly don't know why he doesn't just wipe it out." This thought put Monroe on a roll. They do things to each other in Times Square, he said, that animals don't do to each other. The city is filled with all these gays and lesbians, an image that made him squirm. We have to deal with the impact of the New Age movement and people like Shirley MacLaine, he said with disgust, puckering his mouth. Even so-called Christian churches are repugnant. Some don't even believe Christ is God. "It's amazing to me that God hasn't ended it."

But soon he will. And then justice will be meted out. Satan will run wild. With the saints gone (in the rapture) the rest of the people will be left to their own devices. There will be "pandemonium" and "tremendous destruction." "They'll fall by the sword," he said enthusiastically in another interview, "their little ones will be dashed to the ground, their pregnant women will be ripped open." In the tribulation, it will be worse than "you've ever seen," "beyond imagination." This deferred violence and shift in agency from himself to God allowed Monroe to separate himself from responsibility for his intense loathing for sinners, especially gays and lesbians. He didn't have to kill anyone. He could remain a relatively gentle and genial person. God punishes sinners, and he does it worse than anything we can devise, for he does it twice and forever. The apocalyptic for Monroe thus served as a vehicle for his own violence toward those whom he felt threatened his fragile self and, at the same time, protected him from having to own these feelings in any real emotional sense. Punishment was in the hands of God, who will carry it out with terrible vengeance after history ends.

When I first met Monroe at Grady House he was a handsome man in his forties with neatly trimmed hair. He wore tailored clothes and with his suit on looked the part of the top executive he once was. He had smooth skin, even features, and a highly appealing boyish enthusiasm. He greeted everyone warmly and genuinely. His hearty laugh at Bible study could often be heard across the room. Yet he could be surprisingly naive. He often acted like an older student and talked about himself as still learning the ropes in his new role as a missionary to the rich.

Monroe was somewhat overweight, which he complained about; he said it had to do with getting used to New York. At our four breakfasts together he talked each time about losing weight, his special cereal, and his concern with the calories in the cream cheese on the bagels and in the butter on the toast (as he devoured each time what struck me as surprisingly large meals). As in other spheres, Monroe longed to control his body, harness it for higher purposes, make it serve God. He also wanted to continue looking good. There is no doubt he was one of the most handsome middle-aged men in the Bible study groups. He even had money, despite his austere lifestyle.

Monroe came from a family of five in an upscale neighborhood in western Massachusetts. His father had several small but successful businesses. The family was reasonably close, certainly comfortable, together, and without any manifest problems or crises. Monroe went to a military college because he had always wanted to be a general in the army. He ended up pursuing that goal for seven years, including stints in Germany and Vietnam. After a while, however, Monroe recognized in himself that he was too money oriented and not doing everything he should to stay on track to become a general. He was not "maxing out" on his efficiency reports. It was pretty clear to him that he would have a decent career but would never make it past colonel. That was not enough. "I did not want to be a colonel in the military," he said. It was second-rate, not worth his considerable talents. He had always intended either to be a general or make a million dollars. It was time to move on and make money.

He left the army and moved to New Orleans where he had some contacts. He was recently divorced, but not long after moving south he married a beautiful woman with whom he was very much in love. He established a small business that grew quickly into a multi-million-dollar enterprise. Some thirty people worked for Monroe. He bought a magnificent home with 5,000 square feet outside the city, a 450 SE Mercedes, and began taking long vacations. It seemed on the surface that he had fulfilled all his dreams. But underneath he was deeply troubled. He was also alone. His second wife had left him.

Then one morning several Christian friends took Monroe to breakfast at an elegant restaurant in the French Quarter. They confronted their colleague bluntly: "What would happen to you if you died?" He was struck dumb. Despite all his outward success, he could not answer the question, for he had no sense of anything beyond what seemed to him his utterly meaningless existence. Monroe's friends shared certain key biblical passages, like John 14:6, when Jesus says: "I am the way, the truth, and the life: no man cometh unto the Father, but by me"; and 1 Corinthians 15:26, "The last enemy *that* shall be destroyed *is* death." In such passages Monroe discovered what he believed to be the power of Jesus and the mastery of death. Only in that faith could he find sense to life. It changed everything for him.

After he let Jesus into his heart at that breakfast, Monroe sold his business and his home and car and packed off to Dallas Seminary, the Harvard of fundamentalism, for training to become a missionary. He said even he was daunted by his new enterprise. "We always think of a missionary in Africa going around with shorts or, you know, tramping through the jungle." His parents wondered why he could not keep his business going and attend a seminary on the side in New Orleans. The final straw for his parents was that at some point not long after his conversion he had a good job offer that would have allowed him more or less to maintain continuity between his new and former selves. It was an offer to head up a group of executives in the city who had all been reborn and now wanted to run their businesses according to the teachings of the Bible. His job would have been to advise these rich and powerful businessmen on what it means to run a Christian business, to do something useful and Christian with the valuable resources God has entrusted them with. His "church" would have been CEOs in a crucial part of the new South, a small but select "congregation" that directly influenced the lives of thousands working for them. Monroe, as a former member of this small club of CEOs, would have had a good salary and could have kept his house and connections. It would have been respectable, and not only kept him out of short pants but in his dark suit.

Instead Monroe threw off everything of the world, went to seminary, and volunteered to serve out his life with a Christian organization that has evangelical programs all over the United States and the world. Monroe fantasized he would end up somewhere exotic like Russia. In any event, he would have to work as a true missionary wherever he was sent, and he would have to raise his own salary. His parents were aghast. He was once worth millions; now he would be begging. But it was precisely the totality of the change that had the most appeal for Monroe. He had been stuck in his life. Everything had failed him. Two wives had left him. He felt worthless in a mansion of plenty and utterly lonely in his fancy car. Jesus' story of the camel hit home (Matthew 19:24: "It is easier for a camel to go through the eye of a needle, than for a rich man to enter into the kingdom of God"). For Monroe it was not enough to change inside. His conversion breakfast brought him new life, he felt, but that was only the beginning. He then had to make over everything else, purge himself, be renewed. His life had to have consistency or it would have no integrity. There could be no compromises. His commitment had to be total. He "let" Jesus in and was "saved" and "reborn"; in return he "gave back" to Jesus everything he possessed.

As it happened, however, not as much changed in his financial security or relative status in society as he might perhaps have wished or secretly fantasized. He liquidated his substantial wealth but then put all the money from the sale of his business, home, and possessions into personal savings and CDs at a time of high interest rates.

He was even to remain comfortably associated with business leaders. When he graduated from seminary, he wrestled for a while with whether to go to Eastern Europe where he felt he might be effective. But then he interviewed with Grady House and felt "like, for who I am, this is the place the Lord wanted me to go." Monroe, in a phrase typical with fundamentalists, said he would "do whatever the Lord asked me to do"; that seemed to be with business executives in New York City. Although he was obliged to raise his salary through the contributions of those he converted and spiritually touched—and had strict limits on what he could draw on from his savings—he was given special permission to use the money from his savings to buy an apartment and get himself established in the city. What Monroe purchased was a beautiful one-bedroom apartment in an elegant high rise. Monroe's life and soul were full of contradictions.

That is not to say he was a hypocrite. Monroe had given his life to Christian service. His "work" was to spread the message to executives, and he put in long days making contacts, having lunches, and following up on those he converted. His apartment was lined with various multivolume commentaries on the Bible, and he spent most evenings and all his free time poring over biblical texts and pursuing their subtler meanings. On a washstand in his bathroom was a stack of daily prayers for Christians around the world, each card for a separate country. Card #53 implored the believer to pray for the faithful in Vietnam to remain true in the face of persecution; for the pastors and others now in prison there for their faith; for the growth of a "missionary vision" despite the difficulties; for the planting of churches among "tribal peoples" who have been responsive to the gospel; for the conversion of Vietnamese who have had to flee to other lands; and for the radio broadcasts beamed daily into the country. No moment was wasted. Monroe was only saved from suffocating earnestness by his self-effacing posture and warm, hearty laugh.

The contradictions in Monroe's life were, finally, what made him an interesting, complicated, and appealing figure. He was not making much money, but he also had not divested himself of his significant wealth. He once moved as a nonbeliever making money in a world of secular executives; now he continued in that world in the same costume and with many of the same rituals (lunches in fancy restaurants, golf, vacation retreats) as a missionary seeking to awaken in his colleagues a faith in and understanding of Jesus. He looked and, in most external respects, acted like any other powerful CEO in New York. In New York, he had reduced the square footage of his home but vastly increased the value of each inch of floor space. He had no car, but that is hardly uncommon in New York where it is easier to take cabs than search endlessly for parking places. And he was still without anyone to love in his life. All alone he cooked and ate and prayed in his apartment overlooking Manhattan, just as he once rattled around his huge house all by himself.

But he felt different inside. He wasn't empty; God was within. His life had a purpose, a direction. Most of all, Monroe did not dread death. Like any sane person, Monroe feared sickness and the experience of actually dying, something he went through with his father between my third and fourth interviews with him. I shared with him then my terrible feelings of loss when my father died suddenly when I was sixteen, and how it took me some fifteen years to get over it. Our mutual loss helped bring us together and bridge the gap between the fundamentalist Christian and nonbelieving researcher. Monroe talked at length of his father, what he looked like toward the end, and the joy he felt that his father had converted on his death bed. For Monroe death was not the end of everything but the beginning of meaning. He looked forward eagerly to a future filled with God, his own eternal life, and some reasonable reward for his suffering on earth. Monroe still doubted himself and would forever wonder whether he was performing as well as others. But he remained confident that in the long run things surely would work out.

I asked Monroe why he seemed so acutely concerned with ultimate meanings in his forties both before and after finding Jesus, and what, especially, was the background for his intense sense of emptiness that had resulted in his conversion experience. "Men," he said in reply, "go through, as women go through, a change of life." For the first time in his life he had been troubled by a lack of motivation. He felt "low." He was searching. All the earlier goals he had set for himself he had met (or, in his relationships, realized he would never succeed at). A lot of what he was going through right then was probably brought on by the death of a father, he added parenthetically, though it seemed mostly to come from the larger sense of being halfway through life. And "I'm halfway, by golly," Monroe said in his idiosyncratic way.

Even after becoming a Christian, Monroe told me with an evangelical edge, things don't change overnight. You have to search and study. By way of explanation he reached over for his Bible and quoted to me 1 Corinthians 2:14: "But the natural man receiveth not the things of the Spirit of God: for they are foolishness unto him: neither can he know *them*, because they are spiritually discerned." This passage was extremely important for Monroe—and for many I met and talked with at Grady House. These were generally well-educated people who read their texts seriously. Somehow they want to explain the feeling of greater understanding they have of the words of God after being reborn. They can read and comprehend what the Bible says before their conversion but they cannot fully "know" it unless in the act of reading they are filled with the Spirit; and even then it takes unending effort and continued study to "mature" in belief, to move further along what Monroe called the "spiritual journey." "This will sound hokey," he said, but all you have are words when you read the Bible as a non-Christian. There is no "supernatural sense," no "full understanding of that till you become a Christian."

The Christian world was tightly closed for Monroe in the magical power of the sacred word. When he shared "spiritual-type things" with me as a nonbeliever, "the amount of revelation that is revealed . . . is limited." The sacred word marked the boundaries of the self. Inside of that line for him lay true knowledge, fulfillment, and happiness; outside lay only ignorance and despair. This Manichaean view of things was reassuring at many levels. It defined the possibilities of the new self. Belief brought you into direct communication with the Almighty; it empowered action and banished doubt. A new world of ethics and end time hope opened up. At the same time, nonbelievers can read the same Bible and not take the same truth from it. It's only words for the nonbeliever, while the believer reads with the lens of the Holy Spirit. "It's incredible," said Monroe to me, "how passages and things in the Bible really come together after you've trusted Christ. It's a phenomenon." He really wanted me to see that, to give something to me: "When you come to place your trust in Jesus Christ," he told me with enthusiasm, "you'll remember that and you'll look back on that" and understand.

DOUBLINGS

The early psychoanalyst Otto Rank first introduced the concept of "the double" into psychoanalysis, and it has been a popular idea ever since, especially for literary theorists.[2] In psychiatry, however, it was not until Robert Lifton's work with Nazi doctors that the idea of doubling actively re-entered psychological imagination. As Lifton uses the concept, doubling means "the division of the self into two functioning wholes, so that a part-self acts as an entire self."[3] There is, of course, nothing magical about doubling. Along with several other concepts that have emerged in self psychology in recent years as either new ideas or revitalized older ones (including disavowal and splitting),[4] doubling is used in trying to describe the divisions in the self that are the consequence of dissociation. The self is, almost by definition, a holistic concept. Even in multiple personalities, there remains an essential communication between competing selves. Certainly, in most of human experience the separateness of aspects of experience is a relative concept. "I" am one thing, one person, one being, something William James clearly recognized, even if Freud tended to forget it. But life can seem in parts, even as we yearn for wholeness. "Man is born broken," says Brown toward the end of Eugene O'Neill's *The Great God Brown*. "He lives by mending. The grace of God is the glue." This apt characterization, which was one of Heinz Kohut's favorites, may express the dilemma of contemporary humans.[5] In any event, fundamentalists turn away from their broken, fragmented selves toward a fully separate self that is born anew with its actual baptism.

The reborn self that fundamentalists proclaim grounds their existence. The creation of a new self at the moment of conversion marks a profoundly significant psychological realignment, as Larry demonstrated when he found Jesus instead of jumping into the East River. It brings a new code of ethics, and it changes the style of one's life, as two pastors, Dean and Lester, found in getting beyond their drug-filled adolescence. It brings a new self-concept, as Monroe found in remaining alone and in his suit but filled with God. And it brings a new future in the idea of the millennium, as Otto and Mary imagined, one of goodness and virtue and social equality.

But most of all the reborn self brings salvation from death. Indeed, the transition from old to new selves, as fundamentalists imagine it, is itself a kind of death experience conveyed in the language of rebirth. Whatever else transpires in this vale of tears and hereafter, that new self is eternal and will eventually rest in peace with God. Cynthia thus felt protected against sin in her reborn self. "I'm never tempted to read smut," Cynthia gushed, "because I know that my mind is impressionable," even though she acknowledged watching TV movies and being horrified by all the swearing. "When you accept Christ that gnawing feeling, that uncertainty, that impending fear is gone, is replaced with peace and the guilt is gone and that is the beauty." But death remains. "There is a real freedom in being a Christian. Number one you say I don't have to worry about death and my eternal destiny. . . . But death isn't so bad when my eternal destiny is secure. Right [which she repeats, as if to reassure herself]. Right. I don't fear death anymore. It doesn't mean I want to die. Let's be real. But I don't feel fear is the ultimate." She had, in fact, radicalized the relation between life and death. She once said that as a child she feared the unknown, but "Now I don't fear the unknown, I don't fear death in the same way that I did. But I don't see that second coming of the Christ as death." The return of Jesus is not death, of course, except in a subtextual sense, that is, to save believers from death. Cynthia continued: "But I just see it as an exit out of this life to be with Christ." The return of Jesus, in other words, somehow washes away death and makes her immortal. Cynthia wanted that desperately.

In fundamentalist theory, all important things happen twice. You are born full of evil, separated from God. To enter the kingdom you must be "reborn" in a dramatic act of self re-creation. Jesus returns to earth at the end, making good the promise of ultimate redemption. It will be his second trip. True Christians who have died will be resurrected at the rapture. They will then live again on earth during the millennium, and forever in heaven. A crueler doubling is reserved for nonbelievers. Their sinful bodies are obliterated in a wash of violence during tribulation and their souls rest for a thousand years while the faithful rule the earth with Jesus. They are then resurrected as a kind of living presence to be judged by God and brutally cast forever into the lake of fire. (Revelation 20:13–14: "And the sea gave up the dead which were in it; and death and hell delivered up the dead which were in them: and they were judged every man according to their works. / And death and hell were cast into the lake of fire. This is the second death.")

More than anything else, these doublings distinguish fundamentalism from mainstream Christianity. There are at least three reasons for such marked differences in basic doctrine. First, fundamentalists seem to have to be doubly sure of the apocalyptic precisely because it is so fraught with uncertainty. Repetition relieves uncertainty, and yet reveals an aching doubt that prompts the repetition or doubling in the first place. Faith, for fundamentalists, is not just a part of our being in relation to a transcendent power. On the contrary, "real" faith must be a visible part of self-transformation as we define a personal relationship with God and become a new person. Similarly, one can never be quite sure that nonbelievers will not get away scot-free, so they must die and die again. Maybe then they will really be dead.

Second, the repetition of important things makes difficult and transcendent ideas much more comprehensible for ordinary people. End time theory is democratic, accessible, and imaginable in its literalism, while also being highly evocative in its mysticism. To dismiss fundamentalist theology as the kind of fanciful imaginative scheme fit only for comic books is an elitist judgment that reflects more than anything the anger of mainline Christians who have seen their churches emptied by the message and enthusiasms of fundamentalists. Accounts of faith, Jesus, the end times, the afterlife, and reward make the fundamentalist story immediate and concrete. These are not the concerns of erudite theologians but the narratives of popular culture. Fundamentalists, for example, talk and worry about where Jesus will appear in the clouds at the rapture and whether the Mount of Olives will split when his foot touches it at his descent. One need not learn Greek or Aramaic to reflect on these kinds of problems, and many millions find it religiously rewarding to work their faith at this level of explicitness.

Finally, the doubling in fundamentalist theory touches individual and collective death. Ideas such as the double death of nonbelievers weave the true threats to human existence into the Christian story. Fundamentalist theology is, in this sense, an authentic, maybe even realistic, adaptation to the modern world. If all the bombs go off or we choke ourselves in a haze of pollution, the human story will die in ways that make little sense in a theology based on the compassion of the Sermon on the Mount. The focus on violence by way of tribulation gives the traditional Christian story the edge it needs to fit our crumbling and maybe dying world. As Kathryn, an African American woman in her mid-thirties, said, "You cannot go over it, you cannot go alongside it, but you must go through it. You must go *through the blood.*"

Fundamentalists live with a stark contrast between eternal souls and degraded bodies. Christianity, of course, has always taught such a dualism, but the fundamentalists literalize it in their end time views about double resurrections and deaths. The intermediate period between the final end and the termination of human history—the tribulation and the millennium—imposes similarly contrasting fates on the souls of the faithful and the infidels. Nonbelievers, of course, suffer and die in great numbers during the tribulation, while at the rapture believers are either raised from the dead or taken directly from life to be with Jesus in the clouds and then to rule with him from Mount Zion. During the millennium these "resurrected saints" look, as Monroe said, like Jesus after the resurrection.

The way dualistic death concerns worked their way into the interview process could be surprising. Mary's loose talk of mass death and Otto's numbed counting of those who die during tribulation frankly appalled me at the time; only in writing this book and with distance from the actual interview was I able to gain more empathy for the human pain behind such an easy acceptance of collective violence. In one interview with Reverend Lester, he launched into an hour-long lecture about how people build their security around a wife, husband, or whatever and then collapse when those fall apart.

The gospel, on the other hand, provides a permanent identity and inner peace. Reverend Lester thus set up a contrast between domestic and spiritual peace, a dualistic tension that carried over into a diatribe about the apocalyptic in which he distinguished between those who get the sign during the tribulation and those who do not; the latter are persecuted and hounded and judged and "actually killed."

For fundamentalists, the nonbeliever is death tainted. It must never be forgotten that the nonbeliever (in the eyes of the faithful) lives a constricted life and suffers the pain of death without hope of redemption. There are, in other words, severe consequences for refusing to accept Jesus in one's life. In the immediate and visible present the effects show themselves in a failure to understand the Bible. To the fundamentalist, the nonbeliever is like a preverbal child (1 Corinthians 13:11: "When I was a child, I spake as a child, I understood as a child, I thought as a child; but when I became a man, I put away childish things"). Words are little more than babel. You need time and lots of help to discern meanings, coherence, and grammar. But the larger significance of nonbelievers' failure transcends issues of cognition. Those who refuse Jesus are not only dumb but also different, dangerous, and possibly contagious. The believer is obliged to rub up against the taint in the commandment to convert, which implies a conquering of death. But to stay with that death too long can be a dangerous affront to the self.

Such thinking can lend itself to potentially dangerous stereotyping. People like Monroe tend to believe the Lord is with him in his reading of the Bible and that God speaks directly to him through his word, while all others are doomed to ignorance (and, subtextually, eternal damnation). The difference between self and others is sacralized, which provides a totalistic framework for dismissing all those who do not fit into the holy world in which the fundamentalist is blessed. The fundamentalist's chosenness defines the nonbeliever's abandonment, the one's salvation the other's ultimate punishment. Nonbelievers are rejected by God and thus in some inexplicable way are only tentatively human. As such, nonbelievers are dispensable. If they intrude in the believers' world, the psychological conditions exist to make it possible for believers to accommodate violence toward nonbelievers. I must stress that for most fundamentalists, and certainly for all I met, such violence was nowhere near being realized. But the fact that the potential exists is best illustrated in its occasional realization at the radical fringes of fundamentalism, as, for example, with the survivalist, Aryan, or Neo-Nazi groups in Idaho and elsewhere, or with David Koresh and the Branch Davidians.

Two important factors, however, one religious and the other psychological, mitigate the dangers of fundamentalists acting on or realizing the potential for violence that exists within their belief system or within themselves. Religiously, the fury of doctrinal certainty is softened by an evangelical commandment that fundamentalists take quite seriously (though some much more so than others): One has an obligation to reach and convert others, to help them, to recognize their weakness, to bring them to Christ. Such an impulse within Christianity tends to expand fundamentalist empathy out of necessity and may explain why Christian fundamentalism (as opposed to its forms in some other religions of the world) has so far, except for dramatic episodes on the radical fringe, been relatively free of violence. Monroe, for example, gave his whole life over to saving souls for Christ; during the time I knew her Arlene was actively planning a full-tub baptism for scores of the reborn in the gymnasium of the quarters for women on Riker's Island; and Mary spent hours each week with Jews for Jesus *and* Arabs for Jesus. The evangelist cannot afford a life-style of pristine ideological purity, even if he or she is emotionally drawn toward monastic retreat or violent engagement. The world cannot be disdained. It must be entered or no one will ever be converted.

Equally significant, the fundamentalist shares a specific psychological connection with the nonbeliever that goes beyond the mere fact of their common humanity: The nonbeliever symbolizes the believer's pre-Christian, earlier self. For Monroe I had the distinct feeling that I represented the way he saw himself prior to accepting Jesus into his heart at that New Orleans breakfast. As such I was the discarded part of his being, something that no longer fit as he grew in faith and found new robes in which to dress. The danger, of course, in such symbol-systems is that one will turn on these discredited and abandoned fragments of the self with violent renunciation. The reformist's zeal can be harshly condemnatory; enemies of the state are often purged after the revolution; the newly rich may disdain the poor as lazy; and the recovered alcoholic all too often scorns spineless drunks. But the more tentative approach of Monroe also remains. He looked back with sadness on his life before coming to know Christ, and at times that spilled over into the way he treated me with a note of condescension. He knew me, or at least thought he remembered that part of himself that he saw symbolized in me, and connected empathically with me, despite our rather large differences in background and values.

Don DeLillo, in his apocalyptic novel *Mao II*, notes: "The nice thing about life is that it's filled with second chances." In one sense, this is a thoroughly upbeat statement that reverberates with the American dream. There is hope in our potential for self-refashioning. But DeLillo's comment also touches a certain dread, for second chances are premised on our failing the first time. Who knows what will happen the next time around?

THE LITERAL SELF

Perhaps since the first century, Christians have had a sense that God's intentions and the story of Jesus are directly communicated to humans through scripture. As a result committed believers have always tended to literalize those words. But it was only in the nineteenth century that a theory of inerrancy emerged, arguing for the absolute integrity of every word in the Bible as God's complete truth and thus casting a long tradition of literalism into dogma. Inerrancy, however, does not require that the Bible be taken as literally true in theory or in practice. The erudite (and non-fundamentalist) theologian James Barr has written extensively on this seeming contradiction. His basic point is that, while inerrancy is a "constant factor" in all of interpretation of scripture, literalism may vary "up or down."[6] Clearly some biblical passages must be interpreted symbolically, something fundamentalists generally recognize and accept as part of the complexity of understanding the text. When asked about whether a born-again Christian has to accept the Bible literally, Reverend Dean hedged and said a Christian should read it literally "where possible." He added that he was not a creationist, believing in a literal reading of the story of creation—a belief in fact held to by only a minority of ideologues in the movement. But what the Bible is not, in the view of fundamentalists, is just a great story or a series of theological reflections. There is a "plain" or "right" meaning to any passage that God means to convey in it, even if it is difficult for humans to ascertain that meaning. That meaning may not be literally true but it will be the actual truth of what God said.[7]

The matter of literalism among poor and largely illiterate believers, however, is a bit more complicated than these theological distinctions would indicate. Can one really apply a theory of inerrancy, developed by highly privileged white Victorian Presbyterians at Princeton Theological Seminary, to the educationally disadvantaged masses? If you are illiterate and cannot appreciate the text in its full meaning, can you be a fundamentalist, or, as they might put it, a real Christian? Belief is the first and greatest step; it takes only a leap of faith. But belief is the beginning rather than the end of Christianity in the minds of fundamentalists. At a minimum, you also have to lead a moral life; proclaim the word to others; and learn the word and study it carefully. Reverend Lester, for example, said, "There are 1,700 churches in New York City. Few apply the Bible as a living book. Few teach the Word of God to common people," which was his mission from the first moment of his "church planting."

Intimate acquaintance with the Bible is, in fact, an important goal of the Bible study sessions that are such an essential element in the activities of any fundamentalist church. At Grady House a high level of education was assumed among the participants, and the issue was to walk a fine line between simplistic, literal reading and something approaching what they called "historic Christianity." At Abiding Light, on the other hand, where the congregation consisted of poor whites, blacks, and immigrants from various countries, nothing in the way of literacy or background knowledge could be assumed. Ian, the leader of the Bible group I attended, was particularly good at reminding members of such basic information as who the Jews were, what difficult terms meant, and where key places were located. He often had different people read passages aloud, and then would lead a discussion of their meanings. For the newly or partially literate (and perhaps especially for those for whom English is a second language), this kind of Bible study is highly educational, and spills over into their lives generally in significant ways.

Learning how to read, however, in the context of a belief system that stresses the theoretical notion that every word in the Bible is inerrant tends to reinforce the literalism of the movement in a naive but often touching way. I never met a fundamentalist in the various study groups in which I participated who was too poor not to have his or her often expensive Bible wrapped in a leather case with a zipper. These cases are carried as badges of honor. They protect the sacred text from rain and damage, and ensconce it in what I often felt was a mystical wrapping. A distinctive sign of a fundamentalist on a subway, for example, is the unzipped case with the open Bible on their lap. For many the Bible is the first, and remains the only, book they have really read. Even without a theory of inerrancy, one tends to treat such volumes with special meaning.

Such a learning process by rote with public reading and discussion as its core experience tends to move one toward ever greater literalism. Teachers of Bible groups are necessarily more educated and—at least with Ian, who did not have a dogmatic bone in his body—may be more moderate in their views. He simply passed over troublesome passages (like those dealing with the need for wives to be subservient to their husbands), and never tried to comment on thorny issues of theology. Ian's students, however (that is, the regular members of the congregation of Abiding Light), had a much more literal understanding of the text, which they asserted in discussion. Ian often brought in articles clipped from the *New York Times* to illustrate themes that he felt were raised in the biblical passages under review in a given week. Members of the group, on the other hand, were generally not interested in referring to sources outside of the text itself. If they had a question about 1 Corinthians, they wanted to know what it said in Isaiah on the same issue; or in talking about Revelation how it related to Daniel. Only in extreme cases were they interested in connecting the text to the larger cultural and historical world. The fall of Jimmy Swaggart thus caused great consternation at Abiding Light. It fell to the gentle Ian in Bible study to find biblical passages that could make some sense out of the tragedy. It was, after all, an Assemblies of God church, and several people I met had been converted by Swaggart at a revival he led once on Long Island.

But why is it, one can well ask, that learning to read one book carefully should make one a literalist? Abraham Lincoln learned to read a few books (including the Bible) by rote; he even read out loud in the "blab" schools of the American frontier, but he was hardly a literalist. Most highly educated people, in fact, begin somewhere by careful attention to words, and may have one or a few books to which they remain specially attached. Liberation theology, furthermore, purposely uses its Bible instruction as a form of instruction, and turns the process to political advantage and empowerment of the masses. But with fundamentalism that same process of biblical instruction yields exactly the opposite results. The difference lies in the theory behind the reading and the goals that the instruction serves. Inerrancy, one has to say, matters, and the way it undergirds Bible study always returns the discourse to its literal origins. The process tends to discourage interpretive change; it always returns to the self-referencing text that is imbued with the mystical knowledge of God.

Speaking more generally and psychologically, the move toward literalism and away from metaphor defines the religious experience of the fundamentalist. Literalism means control over sin and badness and ultimately control over death. Anxiety over those issues requires the literalism. Whether one can truly find eternal life in faith, or what happens during tribulation to a believer's nonbelieving children, or how nuclear violence fits into the end time story, reflect the kinds of concerns of greatest intensity for fundamentalists and therefore become the theological areas in which literalism most visibly operates.

The impulse toward literalism leads the more creative fundamentalists into some poignant dilemmas. Frank, for example, lived with his own special terror regarding the second death, the final judgment, and hell. "The worst part about hell," he said, "is what is described, it is a lake of fire, it is torment, but I think the worst torment of all would be having briefly experienced the presence of God [that is, at the moment of the final judgment] and the wonderful, the wonderful personal God he is, and forever being deprived of him."

The literal impulse also prompts fundamentalists to reflect on the concrete future history of the soul. Our body dies and rots but the soul, our divine essence that connects us with God, lives on forever.

Some eastern religions and New Ageists argue that this soul is reprocessed in successive lives until it reaches some kind of exalted state. In Christianity things are more teleological (or directional). The soul is our spark of the divine and somehow at death joins with God in heaven. For the stricter traditionalists such (re)union of the human soul with God requires faith during life, just as they would argue that the soul of nonbelievers dies off, or somehow disappears. But in most of mainstream Christianity, and certainly in all its progressive forms, notions of damnation are blurred, if not explicitly eliminated. We are all open to God's love, and the move is toward theological inclusiveness rather than exclusiveness.

Not so with fundamentalists. They wallow in the details of salvation and damnation. Such a position toward the future has generated not only a whole library of books on the course of the end time (Hal Lindsey's, for example), but also detailed graphs and charts of the apocalyptic that are the stuff of endless hours of Bible study. As with any ideology, people also disagree over specifics, often with doctrinal certainty.

Fundamentalist explicitness about the end time, grounded as it is in difficult biblical texts, requires "experts" at interpretation. You must read prophecy, especially the book of Revelation, correctly or you will not understand the future course of events. That explains the many sermons and handbooks and videos and tapes and Bible studies on the subject. If you learn enough, the most specific details about your future life can be known. How exactly will human history end, who will be the false leader, where will the big wars take place? What can you expect during tribulation? Where and with whom will you be living during the millennium? What will you look like? What will God be reading at the final judgment? What can you expect in heaven? You will also understand the dark side with the proper study. Who does not get raptured to be with Christ in the clouds? How many die and by what methods during the tribulation? How does life proceed for surviving nonbelievers during the millennium? And what really is the lake of fire?

The damnation of nonbelievers offers renewed hope for believers ("The last enemy to be destroyed is death," Otto said, quoting 1 Corinthians 15:26). For it is taught in the churches and endlessly repeated at the level of ordinary parishioners that there is nothing you can do to recover yourself if you die without accepting Jesus. No prayer helps the dead along. No amount of good work will offset a lack of belief. I asked Otto once about Mother Theresa (would she be saved?). He replied hesitantly that, well, he didn't know about her relationship with the Lord, but he repeated that only the saved, or those Christians specifically reborn as described in John 3:3, can ensure their future in heaven.

4

DIVINE
COMMUNION

WILMA. "Anything that holds your head together is of God," Wilma said. "Anything that confuses you is of the devil." Wilma led her life with the constant knowledge of God's presence. He spoke to her as she walked down the street, instructed her, helped her make the right choices. He talked directly into one ear. The Holy Spirit, for example, would tell her to stop watching so much television, because "thou shalt have no other gods before me." But Wilma also wrestled with the power of the devil. He spoke into the other ear. You have to be constantly aware that Satan is a "very strong force." He is "just like the Lord" because he was once the archangel and got to know all the secrets of God. But Satan got proud and was banished to hell where he continues to wreak his havoc. Earthly atheists and agnostics, like Satan, set themselves above God. You can't tell them anything, she lamented. They confuse you, like Satan. "He's the author of confusion," Wilma added. You have to read God's word, memorize it, "hide it in your heart." The word of God is sharp, Wilma said, "sharper than a two-edged sword [her version of Revelation 1:16]. It cuts asunder."[1]

The literal struggle between the Holy Spirit and the devil for Wilma's soul reflected the immediacy of God's unfolding plan in the mind of this fragile woman. "Without hell, God would not be just. Where are you going to put all those people who refuse?" she asked. One must hold on. "He that endureth to the end shall be saved," Wilma quoted, seeking reassurance in a familiar phrase. For her that end is close at hand. Plenty of signs "point to the culmination of an age" and "every two thousand years there's a change." What we are living in now is just like the world before it was destroyed by water. Remember Noah? Wilma asked. "Everybody was doing what was right in their own eyes. That's what's happening today. More and more and more."

A member of Abiding Light, Wilma was a slightly built woman in her sixties who had the appearance of a fragile porcelain vase. She was near to tears throughout most of her two interviews, and once actually began crying when she described the experience of waking up from an emergency operation and thinking she was in hell. Wilma had straight gray hair and wore almost no make-up. During the winter she wore a simple black coat and hat that practically made her invisible.

Wilma's father came from Russia in the early part of the century. He was a Baptist, in fact a lay minister, but as a young man visiting a church with some friends he was once filled with the Holy Spirit and fell down speaking in tongues; this was in the early days of Pentecostalism as it swept the country after its beginning in San Francisco in 1903. That experience prompted her father to join the newly established Pentecostal church, Abiding Light. After his marriage Wilma's father worked hard at various unskilled jobs through decades of struggle. The family barely saw him. But whenever he was around in the evening, he would gather the family together to pray and read the Bible together. Wilma remembered those sessions fondly.

Abiding Light then was a large and active congregation with a charismatic ministerial team that tended the flock. An orchestra played as back-up to the organ. Wilma's father played the violin in that orchestra and later passed the violin on to Wilma for her high-school graduation. She in turn gave it to her eldest daughter but has it back now and does not know what to do with it. The passing of the violin into untrained hands seemed a metaphor for Wilma of the decline of Abiding Light itself from hundreds of enthusiastic worshippers to the few score who come to services now. In her typical way Wilma (as did other old-time members in this church) connected that decline with cosmic purposes: They saw it as a sign of the end because "it is written" that the number of Christians will decrease prior to the return of Jesus. "In the last days," Wilma said, "the love of many shall wax cold."

Wilma had very sentimental memories of her "beautiful" mother who died from a severe stroke after Wilma was grown with a young child of her own. She thought her mother must have been half Jewish, for Wilma remembered that her mother "koshered the meat," though why that proved she was "half" Jewish was unclear, just as it was left unexplained why her mother kept kosher after conversion to Christianity. Wilma's most distinct memory of her mother was praying. "Every time I came in the house, I found her on her knees. She just loved to pray." Her mother also imposed herself on Wilma. She taught her to avoid social conversation, "idle chatter," she called it. She was taught to read the Bible and concentrate on sharing the Lord's word. There was nothing else of significance to talk about. At the end of the interview Wilma gently chided the interviewer (a young woman) for letting her talk too much. She explained that she needed more direction. "I like to be a follower, you see. That's why I loved my mother so much. She was so strong, ooh! She made me afraid."

Most of Wilma's adult life was filled with sadness. She mistakenly married a man with a good job rather than the musician whom she loved. That marriage "ruined my life." Wilma cried all day before the wedding and her mother even suggested she might call it off. That was clearly a portent for Wilma. The husband turned out to be a complete cad, often leaving her alone and finally abandoning her, forcing Wilma to return to work to support her young children. She even had to suffer the criticism of others at church ("Why isn't Wilma living with her husband?" they asked behind her back). No love was between them, and worst of all the husband had no interest in her religion or her church. "We were unequally yoked," Wilma put it (referring to 2 Corinthians 6:14: "Be ye not unequally yoked together with unbelievers").

Wilma's family provided few alternative satisfactions. At one point she mentioned two children but only told stories of her adult daughter, giving the impression that a boy died. The daughter was a constant trial for Wilma. Her sanity seemed in question. "She went into astrology," Wilma said, distressed. In fact, she went into all kinds of religions, suffered serious emotional problems, and lived on her social security disability. She was "very emotional" and "nervous," Wilma said.

For all her submissiveness, meekness, and piety, another side of Wilma struggled for a voice in the interviews. "I do not trust what I am capable of doing," she said once out of context, and immediately referred to the grace of God. Her reasoning seemed to be that a side of her, one fed by the devil, strived for expression and independence. The constant surging of such feelings only reinforced her sense of badness. All her life Wilma had fought back such feelings. To illustrate them she told a story of rebellion as an adolescent. She had demanded that her poor parents purchase a new three-piece suit for her to wear to a party. It became a prized possession, though she berated herself for proving somewhat later to be a "complete ingrate." At a church party with some friends of her parents at which she was also wearing the suit, Wilma was asked to play the piano but instead sat under a tree and refused to budge. She was disobedient. As she saw it, predictably, the devil had gotten hold of her, but perhaps she simply wanted to be something that the strict demands of her faith would never allow.

Whatever that small voice was it died years ago, though not without a struggle. Wilma told another story of feeling guilty as a young woman when she played popular music on the piano. "My heart condemned me," she said. And then, without a break in her associations, she told a dream: "I saw a branch of a tree. And I saw the bark about this big, but the branches were very crooked. One went this way, one went this way. It was orderly, but it was so crooked. None of them [the branches] seemed to be going the same way. One this way, one that way, one that way. And yet the trunk was so even. And I was wondering, how could a tree be so, so diversified. And then on top, in gold, pure gold, on top of the bark with all the branches all around, no leaves, just the branches: 'The will of God' in gold. So beautiful, so even." Wilma's dream seemed to capture the central dilemma of the young woman who felt guilty even playing the piano outside of church, and since it stayed with her through the decades the dream seems also to have spoken to her continuing conflicts over her self-definition. Wilma yearned for the straight and even trunk that reached upward and touched the golden will of God. But in fact she spent most of her life in the twisted and crooked branches.

THE REACH OF PRAYER

No one prays more fervently than fundamentalists. Prayer is one of the central experiences of their faith commitments and is elaborately ritualized in the rhythms of their daily lives. Luke, a young executive who attended a Pentecostal church on Sundays and Grady House for Bible study during the week, lived alone in New Jersey. He rose every day at 6:00 A.M. and sat in his living room facing a large picture window with his heavily marked and underlined Bible on his lap open to a passage from a guide to daily scripture that he reflected on and prayed about, slipping always, he said, into tongues. Any church function begins and ends with prayer, and services themselves return constantly to individual and collective prayer. At Grady House (where Luke was more restrained in his self-presentation), there were four distinct periods of prayer in the course of an evening's activities: before and after Bible study and, with Sam, before and after his sermon/lecture. At Abiding Light, at least once each year members of the congregation gathered for an all-night prayer session, though even the earnest Ian told me he had trouble staying awake. At Calvary each Sunday one of the remarkable sights in Christendom is six to seven hundred people speaking in tongues at one time with all the fervency of black Pentecostalism.

The Lord hovers closely for true believers. They ask God for guidance in matters large and small in their lives, and expect concrete answers. If in their lives it turns out they have chosen badly after asking

God for help in a decision, they reason that the devil has spoken. It is not that their faith is weak, just that Satan has great power. Nevertheless, they see—or convince themselves they see—enough evidence of God's majesty in the world but most of all in their lives to fully justify their confidence in their continued personal relationship with Jesus.

I often wondered, given fundamentalists' belief in the reach of prayer, what were its limits. Clearly, much of what one asks for is denied, from the trivial to the ultimate. This denial is not new to fundamentalists, but fundamentalists, because of what they believe is their closer form of contact with God, seem never to doubt that they are in communion with the divine. The failure of prayer is thus quite personal. It may result from inadequate sincerity in the asking or from God's inscrutable ways that may be temporarily confusing but always have a purpose.

Otto told me of the extraordinary powers he ascribed to prayer. At several points in his life he had such severe chest pain that he thought he was going to die. But at those times, he did not go to a doctor or take any medication. He prayed. And he did not consider that an avoidance or denial of the problem. He was taking creative action. Otto did not even take aspirin for the eight or nine days of acute pain. With prayer, "I was healed from it. It all just completely cleared up." Otto explained to me why prayer could not solve all the problems in the world in terms of God's mystery and our willful ways:

> Okay, God gave us a free will when he created us, and Genesis says, "Let us make man in our own image." I believe that involves intellect, the ability to learn, create things, emotions, so we can feel, love, hate and if you can't hate, you can't love. You've got to be able to have all emotions. And the will to choose. Now God could have made us robots. So that we all live righteous [lives], we never do anything wrong. But God gave us a will, and that involves the ability to choose wrongly.

The intimacy of the fundamentalist's relationship with God, as shown in this attitude toward prayer, shapes much of the subtext of fundamentalism. God is neither remote nor an immanent power in the universe. He is a part of one's life. He cares for the most minute details of our existence and ultimately watches out for his flock, even if he purposely lets things go somewhat awry along the way. In prayer we approach God directly. A bit of God rubs off, and we ourselves become sacred. In the best of senses, this extension of the divine into daily life enormously enhances a believer's self-esteem and nurtures the capacity to live a Christian life. From the moment of faith the fundamentalist says "I believe" and draws closer to God.

But such proximity to the divine can be audacious, if not arrogant. Reverend Lester fully expected to have God on call. "My ultimate purpose is to be like Jesus Christ in my inner character, the qualities that Jesus had," he said. Isaac illustrated a related but somewhat different grandiosity that was common among those fundamentalists I got to know. The line in Isaac's mind blurred between what he thought God might do in his apocalyptic fury and Isaac's vision of what he would do in God's place. Isaac talked, in other words, with God-like omniscience when he described end time issues. He spoke in the rhetoric of Revelation, and filled his speech with phrases from the apocalyptic. He spoke with the certainty of one who has fully divined prophecy: "They [believing Christians] will be spared [at the rapture] because God said he put the seal on them and they will be the witnesses to the world. You see God always has witnesses—even if he takes the church out, he leaves a remnant." He spoke with confidence about matters that even fundamentalist theologians tread on lightly (like what happens to Christians who convert during tribulation), because he somehow felt his intimacy with the divine gave him special license.

GUILT TRANSFORMED

Nigel stressed that life changes when one believes in God and is in intimate communion with him. You don't need to wake up and worry about paying bills next week (said this affluent Wall Street trader) or dealing with tragedy in your life. "In putting your life in God's hands he takes care of those things and he provides for you." We cannot know what's in the future, but if we believe we can relax in the knowledge that "he has designed the future," including "everything that happens in our life." It's all taken care of.

For Nigel one of the added benefits of such close communion with God was relief from guilt over what he considered his abundant sins during the decade when he strayed from the church. During these years after his parents' divorce, Nigel drove sports cars, took drugs, and dated lots of women. When I asked him if he felt regret now over those years, he replied that his only regret was in losing all that time with the Lord. God doesn't punish us for past sins, he stressed. "He doesn't bring it up, and there is no reason why I should either," he said in a quite extraordinary statement about the closeness he felt to God.

In a psychological sense Nigel's understanding of God's involvement in his life served to reverse the shame-guilt mechanism. Normally we feel ashamed or guilty about bad thoughts or actions. Such feelings of shame or guilt help prevent us from straying too far away from the internalized norms of our culture. Conscience, in this sense, serves to regulate behavior in any social setting. But for those who believe in a fundamentalist God, the pangs of conscience fade after they are saved, or so they claim. God absolves them of their sin and frees them from guilt. Such relief is a crucial part of the personal gain that believers attest to in being saved. "Christianity," Nigel said, "is the only faith that offers atonement. There is no other religion that offers atonement for our sins as human beings." At the final judgment, the Lord is not going to look at you and say, "Chuck, you dropped the ball on February 28 at two o'clock in the afternoon when you lusted after this person." That gives you "sort of a license," though you are commanded to be obedient. But then Nigel concluded with the thought that really tormented him: "One of the big things that I look forward to in going to heaven is the end of that struggle against the flesh."

Perhaps they protest too much their escape from shame and guilt. Nigel spent much of his interview with me rehashing his time of troubles and describing in what struck me as loving detail his manifold sins. Fundamentalists often seem to fool themselves about their relief from sin and guilt. In this they are not really hypocrites (though sometimes their self-righteousness can be suffocating). They fully acknowledge continuing temptation in the reborn self, and theologically assume that as long as the soul remains in the wicked vessel of the body, the possibility for sin exists. That was the point of Mary's story about the rotting flesh under her ring. The victory over sin and death is complete in an ultimate sense but more tentative in the immediate human context. The struggle remains. Yet the relative release from sin, even from the point of view of the fundamentalists themselves, is remarkable. As far as I could tell in my exchanges with fundamentalists, they *are* free from sin (as it is normally understood in the Judeo-Christian tradition). If hardly free of guilt, they are at least released from torment, expiating guilt by the constant processing of it in prayer.

The amount of guilt felt, however, often had little to do with actual behavior. A huge difference exists between the subjective experience of guilt and the actions and thoughts that prompt it. Wilma berated herself for playing the piano as an adolescent just for the pure fun of it. One could see Nigel's "sins" that have caused him so much pain as the normal behavior of a college student.[2] Isaac, on the other hand, had been a cocaine addict, and Arlene had been a prostitute, crack addict, and had actually tried to kill her lover at one point. Yet all these fundamentalists struggled in similar ways with their transgressions by collapsing radically different behaviors into the common mold of their pre-Christian, sinful self that they remade in the experience of being saved.

Guilt and shame, in other words, occupy the minds of fundamentalists to a rather extraordinary degree irrespective of the actual behavior that apparently occasioned it. They feel that they were completely sinful at one point but totally freed of guilt after conversion; only their constant harping on the past suggests its continued presence in their lives now. Much of the motivation for conversion lies in getting free of these feelings. Certainly it matters that the saved universally claim to feel different about themselves and to have experienced a transformation of self in relation to guilt and shame after being saved. But where is all that guilt and shame after conversion?

The answer is complex. The effort to reverse the guilt-shame mechanism never fully succeeds, and fundamentalists (like the rest of us) spend a lot of time in self-laceration and expressions of guilt and shame. They also create a *new* source of guilt and shame in their lives in trying to match the extraordinarily high ideals they set for themselves. But to a significant degree, it seems, fundamentalists do free themselves from much of the haunting residues of guilt through a process of externalization. God takes over one's sin. With God's forgiveness, one can forget about sin and trust, as Nigel did, that God will not recall it. This attitude presupposes an intensely personal relationship with God, one that can only be continued by a sense of communion with him as an immediate part of one's daily life. God has to enter into matters that most people would never imagine him caring about. That is the heart of the "personal relationship" with the Lord that fundamentalists constantly evoke.

But shame and guilt, then, become an integral part of the apocalyptic. A striking aspect of the fundamentalist system is that just as individual guilt and shame diminish, collective evil increases. The badness, one might say, shifts its venue. Fundamentalists believe that the number of true Christians will decrease as we approach the end of time, for evil will increase everywhere else. The world implodes on itself from the weight of all its evil. End time violence is the indirect expression of all that accumulated sin, and it helps maintain individual purity as it unloads destruction. Such is the effect in fundamentalist theology of transforming guilt. The purer Christians are, the more sinful nonbelievers become.

5

THE END
AT HAND

▬▬▬▬▬▬▬▬

ISAAC. Isaac represented the extreme edge of end time commitments. Underneath his veneer of good humor and geniality lay a tormented soul. He continued to wrestle with drugs. He had to suppress his own violence and he was always toying with leaving the church in an act of rebellion. The "solution" Isaac found to the dangers within was a kind of cosmic projection. He completely embraced the violent end times and neatly shifted agency. It was not his violence but that of God. It was God who punished pornographers, and God who rained down desolation and made the blood run to the bridles of the horses. The end time script proved useful for Isaac, the actor, as a vicarious expression of his inner conflicts. His immersion in end time destruction served to control his own violence. Antichrist was a useful carrier of Isaac's projections, and he was drawn to the tension created by living on the cusp of destruction without knowing exactly how soon it will occur. The shifting of agency in a very real sense played an important healing role for Isaac. Through faith he had given up his drug addiction, gotten his and his mother's life back together, and found a community in St. Paul's Church. But Isaac's new faith commitments represented a perilous and fragile new set of self structures, something well short of a transformation. As his interviewer keenly felt, despite his friendly facade there was a disturbing readiness for violence in his obsessive attraction to the details of destruction in the end time story.

Isaac was in his late thirties when he was interviewed. He was balding, which made him look older, but fit from his frequent weight-lifting. He was unusually outgoing and an actor who had appeared in various bit parts on TV and in commercials. He was particularly respected by other members of the St. Paul's congregation for his knowledge of the book of Revelation. He even taught a course on prophecy. Isaac had a good sense of humor and could be disarming in his frankness (at one point he described himself as "cocky and arrogant"). When he made announcements at the Sunday service he usually had the entire congregation laughing. But there was also a suppressed violence in Isaac. Tension pulled at the corners of his mouth, contradicting his professed happiness. During one interview Isaac talked at length about the serial killer Ted Bundy (even he "wanted love"). Isaac seemed unduly interested in Bundy, whom he said "represents something in all of us." Isaac was himself a cocaine addict before being saved and he spoke with feeling of the rage the drug can cause.

Isaac grew up in Florida. He was raised a Methodist and was very active in his church. He was president of his Methodist fellowship and during the summers went to youth camp. The religious beliefs he was taught, however, were "watered down" and without much integrity. At least in retrospect, the mainstream Christian church failed to provide that ideological core of commitments that Isaac yearned for. After high school Isaac went into the army. The Vietnam War was winding down, however, and he was not sent overseas. At twenty-one he started college in Florida, but he later transferred to a west coast university. In both schools he majored in acting and proved to be quite accomplished; since he was prematurely bald he was always cast as the grandfather.

Isaac spoke about end time issues with authority. He knew the book of Revelation well and enjoyed rambling on about topics like the ingathering of the Jews, the exact nature of tribulation, the seven trumpets and seven vials, and the plethora of symbols that clutter the texts of prophecy. Isaac attached great significance to the book of Revelation, which along with Genesis are the two books "the devil attacks." Isaac saw the world as a place of marked decay. As in the days of Noah, he saw people drinking and eating and not noticing what was going on right in front of their eyes. But he clearly saw that the signs of the end are everywhere. It is all intensifying, including the vast expansion of knowledge. Along these lines, Isaac seemed particularly impressed by computers, which for him were an integral part of end time process.

Isaac was influenced by people like Hal Lindsey (whom he mentioned specifically at one point) who take the end time grid and apply it to contemporary events. During the cold war, Russia and China played out the Gog and Magog roles in Lindsey's hugely successful books, while the Gulf War brought Saddam Hussein into focus as Antichrist and aroused great passions among fundamentalists about Israel and the Jews.[1] Isaac's special concern in the construction of such apocalyptic narratives was the identification of Antichrist. This charismatic contemporary leader, who wears the facade of peace but is inhabited by the devil and is the instrument of great destruction because he fools people for so long, perhaps symbolized the inner tensions Isaac himself felt.

Isaac had strong views about the liberal drift of politics and ethics in America. He mocked those who insist on access to pornography as a right of free speech and yet turn around and deny fundamentalists the right to worship in school or even educate their children at home. That represents a disintegration in values, according to Isaac, one that marks the end times (and which Antichrist will take maximum advantage of at the end). "I wouldn't want to be you or someone like you," Isaac said to the interviewer, whom he knew to be Jewish and who had steadfastly resisted conversion despite months of fieldwork in St. Paul's. You, he said, speaking both generally of nonbelievers but more specifically of the interviewer herself, will be part of the armies that go up against Jesus when he touches down from heaven and splits the mountain and laughs at the assembled hordes.

Isaac liked the image of that haughty laugh of Jesus, as he did anything that suggested violence. He searched out the bloodiest of biblical passages to quote (which in the book of Revelation is not too difficult). "It says" was a refrain of Isaac's. It says "he called the birds to come and eat the flesh of mighty men"; It says "the battlefields will be covered almost up to the bridles of a horse with blood, that's how deep you can feel the blood will be, you know." Isaac truly lived psychologically in the violence of the end, that time when a third of the vegetation of the earth will be burned up and a third of the water poisoned. He also added his own creative images to more familiar ones about end time events. "The sky," he said, "is going to literally reel up like a scroll, almost like a Venetian blind, and boom!" People will have sores all over their bodies, he continued, because the ozone will be completely gone, and they will stand there helplessly shaking their fists at heaven, demanding God help them, as though he was working the heavens as a short-order cook. Isaac warmed to his topic, leaning forward across the table where the interview was being conducted, pounding the table, hoping to impress his nonbelieving interviewer.

Isaac segued from end time violence into drugs and his own tormented experience with cocaine. All you have to do is look at crack, he said, and you get addicted. It must be "out of the pit of hell, you know." And then he gave his testimony, his experience of degradation that led to his conversion. It came four years ago. He was a cocaine addict at the time, doing two or three grams a day. He went back home, partly to get away from New York but also to see his mother. What he found was awful. She had become almost a bag lady. She had stopped bathing and the house was full of trash. There were rats in the house. He turned from the sight at first, not wanting to get involved because he knew it would take a deep level of commitment to help her.

That was the turning point in his life. Almost absentmindedly, he picked up a Bible and found suddenly that the text was speaking directly to him. He had never experienced those words before in that fashion. He faced what he considered his own evil ("I'm not basically a good man, I'm basically a bad man," he said once, and like Satan he was a "very vain creature"). But somehow the words of the Bible worked on Isaac. He returned to his mother and coaxed her out of her house and into a hospital where she could be treated properly for her diabetes. He then stayed with her for six months and got her—and himself—back in shape. Somewhat later, he moved to stay away from the New York drug scene he knew too well. He found a large fundamentalist church (with ten thousand members) and was baptized. He spent lots of time reading, trying to catch up on his religious education. He was quickly recognized as a good communicator and was asked to teach a course on religious fundamentals. He said it helped him solidify his own faith.

For all this time he stopped his drug use as well, though he added, somewhat ruefully, that he had "slipped" several times. "Becoming a Christian doesn't mean you're going to stop sinning," he said, rationalizing. It only means you will sin less, a sanction he found in Jeremiah: "The heart is deceitful above all things." And he acknowledged in himself: "I'm entertaining sin in my life, I'm entertaining thoughts of rebellion." In general Isaac said of himself that his move into Christianity was a "slow burn" rather than a "bolt of lightning." He constantly struggled with himself, with doubt, with desire. He gets "antsy" and feels he wants to walk away from the church (and probably back into drugs).

And yet Isaac testified to the power of prayer that holds his latent violence in check. He told a story at one point of being home with his mother and sister and her family recently. His brother-in-law was an alcoholic and into drugs. On Easter he totaled his jeep while drunk. Isaac was enraged and told his brother-in-law he wanted to "deck" him but refrained from physical violence and prayed instead. The next day the brother-in-law got into a rehabilitation program. For Isaac it was proof positive of the place of God in our lives.

THE TIMING OF THE END

The Bible reports that Jesus explicitly told his followers he would return, both before his death (Matthew 24:27–31) and during the forty days after his resurrection but before his ascension (Acts 1:4–5). This promise is referred to many times elsewhere in the New Testament (especially in the expansive readings of the Bible by fundamentalist theologians like John Walvoord[2]). Since the apostles watched Jesus ascend into the clouds (Acts 1:9), believers have waited eagerly for his return. But it is not to be talked of; Jesus was quite clear about that (Matthew 24:36: "But of that day and hour knoweth no *man*, no, not the angels of heaven, but my Father only"; and Acts 1:7: "It is not for you to know the times or the seasons, which the Father hath put in his own power"). This dual message of immediacy and uncertainty, of hope deferred, of dreams that may not be mentioned explicitly, creates the central tension in the apocalyptic for fundamentalists. Mainstream Christians tend not to worry too much, if at all, about the Second Advent; fundamentalists are obsessed with it. They want it now and move toward it psychologically, but they also must avoid naming a date. Paul Boyer, in *When Time Shall Be No More*, details the long history of such date setting and its agonized rationalizations from those actually involved in such activity.[3] My fieldwork and interviews reveal a somewhat different picture, for I avoided the noisy leaders of the movement or those at the radical fringe. Among ordinary people, I found more confusion and hesitancy about the world's end, combined with a deep longing. The timing of the end is a complicated matter, but much can be learned about the fundamentalist movement and individuals within it from the way they position themselves emotionally and spiritually in relation to the return of Jesus.

The Second Advent, it should be remembered, is by definition for fundamentalists the event that marks the end of human history and inaugurates the sufferings of tribulation that are then followed by the hope of the millennial rule of Jesus on earth. The "end" stops our historical time and ends evil, but it marks as well the "return" of Jesus and the "beginning" of the millennium. These discrete (and magical) aspects of the end time process can easily merge, however, in the minds of fundamentalists. For their own reasons, fundamentalists focus differently on endings, beginnings, death, renewal, despair, and hope, but all agree that the expectation of the return of Jesus defines their existence. It may be that those who are most agitated about their own death are also the most immediate about the apocalyptic end. The end time process, precisely because it involves so many different events, allows for much variation in self-expression.

For Arlene the end was misty, just as her images of the millennium recycled her memories of her childhood in Jamaica. Reverend Charles brought a much greater sense of urgency to his reflections on the end but also steadfastly avoided any hint of date-setting. Sam was somewhere in between. He put little emphasis on the idea of the return of Jesus or the end of the world, either in his interview or in his sermons at Grady House. He clearly believed in the Second Advent, but he laughed at the idea of setting a precise date for the return of Jesus and saw no significance in the year 2000. What mattered for Sam was that he will appear before Christ whenever he comes (though it was not clear Sam had the final judgment or the rapture in mind). In fact, Sam got quite confused talking about these issues and acknowledged that he just does not pay much attention to the theology of the end time. He does keep straight "the really important things," namely that Christ will return, that there is both a heaven and a hell, and that only those who accept Jesus are "headed in the right direction."

Reverend Dean was a bundle of fascinating apocalyptic contradictions. His ideas were incompletely formulated and conventional; they were also appealingly human. Though a minister, he was not at all interested in or informed much about the theory of premillennial dispensationalism. He was only vaguely apocalyptic. Contrary to all expectation, he once described a "harmonic convergence" New Age celebration held in Central Park with interest, by way of noting that other people as well felt "great changes are occurring." At another time, he referred to Hal Lindsey's *The Late Great Planet Earth*, which he said was a "credible" statement, even though he said at another point that he didn't "see" nuclear war in the Bible (which is the whole point of Lindsey's book). Christians, Reverend Dean said, have always believed in the end itself. "Every generation since Christ," he said, "has believed that they were living in the last days. . . . We live that way because we want an open, active relationship with God. Love compels us to go on." Reverend Dean's apocalyptic style was in general decidedly gentle. He made it clear that he did not like the rabid patriotism of Jerry Falwell but greatly admired Billy Graham.

Deborah asserted that the end times play a very important role in her thinking, though she gave it a typically personal twist. For her living in the end times gave life an "urgency." There is no guarantee, she said, "that we are going to live another day." As proof, in a sense, she told a story of a woman she had met handing out tracts on a bus. Deborah introduced herself, and discovered the woman had stomach cancer. Deborah was impressed that the woman seemed at peace with herself. Deborah concluded: "Here she [the woman] is, who knows how many days she has, if the Lord heals her, but we also have to think of it in [terms of] the time that the Lord is returning." The point seemed to be that end time urgency connected with daily life by making death more real and apparent. God's purpose was apparent at many levels. The threat of actual death sharpened life's focus, as with the woman on the bus. But the awareness of the end times does the same for the young and healthy, like Deborah. We are all living with the equivalent of stomach cancer in the certainty of individual death, but we must also realize the equal certainty of end time finality for human existence. Deborah's small story of human suffering evoked for her cosmic endings, indeed God's purpose.

The end times for Reverend Lester are right around the corner, but what he really cared about was God's judgment at the end. "The judgment has got to come as the sun has got to rise." There is also moral rot everywhere. In fact, if God doesn't bring judgment on America, he is going to have to "apologize to Sodom and Gomorrah" (which led him into a tirade against abortion, and the murdering of 25 million babies). Asked once whether it changed his life in any way to believe the end is imminent, he replied: "No. I'm living one day at a time anyway, giving a hundred percent to whatever it is that God wants me to do." But the image of the end he lived with was terrifying. "The heavens will pass away with a roar, and the elements will be destroyed with intense heat and the earth and its works will be burned up." And he added: "We are talking about hydrogen bombs, we are talking atomic bombs, nuclear war heads."

Such knowledge posed problems for Reverend Lester about how to lead his flock. If he talked too much about the end times in his sermons, he felt people would either get "smug" about their own salvation and the fact that everyone else is damned (it "just puffs people up" knowing that they will have eternal life, he said), or be frightened away. "You have to share truth with love," that is, somehow not ignore the end time message but present it in the context of a ministry of the love of Jesus. Reverend Lester's subjective sense was that he muted discussion of the end in his sermons, which was in marked contrast to the impression I got from his sermons, and most of all from the powerful apocalyptic themes that emerged in the interviews from his church members. The apocalyptic was also expressed throughout Reverend Lester's ministry, sometimes in small but significant ways. After his second interview, for example, Reverend Lester gave his interviewer a six-page newsletter on the church that was prepared for new or prospective members. The newsletter speaks primarily of the loving model of Jesus, whose teachings are a guide for the living and whose death has saved us from sin. But tucked away at the end of the little brochure, in one strategically placed half column, is the note: "Some will enter the kingdom prepared for them from the foundation of the world. Others will not."

Within all this diversity on the timing of the end, I did find one consistent element in the way fundamentalists of different classes view the apocalypse. Working-class fundamentalists, whether African American or white, male or female, tended to see the end within sight and some even connected it to the approaching end of the current millennium. The upper-class fundamentalists I got to know pushed the end well beyond their own lifetime. The poor and disenfranchised, in other words, whose lives approximated the suffering of the early Christians, yearned for the transformation and renewal so basic to apocalyptic theory.

Otto was as specific about the significance of the year 2000 as anyone I talked with, though even he hedged ("I'd be surprised if we reached the year 2000 before he comes back") and told me in quite a different context that he did not expect to die, for he would be raptured first. Certainly, no one I encountered matched Otto's obsession with end time death and resurrection (though Harriet and others also talked loosely about the year 2000 and suggested as well that they expected the rapture imminently). Otto, however, lived in and for the return of Jesus to a remarkable degree, even for fundamentalists. Yet he pressed toward the Apocalypse with dread. There was persecution, war, and suffering at hand on the horizon, and Otto had thought through what all that meant for himself and his family. "Ah," he said sighing, "Well, my youngest is thirteen. I've got two married, one that's on his own, he's twenty-one. So hopefully they won't be in the part [of their lives] where they could be drafted in some war or something. I don't know. It concerns me, yes." But at least he sees a "light at the end of the tunnel." There will be persecution, Otto said, but it won't last long. Nor will it kill everyone. Many will die, including Christians in the vast persecutions,[4] but there will also be purification. "The best and truest will survive."

On the other hand, the fundamentalists from Grady House delayed the end in their religious imaginations. They saw it as vulgar, not to mention blasphemous, to even think about a human dating of God's purpose. One might say they were certain about *an* end but unsure about *the* end. The men in my Bible study group, for example, laughed with scorn at Elizabeth Claire Prophet who dared to make a concrete prediction that the end would come in April 1989; Nigel made unflattering comparisons of her with the Millerites, a group that predicted the end in the 1840s. The end for this group of rich fundamentalists was only imaginable as a real but remote possibility. Their empowered class position in the society appeared to spill over into their spirituality.

The idea of the end for them, however, was not at all one that assured a human future; in this aspect of the apocalyptic they had much more in common with working-class believers than with other upper-class mainstream Christians. Their suits and Mercedes and houses in the Hamptons could be deceptive. They lived with a clear sense of the outer limits of the time left for human history. They were loosely but absolutely apocalyptic. They talked about history not lasting past the time of their children or their children's children. Everyone I talked to in-depth at Grady House dated the end, even if vaguely, along such lines. Two generations, it seemed, was as far as any fundamentalist could see human history lasting.

On that continuum from half a decade to roughly a century, however, there was a crucial point of psychological significance that further distinguished categories of fundamentalists: the point of their own death. Arlene, Otto, and the others, whether or not they at-

tached significance to the year 2000, all believed the end would occur before they died; Sam, Nigel, Monroe, and the members of
Grady House saw the end as coming sometime after they died. The
moment of one's personal death served as a kind of metaphor for a
collective ending, even, perhaps especially, for the disenfranchised.
It actually mattered much more than the year 2000 in figuring the
apocalyptic.

"We don't have much time," said Ivan, an African American fundamentalist of thirty-three who worked two jobs to survive but lived
in a shelter for the homeless. "We don't, you, me, my children, your
children, and anybody else's children." At the most "we have thirty
to forty years" (which is what he could reasonably expect to live),
but even that could be shortened "if things keep increasing at the
rate they're increasing with the drugs, the larceny, the murder, the
mayhem, it's not going to last that long." Later in the interview,
however, Ivan seemed to contradict himself. In thinking about his
future he imagined himself "thirty years from now" with a nice
home in the country somewhere, a fantasy that transcended the effects of the prejudice he encountered in contemporary America. But
he added quickly "if there's a country," which took him back into the
apocalyptic. "God knows all the shit that's going on. He knows the
good that's going on, what little good there is, and he knows all the
evil that's going on. He knows."

Monroe, on the other hand, dated the end in the second generation. In a general discussion of the return of Jesus, he noted the urgency of conversion for all, especially his daughter Jennifer. He was
concerned that his daughter be "prepared." He wanted her to have a
"commitment equal or greater than mine," and was concerned that
her faith was weak. He did not want her to waste her first forty-three
years, "like I did." For there is no joy or happiness in life, he added,
outside of belief in God. Although banal in one sense, Monroe's
ideas about the end were not quite as simple as they seemed. He had
only a vague idea of the end in Jennifer's lifetime, which was part of
his continual immersion in end time prophecies. He was keenly
aware that history seemed to be hurrying along, which he felt could
be God's way of announcing that the end was at hand. He said:
"There are so many of those prophecies that are starting to be ful-

filled in the last thirty, forty years at a rapid rate." The creation of the state of Israel was "the big one" for him, but "there's so many." There are "a lot of things going on" that are highly "significant." What Monroe slid away from was the implication for his daughter of human history ending during her lifetime, and what that meant in terms of her loving, or having children, or doing anything else that committed her to this life, indeed to human existence. Instead, he only addressed the importance of faith in general. It was not easy for Monroe to think about the implications of his end time thinking for himself or those he loved. He could only think about the apocalyptic in the abstract. He was not dogmatic, in other words, but he also was not without his convictions about the approaching end of the world. In this he was quite unlike those who trust, even if ambivalently, a human future. Monroe counted out his own days and envisioned a life for his daughter. But he had no image of his own symbolically immortal self lasting through her and unto the generations.

Mary had some of the same confusions as Monroe. True to form, she stressed that Jesus' return is "imminent, really imminent" and noted that "I don't think there's going to be that many more generations. I honestly don't." In everything Mary said, Jesus seemed to hover over her life, ready to drop in at any moment. However, the only actual date she gave me for his return was one hundred fifty to two hundred years, which seemed a rather long way off for someone as thoroughly immersed in the apocalyptic as Mary. She herself could not really understand it all, but the divine, she said, seemed to have remarkable patience with human evil. God has a "long fuse," she said. Perhaps as well she felt the need to be "historical" with me—she referred several times in the interviews to my profession as an historian—and to appear knowledgeable like her own father, whom she once said was the most informed man on historical events she ever met. But perhaps she also simply changed her mind without conscious awareness, responding to internal cues and various stresses in her life that gave shape to her apocalyptic notions.

THE RAPTURE OF THE CHURCH

"Then we which are alive *and* remain shall be caught up together with them in the clouds, to meet the Lord in the air: and so shall we ever be with the Lord" (1 Thessalonians 4:17). The rapture is probably the single most significant theological innovation in contemporary fundamentalism. It gave new meaning to and helped reshape premillennialism in the nineteenth century and was a crucial part of theologian John Nelson Darby's overall end time schema. It is based on only this one biblical passage, but it is an idea that unlocks many other prophetic mysteries.[5] Obviously, a powerful note of escapism is sounded in the idea of the rapture. The rapture lifts the faithful out of end time destruction, including (as most imagine it) nuclear war, rivers running with blood, strange beasts stalking the land, and general mayhem. The confidence of protection from these disasters in turn profoundly affects the way many fundamentalists think about social responsibility, and contributes to a tendency to opt out of involvement in political and social matters and into a privatized, separatist world. Democracy is not well grounded in the lives of the 60 to 70 million Americans (conservatively estimated) who believe in the rapture.

The escapism inherent in the end time doctrine is also deeply personal. The rapture represents the great triumph of faith for those who consider themselves God's chosen people and in direct communion with him; the rapture justifies the wait and makes everything worthwhile. From the moment of the rapture, eternal salvation is absolutely secure; indeed, as Monroe put it, the "resurrected saints" (that is, the raptured souls of the faithful dead) actually look like Christ after his resurrection. Further suffering and death await the world and all its inhabitants, but true Christians need never worry again. They are on a sure path. Even the brief loosing of Satan (Revelation 20:7) at the end of the millennium for one final battle in no way threatens their royal road into heaven.

But the rapture has a dark side: As the key event on the very cusp of the end of time, it saves the faithful but also represents the point beyond which there can never, ever, be hope for nonbelievers. They may live through tribulation, perhaps survive a while during the millennium, even have children who will make a life and have their own children for many generations. But nothing they do can ever alter their ultimate fate at the final judgment. The moment of greatest hope for fundamentalists is simultaneously one of eternal damnation for nonbelievers. It is quite grim, for it simultaneously means personal salvation and eternal separation from nonbelieving loved ones (Harriet, for instance, was truly haunted that her middle child, who had strayed from the church, would not be raptured).

Mainstream Christians and secularists in general tend to mock the idea of the rapture as a magical, nonbiblical idea harbored by religious enthusiasts. But such attitudes fail to appreciate the centrality of rapture doctrine for fundamentalists, at least as far as I could tell from my work in the churches and from my interviews. The rapture is not just a vague idea that floats in the air; it is a linchpin of the fundamentalist belief system, for it explains why it matters so much that Jesus will come back at one specific point and not another (before tribulation to save true saints or believers for the millennium itself), which in turn is crucial to the concept of phases in the revelation of God. The end of each such revelation, or dispensation, ends in violence, and the last (which is, of course, ours and the one we care most about) must have massive violence—the tribulation—but must also preserve the faithful to remake the world with Jesus as the anointed king. The rapture bothers many informed literalists, precisely because it is not specifically mentioned in the Bible and has to be inferred from the passage in Thessalonians.[6] But in the popular mind the rapture is appealing at many levels, and the longer it remains central to the theory the more sheer weight of historical tradition accrues to it.

What I found particularly interesting in my work, however, were the different ways fundamentalists shape (and sometimes modify) rapture doctrine. One of the more famous, though for some obscure, ideas during the cold war (which sometimes found expression in bumper stickers) was that as the bombs come down the faithful go up. That notion is an example of the general way fundamentalists locate images of the rapture in a decidedly modern context, which can seemed strained to an outsider—and is not always easy or clear for fundamentalists themselves. Cynthia, for example, had reflected anxiously about the specifics of what might happen to planes that were in flight at the moment of the rapture. Some would crash after the pilot was lifted out of the cockpit, but others might keep flying because the plane would be on automatic pilot, which would allow the co-pilot to take over. "Of course, now we've automatic pilots so you know maybe they'll end it. And how is it going to be explained [*pause*] away [*pause*] I don't know?" Clearly, Cynthia was speaking out of a private voice at this point, struggling in a realm within her end time self that was cut off from the interview process.

The rapture has also gotten sexualized in the minds of fundamentalists. Reverend Lester was not unique in this regard; he was only unusually expressive. He was asked in one interview to define the rapture: "There will be, according to scripture," he said, stumbling a bit at first, "we will be with the Lord." Then he was on a roll, relating his version of Revelation 21:2 ("And I John saw the holy city, new Jerusalem, coming down from God out of heaven, prepared as a bride adorned for her husband") and 7:4 about "sealing" the tribes of Israel: "It will be almost like a honeymoon, Jesus the bridegroom comes for the church, the bride, this is the beautiful symbolism used here, and he takes those that are his from every tribe of the earth up to the heavens." The passage in 1 Thessalonians (and a more obscure one in Revelation 1:7) simply locates the Lord in the clouds. But in the imaginative realm of fundamentalism, "the Lord" becomes "Jesus," who is then transformed into the bridegroom of Revelation 21:2 with the church as a waiting bride. Their meeting in the air, which is textual, subtextually becomes a kind of heavenly sexual intercourse. The passively waiting, virginal, and submissive female church gets "snatched up" (a common fundamentalist expression to describe the rapture) by Jesus standing erect in the clouds, which is how he is almost always pictured in popular representations. Reverend Lester, however, pushed beyond even this imagery, and went into a discourse on intimacy. Such closeness with God necessarily precedes intimacy with others, as he put it, and the rapture is like the "ultimate of intimacy." He then made reference to Ephesians on the proper roles in a marriage for husbands and wives (Ephesians 5:22–23: "Wives, submit yourselves unto your own husbands, as unto the Lord. / For the husband is the head of the wife, even as Christ is the head of the church: and he is the saviour of the body"). In this whirlwind of associations, Reverend Lester brought the dialogue full circle, folding a sexualized rapture theory into domestic relations.

But by far the most fascinating commentary on the rapture that I found was from Deborah, a perfectly ordinary believer who struggled valiantly to bring together her decency with the rapture's harshness. For those nonbelievers who miss the rapture, she said blithely, "they still have another chance." Since "every eye will see him" (Revelation 1:7), Deborah concluded that the rapture will surely be on television. "I do believe they're going to maybe record it on film or something. Somebody might get it on film." And she added the *New York Times* already has a headline prepared.[7] Through these media the rapture will be made available to the world just after it occurs. Nonbelievers who missed the rapture the first time around will be able to watch it on TV or read about it in the *Times* and even then accept Jesus and join the church; that is their second chance. Deborah was vague about the details of what can only be called a second phase of the rapture. This wonderfully original notion that bent theory, to put it mildly, and softened it considerably at a crucial juncture, was in the interests of extending the opportunities of salvation for nonbelievers. It would seem she simply refused to fully take in the harsh, apocalyptic doctrine that had been forced on her all her life. She had the main ideas in her head, but they had been quite drastically modified in an age of mass media to suit her more humane purposes.

Nor did Deborah stop revising end time theory with the rapture, part two. She was equally expansive in her understanding of the further opportunities that would be available during the millennium. Her basic image of the millennium was conventional. She described how during it the government, run by Jesus, will work the way it is ideally supposed to, and there will be peace and contentment on the entire earth. But Deborah added a rather significant twist. People, she said, will be so astounded at how good things are that they will finally recognize the majesty of God and accept him as their Lord: "There, again, they'll have that opportunity to make a decision." This *third* chance for nonbelievers, furthermore, would actually be practically open-ended, for the millennium, after all, lasts a thousand years. Deborah even argued that the chances for salvation only begin to diminish at the end of the millennium when the devil is loosed "for a little season" just prior to the final judgment. In her ruminations Deborah was particularly concerned with those children born during the millennium. It was beyond her comprehension that such innocents would not have an opportunity for salvation. So she made one up. Children, she said, will be witness to "the wonderful way things are being done" and "there's another chance for them, too." One can only wonder how many Deborahs lurk in the fundamentalist ranks, humanizing the tyrannical ideas of (largely male) theologians mapping out what they believe are God's destructive plans for a wayward humanity. Her adaptations may suggest a uniquely female use of the magical elements in fundamentalist theory.

GENDER AND FUNDAMENTALISM

I am in a position to offer only a few tentative generalizations about the gender differences I found among fundamentalists. When I was doing fieldwork it was not a conscious concern of mine to search out such differences, and I had no questions specifically about gender in my interviews. It was only later, almost as a kind of secondary analysis of my data (and prompted by the questions of several feminist friends) that I became increasingly aware of some interesting points I could make about gender and fundamentalism. Nevertheless, I offer these findings with caution, and hope they will contribute something to the work already being done in this area by others.[8]

In the broadest possible sense, the men I encountered tended to imagine the end as an extension of their traditional hierarchic and patriarchal Christianity. They often reflected male fears of the breakdown of social and sexual roles in society, and their images of nuclear and end time destruction in general were harsh. Most women, on the other hand, deflected end time violence onto more immediate human concerns like personal salvation and morality. They tended, in other words, to skip over tribulation and move directly into the millennium. Men, it seemed, planned the death of the world at the side of God; women prayed that their children would accept Jesus so that they would have eternal peace with God in heaven.

Otto laid claim to an assertive, macho brand of Christianity with a paranoid certainty. He evoked images of persecution of Christians and had complicated schemes of punishment worked out for non-believers prior to their ultimate damnation in the lake of fire. The end was close at hand for Otto, and he certainly expected to be raptured before his own death. Other, somewhat stereotypical male, themes entered into the imagery of fundamentalist men. Monroe's homophobia, for example, was so extreme he even mocked himself at one point about it. Nigel's form of sexual obsession had to do with a search for the ideal mate and a rigid puritanism. This well-heeled and ambitious Wall Street bond dealer lived an intense celibate life as he sought the perfect Christian mate who would never leave him. Nigel spent two nights a week in Bible study groups besides his church activities. He kept himself under strict control and reined in his lurching desires, which he renounced after his conversion.

Grady House, in turn, provided an institutional setting for pairing true Christians who toed traditional gender lines. The House, among other things, was a kind of Christian singles club. On a given evening, there was plenty of opportunity to mingle before Bible study began (though the study groups were segregated by gender), and a lengthy break with coffee and cookies before everybody from the various groups gathered on the main floor for announcements, a selected testimonial, and the lecture/sermon/biblical commentary that Sam, the executive director of Grady House, gave. Once at announcements, two gorgeously dressed young women urged people to sign up for an upcoming ski trip Grady House was sponsoring. They both giggled a lot as they emphasized the fun and fellowship of the trip but especially the opportunities it would provide for meeting good-looking Christian men. One said that last year there had been three executive ministry marriages that came out of the Aspen trip. The unmarried men I got to know well at Grady House—Monroe, Nigel, and Luke—were all actively looking for mates. I learned indirectly that Monroe married someone from Grady House after I stopped attending. For Luke it was quite a trip to come to the House for Bible study, since he had to return to a rather distant town in New Jersey late in the evening when it was over. When I asked him why he attended, he said honestly and without apology that he sought a Christian mate. What was left unsaid, however, is that such a mate would also be well educated, probably rich, cultured, traveled, and exquisitely dressed. For a boy off the farm and the graduate of a midwest Christian college, even though he was doing well in his business activities and had the prospect of getting rich himself, such a mate represented a rather large leap into the upper middle class.

There was, however, an important male theme that broke from the stereotype. Many men, almost despite their fundamentalism, were complex, ambiguous, vulnerable, quizzical people. Most such men seemed uncertain about their sexuality and lonely (which partly explained the intensity of their involvement in church life). Ian was an ascetic man who played the organ at five services each Sunday in two different churches and was involved in various church activities most other days. He did not care at all for issues of dogma or ideology (he could not remember whether he was to be raptured up before or after the millennium), but built his whole life around preparing for that time with Jesus. In the mid-1980s Ian had been positive enough about the future to put his money into a long-term investment program. Later, however, after the fall of Jimmy Swaggart, he got depressed about the world and how much longer the Lord would tarry. He felt Swaggart's fall was surely a sign that the end would come before the year 2000, and so transferred his money into a savings account with less interest earned but no restrictions on withdrawal. His reflections drew him into end time musings. He looked out the window as he talked of the death and destruction foretold in Swaggart's fall. He grew pensive and sad. He noted how tragic it is that the treasures of the Met and the glorious music of Bach are all of this world and will be wiped away in the tribulation. But, he said, almost as an afterthought, our hope is in Jesus. That makes it all worthwhile.

Women, for their part, tended toward a conventional form of Christian self-presentation. All accepted without question church teachings on issues of morality, and nodded in affirmation when Bible study discussion turned to Ephesians 5:22–23, about how a wife should be to her husband as he is to God, or 1 Peter 3:4–7, about how wives, as weaker vessels, should be in subjection to their husbands. The various ministers' wives I encountered were all dutiful, quiet, supportive women who served as role models to the congregation.

The fundamentalist women I met were also generally more gentle in understanding the apocalyptic. Kathryn turned her attention to the violence of the end times with some reluctance in the interview. She said such violence was "ugly and horrible" and that she found thinking about it "dismayed her." Thelma said she detested the book of Revelation. "I don't understand it," she said with certainty. "I don't think I want to understand it because I think I'd get too caught up [with it] *and* I'm fearful of the thing. And it sounds like an ugly book." For her part, Wilma expressed great interest in the approaching end of the millennium and the many signs that prove we are at the end of the dispensational age and that Jesus is about to return. But she also grew impatient with a question that sought to tease out the logic of her points and tie down a date for the end. "I'm not too concerned about that," Wilma said, "because there are a million interpretations. Everybody has his own interpretation. So I don't go into that too much," even though in fact she lived her life around end time expectations. Deborah, finally, illustrated a distinctly female voice in modifying end time theory altogether, especially regarding the rapture, to soften its harsh treatment of salvation. Deborah also had a wonderful reason why the battle of Armageddon could never be nuclear. The Plain of Jezreel, near Megiddo south of Haifa in contemporary Israel, where the battle of Armageddon will be fought, is too small for a big battle, she said. "It will be difficult to bring heavy military equipment onto the plain of Armageddon."

Among some women, there was as well a sexualization of their relationship with God. Cynthia, who was single, began to cry as soon as she talked about her personal relationship with God. She was too tender, she said of herself, and "his love is so wonderful." She also spent an inordinate amount of time in the interview talking about all the pornography and smut in the world and how she was not tempted to go down to 42nd Street. Wilma, in turn (and also in tears), said in an eruption of associations that we all need to "make love to Jesus." The connection between the individual and the divine is so concrete and immediate in fundamentalism that it lends itself easily to personalization, even sexualization, in the needy. This process is particularly apparent in women, since the figures in the pantheon are all men and the discourse patriarchal.

There were, however, some interesting variations on the female apocalyptic. For some the totalism of the church environment and the literalism of their religious commitments caused them to strive toward a mythical image of purity. Harriet's monastic life was perhaps the most interesting I encountered in this regard. A quite different female variation was illustrated by Mary's muscular Christianity, which came close to a mocking of the male style. Her special obsession with the signs of our decay, the nuclear and other violence of the end times she evoked with such vigor, and her imagery of a reborn millennial world were much more typically male in the fundamentalist world. Mary adopted this male style in an aggressive way that made her the leading end timer in her church, the analogue of Isaac in his congregation. Mary, also, in her appropriation of the Christian male role, was disdainful of America's men. All our men are on the couch, she complained, wimps and helpless beings who could never repel a Russian invasion. Psychiatry has destroyed us, Mary concluded. Kathy, in turn, a severe young woman interviewed in a Christian bookstore, relished the most phallic of patriarchal images. Jesus, Kathy said, would keep absolute peace during the millennium because he would rule with a "rod of iron." Anybody who disobeys or does anything wrong will be "zapped," she said. "And that's it."

Finally, the women in Calvary Church in Harlem clearly represented an altogether different female style. For one thing, their gritty lives made some of the concerns of wealthier white women seem trivial. They told stories of AIDS and drugs, absent and murdered husbands and sons, and fierce struggles to keep their families and neighborhoods together. These proud women seemed to have weathered trials that prepared them for God's mercy. They had already suffered tribulation; they are the surviving remnant. There was nothing separatist about these women. They adored their charismatic preacher, Reverend Charles, and prayed with remarkable enthusiasm. They were clearly the heart and soul of their church and reached out from it to include men. They pulled their children along by the scruff of their necks and applauded their men if they made it to church. But it seemed clear to me that from this congregation, it will be the women who lead the faithful into the millennium.

6

THE
WORLD
AND ITS EVILS

▬▬▬▬▬

REVEREND CHARLES. The story Reverend Charles had found to make sense out of his life history and commitments was that of Jonah. This "first and greatest evangelist" was a messenger of God sent to warn the citizens of Nineveh that they risked destruction unless they repented of their evil ways. Jonah, who at first resisted carrying out God's commandment by fleeing (just as Reverend Charles delayed his "calling" to the ministry), eventually accepted his responsibility. He then reached Nineveh in time and convinced its inhabitants of their impending doom and the urgent need for them to repent of their sins. The citizens of the city fell down and worshipped, and even the king put on sackcloth and sat in ashes. Similarly, Reverend Charles saw his role as that of warning a doomed people of the need to beg God's forgiveness. "I think one of the roles of our church or any end time church is to make people aware." They then must change their "life-style and their attitude toward life, and their attitude toward God, and their attitude toward each other." It is only the pressure of destruction that can force such a radical transformation; standing at the edge of the Apocalypse, Reverend Charles felt, was a powerful motivator.

The ironic end of the biblical story, however, which was hardly lost on Reverend Charles, is that Jonah's success and the repentance of Nineveh only bought some time. As the book of Nahum, which is the sequel to that of Jonah, makes clear, after about a century God in fact carried out his destruction of the city so totally that it disappeared from the face of the earth. For Reverend Charles, who commented on this final end of Nineveh in a near whisper of terror, such is the paradox of faith and action. He sought to instill hope within awareness, or soon someone without "God in his heart" will "push the button." At best we can only buy time, and even that takes a huge effort and commitment. But we cannot give up, even though our ultimate destruction is assured. We must and can only act in a godly way to make a human future worthy of muting God's fury. It is an ambiguous lesson, it seems to me, but perhaps it is the only spiritually honest position in an age of real and evil threats to human existence.

Reverend Charles had a wonderful sense of humor, was articulate, and kept his vast church together as a dynamic force in the neighborhood. His hour-long sermons each Sunday were masterpieces of performance and conviction. His timing was perfect as he mocked his own sleepiness while once driving a bus (as a way of waking up the congregation), or mimicked the turning of the microphone head as an imaginary camera to keep the Lord "in focus." One could feel the expectancy in the air as his sermon approached, and the great sense of joy people took in having listened to his words and shared in his message. He had profound influence over the lives of his parishioners but used it to bring them out, to help them realize themselves, never to demean them. Reverend Charles was a consummate leader harnessing the collective will of his followers for the glory of God and the good of this deeply troubled and threatened community. These general assessments were made after some five years of my own intermittent participation in his church and three supervised interviews with Reverend Charles by a young African American researcher.

Born in 1930, not three blocks from the building that was the current home for the church, Reverend Charles was a taut and wiry man. At the time of his interviews, he was in his late sixties and had strikingly large and intense eyes. During the interviews he stared so closely as to seem almost glaring. "My folks were poor," he said. In his crowded family and later at school Reverend Charles seemed to have been particularly active and full of mischief. "I was the least likely to succeed, not because I didn't have brain matter, but I was prone to get into mischief and trouble, and my parents came back and forth more often than any parents should." Yet he carried a kind of secret mark, a special relationship to God, for his mother converted while he was in the womb. He seemed to see that as a kind of magical blessing, like being born under the caul. "I couldn't conceive that I would maybe have a hand, some small part in helping to upbuild this community," he continued, "and that's the thing that marvels me at what God is doing and has established me here three blocks from where I was born and spent over twenty-odd years, almost thirty years of my life, and then bring me back and then put me in a position where I can help to bring about some change."

Reverend Charles was brought up as a Christian, and most members of his family seem to have been believers, but sometime in his youth he himself strayed from the faith. He related this falling off to the influences of his environment. "I came up in a rough block," he said "a rough area, a rough environment and you know the right way but I'm saying get caught in the tide, and you know, I got caught in the tide for a while." As a child it became clear to him quite early that he would never succeed and get an education unless he worked. Throughout his childhood he held a succession of jobs, including tarring roofs and working in the electroplating field. At twenty-one he was drafted into the Army during the Korean War. During the training period of the war he revealed some of his significant leadership skills and was put in charge of a training program. He found he derived a good deal of satisfaction from this experience, even though he found the racism in the army at that time detestable.

For thirteen years, Reverend Charles held a succession of jobs trying to find one that would give him some satisfaction. As he noted, "I was never ever fired from a job in my whole entire life. But I went from one job to another, because I just didn't feel this was it. I didn't find that fulfillment." At last he was "called" to become pastor at the church, something he accepted with great enthusiasm, despite the fact that it meant a significant loss of income.

Reverend Charles was an impressively well-read man on current affairs and about events in general. He read the *New York Times* every day, along with two or three news weeklies to which he subscribed. His conversation and sermons were factually accurate about world affairs, and when he discussed events as signs he brought to them a subtlety of thought and imagination that was indeed impressive. He also qualified everything. He believed the end was imminent, that it could even occur before the end of this century; he also had printed on the front of the church's program (at least during the 1980s) the slogan that Calvary was "an end time church with an end time mission." But he added in his interview: "God has the prerogative to take us into the twenty-fifth century, to the thirtieth century if he wants to."

Reverend Charles's immediate family life seems to have been relatively stable and without much death or loss. The exception was an aunt, whose death when he was quite young hurt him keenly. "My aunt, she was a missionary and she had given so much of her time. I said Lord, let her live. Our family was close because two sisters married two brothers and lived together and my aunt was like my second mother. I was raised with two fathers and two mothers. I called my aunt, Momma, and called my mother, Mother. I said, "Lord why did you allow her to die? God, what kind of God are you to take a sheep?" But despite the relative stability of his family life Reverend Charles came into frequent and immediate contact with death as a part of his experiences in his world of Harlem. As he said painfully: "I watched a lot of people around me die."

He recounted that as a child he was almost killed in three different incidents. In one of them he was hit on the head and had to have a number of stitches over one eye, while in another incident that he vaguely described he was caught in the hallway while some sort of fight went on around him. He also had an extensive experience with fighting in the "clubs" or gangs that flourished in his neighborhood. He had to take "unto myself" a kind of "survival violence" to make it to school each day with his lunch money. He soon internalized the violence. "It was easy for me," he said, "to destroy."

With his gang he often beat people "to a pulp," because that's what he was trained to do as part of the "club." He was under tremendous peer pressure to act violently. "Something that takes place [and] you've got to go out there, you've got to get out there, with the rest, when they call 'let's go to war council.'" Then you "lie to your mother," and "do whatever you have to do and be down at the spot and they'd outline, 'well this is what we're going to do down here.'" No matter how reluctant you might be, you have to follow what the gang leaders tell you to do. It breeds violence in you. You learn how to "crunch a dude," which becomes easier and easier each time you do it. "So, you begin to think violently. Let's change this thing *violently*, you know."

Death, as well, haunted his existence in the gang. Everywhere there was a sense of killing, violence, and death from which he felt he was spared only because he accepted Christ into his life. "As I look back and watched what was happening to my contemporaries, the fellows I was running with, the fellows and girls, I knew then beyond a shadow of a doubt that I had made the right choice [that is, accepting Christ]." Looking back at them, he saw that most of them were not only dead but that they died violently. Others died as a result of drugs, and the rest were just "empty shells waiting to die." And he reiterated the saving power of his faith: "My survival depended only on Christ coming into my life, my receiving him."

Much of the sense of destruction and death that Reverend Charles felt was fueled by racism, a theme that resonated in the lives of his congregation. He mentioned it often in his sermons, often by allusion, not to stir up anger but to give voice to the real and in the end to move toward some kind of healing. Reverend Charles was also quite concerned with the way whites are buying up Harlem and pushing blacks out. In the long run the process was a direct threat to the future of the church, and he felt it keenly. Such real threats to existence at so many levels lent Reverend Charles an emotional tone of uneasiness tinged with marked suspiciousness toward the outside world: "I feel that *they* let it [Harlem] run down like this," Reverend Charles concluded. "That gets rid of most of the blacks, that disperses most of the blacks." Such a keen sense of danger kept Reverend Charles in a state of preparedness that made him alive and vital, but it was not without its psychic consequences.

Reverend Charles's fears ran deep. "I watched drugs," he said, "take more and more of a grip, and a generation of promising, promising young people [get] wiped out." It seemed to have no end. "There's been times I've felt in my heart that this drug thing is a planned genocide by the white man to just wipe us out." Despair grips the community. "Our fathers and our husbands are in jail . . . out in the streets." It's hard to know when it will stop. "Our black men," he said, "will not live past their forties." The world of Harlem is also clearly getting worse, fast approaching the end time: "I feel its end and end time. And I feel whatever I must do, [I must] do it quickly, do it with all my might." Jesus may not choose to come for another hundred years. That's his choice. It is not within human province to dictate the time of his coming to God. But Reverend Charles did feel, in the light of what he's seen "as a lad" and watched from the time he was "old enough to understand," that "these things have just grown increasingly worse." People seem unusually brutal and inhuman. "We have crimes and deaths now that we've never heard of," Reverend Charles said with feeling. "I mean folks cutting people up in little pieces, stuffing them in plastic bags. Man's hard, man's turning almost worse than animals."

From Reverend Charles's perspective the signs of the end of human history were evident. "On all fronts, it looks dark, it looks dark." Things seemed to be getting even worse than he knew as a child. "I don't know how we're going to survive to the year 2000 at the rate things are going now, unless some things really take hold." Something must happen. "In the light of what I see and read, I feel that we're nearing the end." There is only one solution, and that is for "Christ to return and bring about an end to all the chaos." We have every "conceivable plague," especially now with AIDS. "They say the nearest solution they see may be ten, fifteen years down the pike, and they say 'we have no idea as to the depth of this epidemic.'"

The signs are grim as well in the world as a whole. There is unrest in Israel as well as in South Africa. "There's turmoil, tension, you just sense that the world is headed for a climax."

In a typical sermon, in January 1991, Reverend Charles discussed the Middle East and the issues of the Gulf War then in progress. He noted that with the war we were hearing more about the Apocalypse. It's all part of the "signs of the times." The war sets the stage for World War III, he said, and "even ungodly folk" are talking about Armageddon. The nations are being "positioned" for the end time. The time is short, he noted repeatedly, "perhaps shorter than we think." Jesus is about to come back, the harvest reaped. The segment of the sermon dealing explicitly with apocalyptic and end time issues followed a reading from the Bible in Mark 9:30–37 and bracketed what was to occupy most of his sermon on the biblical passage.

In the verses from Mark, the disciples talk among themselves about who is the greatest after Jesus tells them of his coming death and resurrection. Reverend Charles talked at length about this problem of losing focus on what matters and straying from real concerns. He referred often to the signs of a deteriorating world and of our own sins within it. He noted the circumstances of the community where God had planted Calvary Church, namely in a world full of drugs and crime and despair. His message was that God had entrusted this congregation with a "special mission" by placing it there. "There are souls for us to reach before the end comes," he noted with a passion.

The apocalyptic ran through Reverend Charles's sermon like a red line. It was there in the biblical passage when Jesus tells his disciples about his approaching death and resurrection; it was there in the framing comments about the end times and the current war; and it was there often in the references to the people dying around us in hopelessness and despair in Harlem. And yet, despite his end time themes, I never heard Reverend Charles give a sermon that lacked hope. Somehow he used the apocalyptic to energize his congregation rather than deaden it. Surely his own skill and humanity played a role in this remarkable transformation. But, as I suggested earlier, perhaps the more one's current life approximates the original experience of oppression that led to the book of Revelation, the more apocalyptic themes can authentically speak to personal renewal and transformation.[1] Life in Harlem fit the bill. Despite all Harlem's despair, Reverend Charles maintained a curious and hopeful sense of efficacy and commitment to the human experiment. As though he was energized by standing on the brink of the end, he seemed to draw strength from the approaching Apocalypse. His response was not to be passive or to withdraw (in contrast to many white fundamentalists), but to be highly engaged and connected with life now precisely because of the imminent threat of collective death. As he said: "While I've got the people we are out on the streets, the whole building, everything is dedicated to trying to reap this harvest, because I am gripped with a sense that it is not as much time as we think." And he continued: "This is the time to get *involved*. I'm not saying, well, I've got insurance, I plan ahead, I plan for twenty years from today if I never live to see that Jesus comes next month, next year. I continue to occupy, but I occupy with a sense of urgency."

This urgency bred a spirit of social activism throughout the church. The building, which had been taken over and refurbished by the congregation, was ideally suited for a variety of programs serving the community, including day care programs, a soup kitchen, and an adolescent youth center. Reverend Charles believed with a passion that he must combine saving souls, building bodies, and revitalizing the community. He told the story of a woman whom he helped find God. She had been a hopeless drunk until he brought her into the church. She was living in the park "from pillar to post, stinking up the place." He helped her find a job and a home, and the drug support group in the church gave her new confidence. "Here she has a car in the street, [and before she was] a hopeless drunk. She has a six-room apartment, money in her pocket, money in the bank that God—the Lord has allowed her to lift not just her soul out of sin but the whole mold." She herself then became an active convert and helper in the community. "She's walking straight now, she's working in the program to help folks who are drug addicts and so forth that want to get squared away, putting them into programs, getting them jobs, rehabilitating the whole mess."

At the same time, even Calvary had an intolerant side when certain issues were touched. In the fall of 1992 in New York City an intense debate took place over a proposed new curriculum for first and second graders that in part sought to enhance tolerance for gays and lesbians (stories about having two mothers, for example). Two weeks before Thanksgiving I attended the church to see how the debate was playing out in this congregation. Calvary had lined up solidly against the new curriculum, presumably because the biblical injunction against homosexuality is simply too explicit (Romans 1:27 and especially verse 32, which notes such "sin" is "worthy of death"). One of the assistant pastors gave an impassioned plea for everyone to sign a petition against the curriculum after the service. Other speakers followed (Calvary always had some four to six assistant pastors on the stage with Reverend Charles), and one conducted a prayer for "homosexual sinners." It was for me, frankly, a painfully ironic show to watch. My experiences with Calvary's members had led me to think that they would have been able to show greater tolerance for other oppressed groups and been able to distinguish tolerance for homosexuals from an endorsement of their life-style. The proposed new curriculum did exactly that, and also included multicultural awareness and sensitivity as a much more prominent part of the changes it recommended than anything to do with homosexuality. Calvary, I felt, had gotten suckered into the wrong fight. It was interesting, however, to note that Reverend Charles himself never said anything. Some years earlier (1987) I had heard a sermon by Reverend Charles in which he stressed concern, compassion, consecration, and contact of the Christian for sinners, some of whom—"like drug addicts and homosexuals"—will be difficult to deal with. Perhaps he felt some ambivalence and left it to subordinates to oppose the curriculum.

Reverend Charles always interpreted the Bible for his literal believers in ways that connected it with their lives in Harlem as disadvantaged blacks in a privileged white world. In one sermon, for example, he took the image of the raven—a black and usually disdained bird—and turned it to his purposes. He took an Old Testament passage in which the raven played a helpful role feeding Elijah, who was hiding by the River Cherith (1 Kings 17:2–7), to explain more generally why the Lord sometimes uses the evil raven as the bearer of good. He said he had once been hit by a car and was on crutches (as he began to limp around the stage). Before the settlement came through, he was desperately short of cash and unable to work. He was out trying to exercise his leg and stopped by Big John's Candy store for a cup of coffee. A pregnant pause at this point and raised eyebrows brought instant recognition to the congregation of the nature of "candy" sold at this store. Reverend Charles noted that he knew Big John from his days driving a bus, when he would stop on his route to chat and also then have coffee. Big John, in sympathy for his old friend on crutches, gave him $100. Reverend Charles hesitated to take the money, for he knew well the source of the funds from the real activities in the back room of the store. He went through various contortions to demonstrate his ambivalence but in the end grabbed the money from the imaginary hand of Big John and limped quickly away across the stage. Sometimes, he concluded, the Lord sends gifts via the raven. We at Calvary cannot pretend not to be a part of Big John's world. We cannot retreat into our sanctuary and expect to remain a vibrant congregation. We are part of the community and we must reach out into it. Besides, he suggested by ending his story with taking the money, such interaction can be personally rewarding.

As he was well aware, Reverend Charles's program in the church and his beliefs distinguished him from most other fundamentalist churches that focus much more closely on ultimate issues to the exclusion of social and especially political concerns. Reverend Charles's end time message, on the other hand, explicitly included what is traditionally called "social gospel" *and* a commitment to long-term change in the surrounding black community: "You know," he said of his goals for the congregation, "this is really black power. I can't tell the members [of his church] that because they would back off. It is biblical. Everything that we're doing is based on scripture. But it is [also] black power. We're pooling our resources and helping each other." The black church, he said, "has always been our strength. It's been our rallying point." This sense of Reverend Charles's end time ministry as a form of black power drew on what was clearly part of his early political activism: "Had I not made a commitment to Christ," he said "I would have been a revolutionary."

SIGNS OF THE END

Just as fundamentalists are obsessed with the timing of the Second Advent, so, too, they search everywhere around them for signs that the end is at hand. The concept of such a search is biblical. Jesus thus tells the doubting Pharisees and Sadducees: "O *ye* hypocrites, ye can discern the face of the sky [that is, tell what the weather is]; but can ye not *discern* the signs of the times?" (Matthew 16:3). The world, in other words, is collapsing around us, and if our eyes are open, it should be easy to discover the truth. But if people are enjoying themselves (though falsely and full of evil), that also is a sign of the end (Matthew 24:37–39). In fact, nearly everything is a sign of the end, when Jesus will return to defeat evil and bring salvation. That is the hope in the apocalyptic. Again and again, throughout my interviews, I was struck by how dread and hope are intimately connected in the Christian apocalyptic.

Fundamentalists talk of "signs" with disarming ease and frequency. There are two levels of such signs, natural and human, a complexity that exists in the single most popular biblical passage on the subject (and, in my experience with fundamentalists, one of the most commonly quoted passages in the Bible): "And ye shall hear of wars and rumours of wars: see that ye be not troubled: for all *these things* must come to pass, but the end is not yet. / For nation shall rise against nation, and kingdom against kingdom: and there shall be famines, and pestilences, and earthquakes, in divers places. / All these *are* the beginning of sorrows" (Matthew 24:6–8). These signs detailed by Jesus in response to his disciples' question, "What *shall be* the sign of thy coming, and of the end of the world?" (24:3), range from the purely political (nations rising up against nations) to demographic, social, and economic catastrophes (famines and pestilence) to purely natural disasters (earthquakes). The specific mention of earthquakes in Matthew is why fundamentalist anxiety rises immediately after any major earthquake or other natural disaster. But of equal interest among the signs Jesus mentions are the more political examples of kingdoms rising up against kingdoms (which are more urgent than wars) and what might be considered by-products of political discord (famines and pestilence). Signs, of course, must be interpreted, and in the modern context the search for understanding has generated an expansive attitude toward technology. In this regard fundamentalists are hardly backward. In their search for empirical evidence of the unknown, which feeds their hunger for symbols, they stay abreast of modern technological culture and all aspects of the mass media revolution.

For Deborah the single most important sign was abortion. It's "pagan" and "uncivilized." And yet it continues unabated. "In our day and age, we are supposedly civilized people, and we're allowing people just to openly commit murder." Abortion, it is worth noting, is universally opposed by fundamentalists and regarded as the murder of children with eternal souls—before they have a chance to hear the word and be saved. As a result abortion is often mentioned in the same breath with wars and earthquakes as an important sign. There appears to be no room for compromise on this issue, which makes abortion quite unique, and different, for example, from the debate over creationism. Only the ideologues (like Otto in my study) insist on the teaching of evolution in the schools as a sign; I never heard anyone else mention it. A moderate position allows fundamentalists to accept the theory of evolution ("days" are metaphors in the creation story), which is consistent with the theory of inerrancy as it took shape in the 1880s. At the moment, however, given the way the debate over abortion has taken shape in the last two decades, it is difficult to imagine a biblical position on the subject (and, given the orientation of fundamentalists, any argument would have to have a biblical grounding) that would allow for the emergence of a moderate fundamentalist stance on abortion analogous to the range of views that exist within the movement regarding creationism. For progressives on this subject, the primary task at hand, it seems to me, is to identify just such a biblical rationale for a pro-choice position. It would have enormous political implications.

In any event, the fundamentalist stance on the world in general is that it is deceptively appealing because Satan works within it. Cynthia argued that you must never let down your guard as a Christian, and you must look under every rock to locate signs of the end, like earthquakes and wars, AIDS, pornography, child abuse. But Cynthia also talked vaguely of the Common Market and associated it directly with the Beast of the tribulation, which, she said, "will have everyone's identity" and put the 666 number on their foreheads. Now that's "really interesting," she said darkly, "because right now in Brussels, Belgium, the huge computer system there that controls the Common Market and everything is called 'the Beast.'"

A sign, however, can be a process as well as a thing. One such phenomenon is the quickening pace of change in the world. Brother Heflin, from a black church (he was a visitor at Calvary when interviewed), said such acceleration was one of the clearest signs. "You know you'd have a major event that might take place once in a month. Now you have major events that take place once a day almost." Frank echoed this fundamentalist response to the *rate* of change in the world as much as the evils within it. The quickening pace stimulates the apocalyptic. Frank lived with the conviction that "things are not going to get better but worse," and "there is a pattern there of things getting progressively worse and worse and worse." His metaphors in this regard were both sublime and ridiculous: he noted that microwave ovens can now cook a turkey in an hour and forty-five minutes, on the one hand, and nuclear power and aerospace technology may change our universe, on the other. "The progress we've made, it's exponential, it's beyond just gradual growth." Soon Jesus will return, he said, because things are "utterly and completely hopeless."

Otto gave this idea of the quickening pace of modern life as a sign an interesting historical twist: He argued that it began with Hiroshima and the beginning of the nuclear age. He was careful not to say with certainty that Hiroshima marked the beginning of the end times, but with that qualification, which really served merely to cover himself against overly precise statements about God's actions, the beginning of the nuclear age was definitely when Otto saw the breakdown of things begin, when human history began its downward course. He seemed to understand that ultimate issues became something forever different with Hiroshima, that nuclear power in all its dimensions altered the very shape of contemporary life. In a curious way, Otto's view reflected Robert Oppenheimer's famous statement that physicists knew sin in creating the bomb.[2]

Sam, from his position of privilege, saw the main problem in the world as the move toward a "secular and humanistic point of view where God is looked at lightly." Nigel, for his part, got visibly angry in talking about the agnostic idea that the universe began by accident rather than as a willful creation of God. It is unbelievable, he said, that someone would try to pass off such an idea. "It takes a lot more faith to believe that than to believe that God created the world." The seriousness of the challenge posed by humanism was not related to the upper-class world of Sam and Nigel, for it struck fundamentalists at all social levels. Kathryn said in this regard: "I think we have come to a culmination here of seeing just number one as being all important. Humanism is based on number one being all important. That New Age sort of thing. Seeing how you can develop the inner self to its fullest. Develop the self. So that you can become like God." Humanism, in their eyes, is the direct opposite to true belief, which takes you out of yourself and connects you with God. Humanism is selfish, inner-directed, and, as Kathryn suggested, grandiose ("So that you can become like God"). It is also linked to the New Age movement, which to their mind gives it an organizational base, a kind of church, from which it can reach out to infect the society as a whole.

One sign of so much evil in the world is that Christianity is on the decline in America. "We are very quickly losing influence," Otto said. If "we" were more powerful, "I think we'd see more righteousness in this nation." There would certainly be less drug use, fewer killings, less pollution. We might even be able to stop the "abortion crime wave." It's not church and state that is separated in Otto's view but the separation of "God from state activities." The world presses in with all its evil ways, and true Christians keep losing power and authority, though the persecution of the church is a biblical part of the end times. Otto was systematic and even scientific in his search for empirical evidence of the end. "Never just accept something because someone tells it to you. Prove it," he said, fondly quoting one of his engineering professors in college. I pushed him on why he thought the end was so close at hand. He responded: "Well, I think the scripture in Timothy says that in the last days perilous times would come. Then it lists a whole bunch of things, like lovers of self, boastful, unthankful, unholy, different things, that I'd say were getting worse roundabout us.[3] I remember growing up on Staten Island. We never locked the door, my dad left his keys in his truck. He's got locks on every window now, and even then he's been broken into."

One response to the signs proliferating in the world is to erect barriers against the world. Reverend Lester thus complained bitterly of the inadequacy of the school system to teach children how to live their lives. There are no values taught, and the system itself is loaded with drugs, crime, and corruption, he said. That's why he started the K through 12 school attached to the church. But the school was only part of the protected and sacred space Reverend Lester hoped to create at St. Paul's. He saw false prophets everywhere (alluding to Matthew 24:11), which aroused great fears in him. The evil ones are out there now "becoming part of the system," pocketing money. They are even "representing God," which was a rather nasty dig at the mainstream church. Reverend Lester's goal was to create as self-contained an environment at St. Paul's as possible. It is not possible to be hermetically sealed from the world in New York City, but one can tighten the bonds within to ward off the perceived dangers without.

Analogously, an acknowledged objective of the operation at Grady House was to encourage the rich and powerful to make their businesses Christian after their own conversion. The theological and practical issues were complicated. Jesus was quite clear about the need for the rich to give up their wealth and distribute it to the poor (Matthew 19:21, 24), though a whole discourse (based more on 2 Corinthians than on Matthew) was developed arguing that the biblical commandment was only to abandon the love of money, not money itself. The figure held up by Grady House as the epitome of evil in this regard was Donald Trump. Instead of loving money, you were to use your money and power to spread the word of God, even though evangelism in their world presented its own special problems. One highly successful midtown dentist who gave his testimonial one evening in early 1989 described with self-congratulation how he had made his practice Christian by hiring only believing assistants and working only with converted colleagues. He was vague, however, about whether he intended to put his hands into the mouths of infidels. A more interesting ambiguity emerged in a discussion I once had with a man named Morgan, whom I got to know in my Bible study group but never formally interviewed. He had made a fortune in his merger and securities business but was left feeling a tension between his faith and the godless world of Wall Street. He had made the decision to make his business Christian. I genuinely wanted to understand the specifics of what it meant to create a Christian merger and securities business, but probably questioned him too directly when he was himself in doubt about what he was creating, for he literally backed away from me and my questions. As far as I could tell, what he meant was that he would employ only Christians in his business (like the dentist) but also use his profits largely for Christian purposes. He had no intention of only consummating Christian deals, which would have been impossible anyway. That reasonable business decision made him aware of the highly limited impact his new commitments would make on Wall Street. I think he felt unclean and saw me as an accuser; in any event, he turned away from me in our group and left the mansion immediately after Bible study.

At a personal level, fundamentalists feel the dangers of the signs of the end acutely, and their lives alter accordingly. Commonly, some retreat from the world (though many more than is recognized also move into the world); others intensify their own ethical commitments to stay pure in the very face of the world's corruption. As a child, Deborah's life was often confused by the need to maintain her religious morals and her desire to fit into the sinful world at large. She refused to take square-dancing lessons at her school, for example, because there was doubt in her mind whether she should be dancing. She was allowed to study in the gym by herself during those periods. "I do think I missed out on some things," she acknowledged. Even as a forty-five-year-old woman Deborah positioned her life in opposition to contemporary American culture. She had lived in New York City for a decade and a half and only seen two movies. One was *The Last Emperor*, and "they could have left some of [the trash] out."

Such attitudes have led to the common perception that fundamentalists are separatists, withdrawn from a society they see as corrupted. At the extreme edges of the movement such separatism is total, as with groups like the Branch Davidians, or the Church Universal and Triumphant led by Elizabeth Claire Prophet, or in quieter ways with many smaller church groups in communities around the country. But to label Christian fundamentalists generally as separatist would be wrong. There are, in fact, many exceptions. As I mentioned before, Calvary was a very socially involved church, with its programs for adolescents and drug addicts, its soup kitchen and counseling. And it was not alone. Most members of Abiding Light and St. Paul's (two lower-middle-class and working-class churches with many African American and Hispanic members) worked with the poor and the homeless. St. Paul's ran a soup kitchen, Abiding Light ran a special program for kids in the projects, and generally ministered to homeless people. Abiding Light also regularly had special collections for a drug treatment center for adolescents it ran elsewhere, and often the rehabilitated (and saved) kids came to sing and testify at services.[4]

Even at the upper end of the social spectrum I found some evidence of involvement in the world that went beyond evangelical work. It is true that most of those who attended Grady House deplored New York as dirty and dangerous, a city of sin from which they escaped to the Hamptons whenever possible. Many whom I knew directly worried no more about the world than the dentist who reported making his practice a Christian one. But a few people I got to know at Grady felt rather more empathy for the poor and sought to reach them. Larry struggled to define a world of modest social action for himself that went beyond the boundaries of Grady House. "Your faith without works is death," he said, trying to remember in his uncertain way where the commandment is in the Bible (in James 2:14: "What *doth* it profit, my brethren, though a man say he hath faith, and have not works? can faith save him?"). I asked him what constitutes "works" and he listed feeding people who are hungry for food and fellowship, visiting the sick, relating to the depressed. And he made his commitments real. Every other Sunday afternoon he and his wife went down to a mission in lower Manhattan to work and minister. It was a form of social activism that overlapped with his evangelical commitments, but it also went beyond merely saving lost souls. It was a fairly substantial amount of time for a busy broker who was in school and active in both his church and at Grady House.

ANTICHRIST

Despite these efforts toward good "works," though, the world remains corrupt, full of "false prophets," deceivers, and evil of all kinds. The obvious signs of evil for fundamentalists—crime, abortion, pornography, AIDS, humanism, the acceleration of change itself, the existence of weapons of mass destruction—resonate with scripture and serve as direct reminders of the approaching end. But even beyond such signs the real evil in the world is that which lies unseen or masked by apparent goodness or harmless pleasures—the devil, about whom fundamentalists have a lively image. The devil is at hand, speaking, as Wilma said, in one ear while God speaks in the other. Isaac, in turn, believed the devil is the "most beautiful creature ever created in God's universe." In Ezekiel he is described as a "beautiful cherub, one of God's highest angels." Some people think he was the "choir director" of heaven, but in any event he is a "very powerful, powerful creature." And he is nobody's fool. Never underestimate him, Isaac warned. He will come as the "angel of light," not as some "deformed thing with a red tail." Deborah noted: "And I believe there is a real devil. It's not just a, you know, a way of saying, 'This is good and this is bad.' This is God at war."

The devil manifests himself in human form most concretely as Antichrist, who comes as the great deceiver, the messenger of peace. Most fundamentalists believe he has already been born, and, like Monroe, allude to 1948 (the creation of Israel) as the beginning of the end times in which Antichrist plays such a crucial role. In the scheme of things, Antichrist makes world peace, including most of all with Israel, before revealing himself in all his horror. The subtextual message is beware the peacemaker. The greater the world leader, and the more he speaks to global issues of peace (for example, Gorbachev), the more he is ultimately to be feared as the probable Antichrist. One day, Cynthia said, people will turn on their TV and this "great leader" will appear to tell them everything is okay. They will be fooled into accepting his message. Thelma noted (referring obliquely to Jeremiah 6:14): "The Bible warns us that when men cry peace, peace, then sudden destruction [is certain]. I'm not interested in world peace because I know it's not what God says will be. He has never lied. His prophecies have come true. They're written down." Reverend Matthew had an expansive understanding of Antichrist that included the institutions within which he worked: "Now, the man [Antichrist] again, who, as I said, could be a system, but could well be both: a man with a system, a system that is so subtle that it sounds logical. For example, even the financial structure . . . the World Bank and all the things that are focusing on getting things with some brain, so-called, behind it. And one who can befriend everybody, no enemies. The best way to judge Antichrist is to recognize he is the opposite of Christ."

Carl Jung, in his perceptive ruminations on Antichrist, begins with the idea that the image of Christ parallels the psychic manifestation of the self. In that sense, Antichrist corresponds to the shadow of the self, the "dark half of human totality." The psychological concept of the self cannot omit the shadows, for without it the archetype of Christ lacks "body and humanity." He adds: "In the empirical self, light and shadow form a paradoxical unity." But the self, as expressed in the archetypes of Christ and Antichrist, is "hopelessly split" between the irreconcilable halves that find expression in the metaphysical dualism of the "kingdom of heaven and the fiery world of the damned." Antichrist is the "counterstroke of the devil." It only became Christ's adversary after the rise of Christianity. The image of Christ is so sublime, so perfect, so spotless, that it "demands a psychic complement to restore the balance." If you speak of high, there must be a low, of right and there must be a left, of good and there must be a bad, of the one and there must be the other. The devil is necessary to the image of Christ; in early Jewish-Christian circles the devil was seen as Christ's elder brother.[5]

Perhaps Christians in general but certainly fundamentalists in

particular need the idea of Antichrist to balance the absolute goodness embodied in their image of Jesus. They make abundant use of
Antichrist in this psychological and spiritual sense. Fundamentalist
images of Antichrist can be quite varied and creative, partly because
the two direct references to him (1 John 2:18, 22 and 2 John 7) and
the two indirect ones (2 Thessalonians 2:9 and 1 Timothy 4:1) are
thin. As a result, these references have been fleshed out with other,
vaguer ones, especially Matthew 24:24 ("For there shall arise false
Christs, and false prophets, and shall shew great signs and wonders;
insomuch that, if *it were* possible they shall deceive the very elect"),
and made into a wonderfully picturesque, malevolent figure.

Cynthia stressed that Satan as Antichrist appears as an "angel of
light," which is why he is so confusing. We believers know "who the
final deceiver is going to be," she said—not according to script—but
everyone else is bound to be fooled. Isaac, for his part, said Antichrist would be like John F. Kennedy or Adolf Hitler, both "amazing
men." Antichrist will be so powerful as to mesmerize us. He may
have telekinetic powers. Searching for another metaphor, Isaac said
Antichrist will be like a slum landlord who lets everything get run
down. "But the real owner is going to come back." Brother Heflin,
finally, as most fundamentalists, believed Antichrist has already
been born. In him all sin and chaos unite. Furthermore, he will set up
his kingdom right here in New York at the United Nations, with
branches in Europe (the Common Market) and a third in Jerusalem.

Otto felt that Antichrist works through religion. He uses false
faith, in other words, to draw people in, "then, after he consolidates
his power, then he will outlaw all religion and just say 'I am God, if
you're going to worship someone, worship me.'" The "religion"
that concerned Otto was less secular humanism than the New Age
movement, to which he ascribed some rather surprisingly malicious
motives. For one thing their goal, he said, is to reduce the world's
population to 2.5 billion people by the year 2000 by using euthana-
sia and forced abortions and encouraging homosexuality. In time,
Otto feared, "they may decide Christians are not useful if circumstances were right."

Things were always ominous for Otto. He thus had some quite
specific fantasies about how Antichrist will subtly take over. It will

begin with a consolidation of all the numbers in our lives—social security, bank, license, car—into one computer chip that "they" can put in the back of your hand, "and then just put you under a scanner, or whatever they use, and it could tell who you are, how old you are, where you live, how much money you have in the bank, what bank do you work with, and all these things." Perhaps, he said, they could just as well use a "laser-type tattoo." But since "it talks about not being able to buy or sell with that mark" it will pose a severe problem for believing Christians. Antichrist will not allow you to live in the world without the mark, but Christians will know they cannot take it on. Reverend Lester, like Otto, believed that during the end times people will have to take on signs on their foreheads to buy or sell anything, "almost like a credit card." He had even thought through the bureaucracy of the beast. "Instead of carrying a plastic card you'll go to some place and you'll get a number on your forehead that can be read by some machine. It won't be visible, I don't think, but it will be very clear that that's your numerical entry into buying and selling. It's like having credit cards."

Such modern concreteness about the passage from Revelation brings the end times into direct connection with modern technology in an almost humorous way. It is exactly such contextualization that makes end time imagery real and evocative for fundamentalists. Once the metaphor is literalized, it makes psychological and even spiritual sense to ground it in the specifics of the known world; at the same time, the dimension of absurdity that adheres to literalized end time ideas within a modern world may begin to undermine the whole elaborate structure.

TWO

PSYCHOSOCIAL PERSPECTIVES

7

THE
PROBLEM
OF ENDISM

———

THE REACH OF ENDISM. Endism, it could well be said, is the
shadow side of our firm belief in renewal and second chances. It is
our counter-narrative that competes with the boundless optimism
we have in the future and our remarkable confidence in the capacity
of our political system to correct itself for its own excessive enthusiasms.[1] Endism, which demands a special hearing as we approach the
end of this millennium, opposes such optimistic commitments,
foolishly perhaps, but always with conviction. It cares little about
adjusting for small swings from center right to center left, or making
more equitable use of resources, or allowing creative forms of
expression, or, indeed, about sacrificing today to build a human future for the sake of our children's children. The Christian apocalyptic, as one expression of endism, seeks renewal through ultimate violence and God's cleansing of the earth, through faith rewarded and

evil punished, and most of all through the miraculous return of Jesus.

The principal apocalyptic text of Christian fundamentalist culture, the book of Revelation that so many of my respondents quote, is also the one written last, in A.D. 95, after the destruction of the Temple and the Roman massacre of as many as a million Jews. God's revelation, as disclosed to John of Patmos, comes in the form of a violent and destructive end of human history, followed by some kind of parenthesis that fundamentalists read as the millennium, and the great climax of the final judgment which sorts out those who go to heaven while nonbelievers are thrown into the lake of fire. The apocalyptic, in other words, relates the specific forms of our forthcoming destruction, including the seven-year period of tribulation with its ferocious and unfolding violence of trumpets, seals, and vials that ends with the great battle of Armageddon between the forces of good and evil on the Plain of Jezreel near Megiddo in part of what is present-day Israel. One might say, following Revelation, that the apocalyptic connotes the violent, the redemptive, the vengeful, and the hopeful.

But the term "apocalyptic" also has a series of looser and more secular meanings that have accrued to it over the centuries that, like it or not, have become part of its associative meaning. Thus the apocalyptic is also the predictive (as that which foretells what will happen), the terrible (or any imminent disaster or final doom), the grandiose (or any wild and unrestrained predictions), and the climactic (or anything that is ultimately decisive). In this broad sense the Civil War, Hurricane Andrew, and the return of Jesus can all be quite accurately called apocalyptic, or, more broadly, endist.

Endist thinking, in other words, moves in many directions—including, most of all in America, race relations. The Los Angeles riots of 1992 struck terror in this country. "The City of Angels," said John Singleton, producer and director of *Boyz N the Hood*, the morning after the rioting began, "is turning into the City of Armageddon."[2] And New York has its own brooding tensions. In the Crown Heights section of Brooklyn a Hasidic Jewish fundamentalist group of Lubavitchers lives uneasily among Caribbean and African Americans. In the summer of 1991 a young rabbinic student, Yankel Rosenbaum, was stabbed and later died in a riot after a car in the entourage of the Lubavitcher Rebbe, Menachem Schneerson, hit and killed a young black male. Some radical Jewish leaders complained later that the police were instructed to go easy on rioting blacks, a complaint that was given new life when the person accused of stabbing Rosenbaum was acquitted. The accusation was that Mayor David Dinkins created a climate of fear about black riots after Los Angeles that made it impossible for a jury to convict Rosenbaum's accused killer. Even more specifically, former mayor Ed Koch sharply criticized Mayor Dinkins for talking about the danger of black backlash. When Dinkins makes such statements, Koch said, "he's threatening us with violence."[3] In this case the apocalyptic worked its way into the terrain of fear and code-words that make up American race relations. With a phrase a Jewish former mayor conjured up the Holocaust and pogroms and the whole scenario of racist imagery about black violence for political use against an African American mayor trying to control just such tensions, to stave off further violence, and to prevent white flight. The Los Angeles riots have altered the racial climate in New York and across the country, as fear of racial violence has itself become part of the apocalyptic, renewing the deeper hatreds and fears that always lurk below the surface of American culture.

Endism is deeply rooted in human experience and human history. Henri Focillon, in his brilliant historical and avowedly psychological study, *The Year 1000*, notes that the decline in cultural and artistic activity in the monasteries toward the end of the tenth century was "an evening of the world" (*mundus senescrit*) in people's imaginings.[4] The conclusion of the first millennium seemed too precise a fulfillment of *millennial* anxiety. It took no elaborate calculations, or year-day equivalents, or any special knowledge to feel secure in the approaching end of history. The end (followed by renewal) had long been associated with thousand-year cycles and was in fact known to *all* the ancient peoples "as a basic element of their religion or philosophy." The only change Christianity introduced via John of Patmos was to be specific about the thousand years (Revelation 20:4: "And I saw thrones, and they sat upon them, and judgment was given unto them: and I *saw* the souls of them that were beheaded for the witness of Jesus, and for the word of God, and which had not worshipped the beast, neither his image, neither had received *his* mark upon their foreheads, or in their hands; and they lived and reigned with Christ a thousand years"). In medieval Europe's thoroughly biblical culture, and one brimming with superstition and general illiteracy, the apocalyptic had a kind of democratic flavoring. No experts were required to foretell its coming. Most people (at least as far as one can tell from the fragmentary evidence available) assumed the world was about to come to its logical conclusion. A "nameless fear gripped mankind," a dark mood fell on the age.[5]

When nothing happened there was at first confusion (was the date wrong when Christ was born?), then astonishment, and finally a dawning sense that it was not going to end after all. A great weight seemed to be lifted. The monk Glaber wrote: "About three years after the year 1000, the world put on the pure white robe of churches."[6] Life began anew, especially in the monasteries where virtually the only written evidence of the change in attitude then existed. Dutiful monks who had stopped copying manuscripts resumed their tasks. Men thought again about religious and ethical issues. Long-delayed architectural projects were renewed, which in turn required money and spurred economic activity. Many factors fed into the great awakening that came to be called the Renaissance, and its full flowering was several centuries off. But its early stirrings in the eleventh and twelfth centuries make no sense except as part of a renewal of the human spirit after the grip of the apocalyptic was broken. The extent of the renewal serves indirectly to suggest the degree of psychological bondage in the apocalyptic experienced by a whole generation before the year 1000.

Focillon further argues that the more broadly secular meanings of the apocalyptic arose in the series of crises in the late medieval and early modern period in Europe that included the Reformation but also brought recurring plagues, witch burnings, and seemingly endless wars that dragged out over decades. "We may say," Focillon concludes from a look at the endist imagery in that period of history, "that every time mankind is shaken to its depths by a political, military, or moral cataclysm, it will evoke the Apocalypse."[7] Focillon also notes that there might well appear to be a contradiction between the humanism of the Gospels, which breathe love and peace, and the apocalyptic violence of Revelation. In fact, however, "each of the two satisfies certain needs of the human soul, and it may even be said that they complement each other."[8] Love and hate, one might say, as well as their extensions into peace and violence, are both potentials of the self.

The diverse meanings of endism, however, should not obscure the fact that we know of it directly because we all die. We are the only animals with such knowledge, even though it keeps fading away. It can well be said that human culture itself depends on the struggle to become aware of death. A primary task of religion is to provide some meaningful sense of endings and beginnings (which is why images of the millennium so often draw on those of the Garden of Eden, or, as Freud put it, our images of the future are molded by our indestructible wishes from the past).[9] Our children and forms of work symbolically immortalize the self. And all types of art, but especially literature, seek to define continuities and at some level are always about what Frank Kermode calls the sense of an ending.

No one argues more strenuously than Kermode for what I might call eternal endism.[10] He dismisses as "childish" any attempt to attach special significance to the terrors of our modern age, arguing that apocalyptic thinking is too firmly rooted in human experience. Only the naive, he argues, would privilege one's own time as uniquely dark and set it off as a cardinal point in time. The anxiety itself is not new. Cultures since the Mesopotamians have been dealing with it. Only the patterns of creative response to that anxiety have been different.[11] Kermode would also dismiss as heated imaginings the brooding anxiety aroused by the approaching end of the millennium. It would seem a form of "centurial mysticism," or, as Don DeLillo calls it, "millennial hysteria."[12] To the extent that we feel we now live in a state of perpetual transition, Kermode argues, we elevate our period of ambiguous ending into an "age" in its own right.[13]

Much wisdom lies in such a deep appreciation for the enduring, human attachment to the end. It has been part of culture since its beginnings some six to eight thousand years ago. Most scholars would agree with Focillon's discussion of the decline in creative activity in the half century before the year 1000 (though the evidence is inevitably thin and has occasioned heated controversy).[14] Norman Cohn has shown how widespread the manifestations of the apocalyptic were in social and religious movements throughout the Middle Ages.[15] And much in modern life continues these diverse forms. Apocalyptic eruptions reminiscent of tenth-century France or nineteenth-century New York state (the Millerites) often puncture our sense of calm, from those who mark the end (Elizabeth Claire Prophet in 1990; the Mission for the Coming Days, which forecast the rapture on October 28, 1992),[16] to those who claim divinity (Menachem Mendel Schneerson and David Koresh in early 1993), to the more simply, if terrifyingly, psychotic (Jim Jones). Modernism, it might be said, merely alters the shape of endism. It becomes democratic and somewhat chic, especially in a time of mass communications.

But such continuities may be misleading. To note only the eternal aspects of endism may prevent an appreciation for its more specific historical manifestations, compromising in the process specific moral and psychological insights. Based on the interviews I did for this book, I would argue that our historical moment is fraught with a new kind of dread, for we live with the real, *scientific* possibility that either through nuclear warfare, or choking pollution, or vastly increased rates of disease, especially cancer, we could actually end human existence. Millennial anxieties were quite real in the latter part of the nineteenth century—the term "fin de siècle" originated in the 1880s—and were grounded in the pervasive dread of a transforming modernism.[17] Yet Americans remained optimistic, expansionist, and assertive about the great virtue of their newly forged political institutions. But in the last half century things have begun to change in society, in the family, and most of all in the self. One can no longer trust in a human continuity; it matters that such an ending is scientifically possible. We no longer need poets to tell us it could end with a bang, or a whimper, or in the agony of AIDS.[18] Consciousness of endings haunts the psyches of quite ordinary people.[19] This is what Robert Lifton has called the "shadow" of nuclear threat. It changes nothing in particular but influences everything, and it is surviving astonishingly well after the cold war (just as nuclear threat preceded the beginnings, in the late 1940s, of the cold-war phase of American-Russian rivalry).[20] Before the nuclear age, conjuring up an idea of the actual end of humanity took a leap of imagination. But human endings now lurk in everybody's minds. No one can escape it; indeed, to completely ignore the forms of our potential destruction itself requires an act of imagination.

Furthermore, the emergence in the last half century of a mass movement of Christian fundamentalism, energized by the apocalyptic, has moved the endist impulse into the center of our culture, where it works directly on large numbers of Christians and spills over in unpredictable ways into other cultural forms. The task of the next chapter is to understand specifically how we arrived at this mass movement of apocalyptic fundamentalism. But for the moment, I want to further reflect on the larger implications of fundamentalism for American culture, and how the experience of fundamentalism can work on each of us.

COMMUNITY AND TOTALISM

It is by no means obvious what "being saved" means to ordinary members of fundamentalist churches. Cynthia literalized the metaphor: "You can't possibly know the answers to spiritual life until you're born again." And at another point: "You can't expect to see and understand things of the Spirit until you are born again." And a third pass: "You can't possibly expect to have all the answers when you are still in the birth canal; you have to be born again." All of these versions of the same idea came in one of Cynthia's breathless harangues, and were not dissimilar in content from Monroe's earnest efforts to convince me that only through belief could I get answers to my questions about end time things, or the grounds on which Mary finally refused me a third interview (I could learn more by talking directly to Jesus, she said). As discussed in earlier chapters, the idea that you truly understand what is in the Bible only after being saved is quite conventional among fundamentalists. The words of God are readily available. Anyone can buy a Bible and read them. But those words will be without meaning, or integrity, until you read them as a believer. Then the ideas become clear, the mysteries are solved.

Born-again reading thus casts most discussion of the Bible into a mystical framework, with some important consequences. Many fundamentalists, even recent immigrants for whom English is a second language, insist on reading Scofield's King James version of the Bible with its beautiful but old-fashioned English phrasing. The KJV overall is in a distinct minority among Bibles actually read by fundamentalists (there are some four hundred fifty English-language versions on the market),[21] but it remains the standard in their minds, the ideal to be reached if at all possible. In born-again reading you simply let the text wash over you, bathing your soul. Your task as a believer is to enter into the deeper sense of the words, which represent God talking directly to the reader. If you believe by definition you understand, which is not exactly the hermeneutics we try to teach in the university, and why it took me so long to figure out that my innocent questions about the meaning of difficult passages were often experienced by fundamentalists as intrusive and threatening.

Mystical reading of the Bible also binds the fundamentalist to the community of the church in ways that can be distinguished sharply from most other social institutions in America. They are all born again, and the kind of reading and understanding that they believe flows from that experience grounds their rituals of togetherness. There are, of course, personal and psychological factors in the born-again experience, but accepting Jesus also brings the believer firmly into a tightly cohesive community, which I suspect is as much a motivation for as a consequence of conversion. Friends, entertainment, ethical guidance, and personal integrity all meet in the community, which in turn shapes a parishioner's sense of self. In a world of often intense loneliness (perhaps exaggerated in New York City) and disintegrating families, the vitality of the communities created in the fundamentalist churches is one of their more salient features. At a place like St. Paul's, for example, parishioners often ate together, they spent much of Sunday and at least three nights during the week together, and their children attended the church school. Pastor Lester also played a fatherly role toward them, and he and his wife often had people over for meals. He advised them on minute details of their lives. From the outside it all seemed rather suffocating and infantilizing, but for the members of that community it clearly provided a togetherness that gave meaning to their lives. Even at Grady House, the involvement in the affairs of the community could extend to several days a week including special events like the ski trips for singles or religious retreats over whole weekends.[22]

But the dissolution of self in community can have an apocalyptic downside. At Abiding Light, something was seriously wrong, since from a once huge congregation in the first five or six decades of this century, by the late 1980s Abiding Light was a decidedly dwindling institution. That decline struck terror into the hearts of many parishioners who found it difficult to simply move on, or to understand such changes in anything but cosmic terms: the decline of the church, as everyone who was interviewed told me, was yet another sign of the end. The psychological investment in the church was too great. Its decline made no sense. God must be willing something, revealing his majesty through such ironic means. In this way, a kind of greatness (and mystery) returned to the church. God would never idly let one of his precious institutions disappear.

The mere fact of spending time together means virtually nothing in terms of the psychological experience of participation in a group. It is easy to be lonely in a crowd, or, conversely, to feel richly connected in the mutuality of a close relationship with one person. What defines the fundamentalist church experience is the intensity of its group interaction and the way it draws the individual into its rituals in an active way. Participation is never casual. If during a service you try to sit in the back unseen, there will suddenly be someone at your side, who will afterward take you to the coffee hour and invite you to Tuesday Bible study and Wednesday prayer meeting. At that coffee hour you will be asked directly where you stand with Jesus, along with many facts of your personal life that relative strangers in most group situations would wait months to ask about.

The benefits of such a strong, cohesive community are significant. Friendships are often intense. One is assured support in times of personal crisis. There are as well enhanced feelings of self-worth from participation in religious rituals. I learned quickly in my interview work that one good entry into a person's story was to ask them about how they found Jesus. Frequently, at the end of the interview people would give me a tape of their "testimony." Finally, it matters to one's sense of personal worth that the experience of the divine is shared. Otherwise, it suffices to stay at home and watch a televangelist.

On the other hand, many are repelled by such close encounters and dismiss the group experience in fundamentalist churches as cult-like, though the term "cult" is perhaps so loaded today that it may be losing its significance. A better conceptual question might be whether the fundamentalist experience is "totalistic" in the mind-numbing ways defined by Robert Lifton. Based on his interview work with "brainwashed" dissidents in China during the 1950s, he developed a number of criteria for defining the totalistic environment. These include the control of communication so that the balance between self and world is disrupted; manipulation of the individual around basic issues of trust and mistrust; the demand for absolute purity, which is contrasted with an outside world of pure evil; the obsession with personal confession as the vehicle for obtaining purity and merging the individual with the community; the maintenance of an aura of sacredness around basic dogma; loading the language with highly reductive, definitive-sounding phrases that can be easily memorized and repeated; the subordination of the individual to the claims of the doctrine; and drawing a sharp line between those who have a right to live and those whose lives can be dispensed with in the name of the movement.[23]

There are, to be sure, totalistic enclaves in contemporary fundamentalism. In David Koresh's Branch Davidian compound near Waco, Texas, for example, four or five score followers of this self-proclaimed messiah moved in a trance-like state as they gave over their lives (and the women and girls their bodies) to their leader's extravagant fantasies. The group was cut off from the evil world and armed to the teeth to ward off its potential intrusions, fears that in the end proved quite realistic. Koresh himself developed rituals of immersion into his dualistic world, as when he divided his followers into two groups, the first of which said, "Who's gonna destroy the Babylonians?" and marched three steps in place, to be answered by the second group, "We're gonna destroy the Babylonians." Certainly, Koresh's apocalyptic ideas were sacralized, his language loaded, and evil outsiders were to be dispensed with in the climactic events he foretold. David Koresh was unusual in his charisma, in his disregard for the psychological or sexual separateness of his followers, in his violence, and in the immediacy of his apocalyptic aspirations. But as the leader of a fundamentalist cult he was not alone, nor even that unusual. There are anywhere from 1,000 to 1,500 mostly nonviolent but separate and totalistic cults in contemporary America.[24] The actual number depends, of course, on how you count, but no one with experience in this area would claim the number is negligible.

But is the Branch Davidian sect in Waco—or Jonestown, or the more extreme survivalist and end time groups in places like Idaho[25]—the appropriate model to use in analyzing the typical fundamentalist church? It would be easy to do so, especially if one had a desire to malign the movement, to collapse its wings and use the totalism of Waco as the standard for defining fundamentalism everywhere. It would also be wrong, and certainly contrary to my experience in the churches. Fundamentalist dogma has a totalistic core, even if one has enough breathing space to live in the world as well. But what sustains that core can be complex and very human. Most of the time in my fieldwork I actually enjoyed myself. In all the churches I became friendly with a number of people, and felt I touched lives in a real, human sense as I developed enough closeness to conduct interviews in a private space with a tape recorder. I was invited into their homes, fed, and told of their deepest fantasies about end time matters. I often felt assaulted by their relentless efforts to convert me, but it soon got easy to endure "the pitch" as something their faith required of them. It would be highly dishonest to suggest that I experienced fundamentalists in any way as mindless, thought-controlled cultists.[26]

At the same time, it is important not to be fooled by the ordinary. Significant areas of continuity exist between the mainstream fundamentalist movement and its more extreme manifestations. In terms of ideology, in fact, little separates the two. The Branch Davidians in Waco were firm believers in the theory of premillennial dispensationalism (as are most survivalist, Aryan, or Neo-Nazi groups, whatever else they are). In terms of the rapture, Koresh and his followers were "mid-tribbers." In other respects, David Koresh understood the return of Jesus in ways quite familiar to mainstream fundamentalists, though to be sure, he added a few wrinkles to the end time story. His name, which was the Hebrew version of King Cyrus of Persia, connected with various apocalyptic themes in the Old Testament (it was in the third year of the reign of Cyrus that Daniel had his vision and Isaiah defines Cyrus as an instrument of God), and Koresh in general placed a great deal of emphasis on his symbolic tie to Jews and Israel. A flag with the Star of David on it flew over the compound, and as the flames consumed the buildings one of the last visible images was that of the flag falling into the fiery apocalypse. Koresh also believed that the House of David would be reestablished in Jerusalem when Jesus returns.

In tracking my feelings in the churches, I also noted, often reluctantly, that the pull toward totalism always exists in fundamentalism. When the ideological basis of their belief system is so apocalyptic, it matters that fundamentalists spend so much time together in worship, study, and prayer. The world, they believe, is an evil place to be resisted, and it is in any event on a sure path toward imminent destruction. Everything about their experience tends toward a psychological closing down. After extended contact, I often experienced such attitudes as oppressive. I personally have a lot of hope for the world. For all its suffering and gloomy potential, it is a wonderful creation that we have a responsibility to preserve for future generations. Fundamentalists believe otherwise, which I respect but found distressing and frankly irritating in large doses.

I had even more difficulty accepting the forced immersion of children into the fundamentalist world. Adults make the beds they lie in, but I always felt a pained empathy for the gloomy apocalyptic that surrounded the lives of the children in the churches. Philip Greven, in *Spare the Child*, argues that the authoritarian tradition in Christianity itself finds new vigor in the violence and abuse against children in fundamentalist families, which in turn creates the psychological conditions that attract damaged selves to the apocalyptic.[27] Although he exaggerates, Greven has identified an important psychosocial dimension of contemporary fundamentalism. Even if it is not expressed in physical violence, a violation of children's wills occurs in forcing on them an ideology that makes the world an evil place, in dragging them into a closed faith system without exit from an early age, in loading them with guilt, and in insuring that conversion occurs early enough so that they are bound to the community of believers before they are really ready to make free choices.

There is also a potential for violence in fundamentalism that I often found troubling. As we have seen, violence often defines their discourse. They talk and sing of washing their robes in the blood of the Lamb (Revelation 7:14), and warm to the cascading images of destruction and death in Revelation as trumpets are blown, seals opened, and bowls emptied in the heavens. These waves of violence form a rising and interconnected spiral, for the seventh of each includes and opens up to the next, until it all culminates in the final judgment. The churches themselves are awash in this imagery.

With most fundamentalists, however, this violent undertow remains an unseen counterforce beneath a relatively calm demeanor because of the shift in agency to God. The violence is ultimate rather than proximate. It comes from the heavens rather than from within us. Believers alone will be saved and all others killed. Believers are pure in faith. And in that faith they can overcome death *and* the sins of everyday life. Such a shift in agency allows individual fundamentalists to separate themselves from the violence that suffuses their ideology and present themselves as decent, kind, law-abiding citizens with enduring family commitments. But I found that at important psychological levels they move toward the violence that distinguishes their elaborate system of belief. Under individual or social duress that violence can turn from latent to overt forms. A group like the Branch Davidians in Waco represents that potential realized.

These general considerations, which constantly occupied my thoughts in and out of the churches, found personal meanings in my encounters. In Ian's Bible study, for example, I once let slip that I was married and had three children. Up to then I had studiously avoided mentioning my family. I sensed such knowledge would somehow be used to invade my privacy, indeed my separateness as a person in the interests of trying to convert me. It was. From that moment I was asked on a weekly basis about my family and strongly encouraged to bring them to church. It was suspect that I never brought them to church with me, especially as I clearly was not converting. Why was I there? What was I up to? One day I made yet another mistake and indicated my wife was pregnant. That piece of personal news opened me to the insistent intrusions. Ian immediately asked the group to pray earnestly for the unborn baby, for its future salvation, for the life of its mother, for me, for my faith, and for all unborn babies whom ungodly folk abort. I was appalled at what I had gotten myself into, and found myself praying against Ian and the group and all their dangerous ideas, vowing to myself that if something happened to my unborn baby I would hold them accountable. It was one of the few times I actually prayed in all my fieldwork (and, alas, in this study, prayer usually had this defensive quality for me). I was genuinely scared by the intrusiveness of the group and the danger of potential taint they seemed to pose at that moment in a matter of such enormous personal significance. (The baby, a beautiful little girl, was fine.)

Clearly I have no simple conclusions about the fundamentalist encounter from this analysis. The fundamentalist experience ranges across a continuum from Waco to Harlem, from complete surrender of the individual to the demands of a totalistic group and a charismatic leader to the empowered experience of building self-cohesion and salvaging community, with every kind of nuanced variation in between. Most fundamentalist churches are not totalistic. Believers are too much in the world and themselves to imagine they are under some mind-bending system of control. People come and go from these churches easily (sometimes to the consternation of the ministers). Adults entering the churches make free choices about participation. The vibrant and large fundamentalist congregations are well led and tightly organized. Others, like Abiding Light, are dwindling and often rather pathetic in their failure to attract people. But for all that the potential to move toward totalism still remains. Social crisis, or a big war, or a disaster like nuclear terrorism could transform the movement overnight into a potent and active apocalyptic force, and so transform the American political and social landscape. The consequences of such a transformation are unpredictable, but it is probably not unreasonable to guess that they would not be welcome.

8

A HISTORY OF
AMERICAN ENDISM

Endism is not without a history. Its medieval roots were suggested in the last chapter. In America, the story begins around 1820, though of course it has antecedents: the colonists' struggles to create the city on a hill in the seventeenth century encountered truly great odds;[1] and our own revolution was more radical than most people realize.[2] One could also note that the very discovery of America began in a kind of phallic apocalyptic. The feminist theologian Catherine Keller thus deconstructs the image (from her school days) of a blond, blue-eyed Columbus gazing out at the oceans as a masculinity looking forward, "penetrating its own future, piercing horizons," a gaze that will "render the planet endlessly available to cartography, to conquest, to control, to commodification." Basing her study on his *Professies*, only recently published in Spanish and not translated into English until 1991, Keller notes that in fact Columbus harbored extravagant apocalyptic dreams about the Americas and his relation to them. By his own calculation the world was to end in 1650, an imminence that lent urgency to his "discoveries." He was also the "Christ-carrier," as he began signing letters during his third journey in 1498, selected by God to fulfill ancient prophecies. "He would be the one to rescue Christianity before the Apocalypse," Keller notes, summarizing Columbus's *Professies*, "by spreading Christianity to the unsaved pagan populations around the world," finding the gold "for financing the crusade to recapture the Holy Sepulcher from the infidels." He was to be the new Christ who would discover Eden and rejuvenate the faith at the moment of the world's transformation into the millennium. At some level Columbus confused the line between himself and Jesus.[3]

But endism as we know it in contemporary America, specifically in its Christian form but equally in its broader cultural expressions, began to take clearer shape in the early nineteenth century. Any such historical—or psychohistorical—dating is arbitrary. One could begin elsewhere, and certainly emphasize different dimensions of the story. I have chosen here to narrate the historical unfolding of the Christian apocalyptic in the last century and a half. This narrative began in our crisis over slavery, was forged in war, took ideological shape within Christian theology as a response to modernism, was turned into dogma in the early twentieth century, and became a mass movement in the nuclear age.

LINCOLN AND THE CIVIL WAR

Antebellum America was obsessed with apocalyptic anxieties. This era of rapid social and economic change seemed to spawn great confidence, and yet, as de Tocqueville and many other European visitors noted, the boisterous claims made for the superiority of American life and land and democratic institutions had a distinct note of insecurity to them.[4] Underneath everything lay the great moral blot of slavery that at last began to push many whites to feel radical social change was necessary (or at least inevitable, even if regrettable). The sensitive founders, especially a Virginian like Thomas Jefferson, had recognized the immorality of slavery and the contradictions of their slave-owning lives as they wrote impassioned documents of human freedom. After the 1820s such tortured hypocrisy was a thing of the past, as the institution of slavery itself changed in the first half of the nineteenth century, gaining a new economic vitality and bringing vast wealth into the South. Its apologists became increasingly brittle. In the North the voice of dissent gained new moral ground, connected in part to the spirit of intense revivalism and religious fervor that swept the land from the 1820s on. Preachers like Charles Grandison Finney had remarkable evangelical successes in upstate New York and whole new religions (like Mormonism) appeared in the country. It was also a time of widespread apocalyptic predictions. William Miller, the most famous such prophet, had fifty thousand devoted followers and may have had as many as a million people more loosely associated with his movement in the early 1840s, though after his failed prediction of the return of Jesus on October 22, 1844—called the Great Disappointment—his movement rapidly disintegrated.[5]

The wait for some kind of dramatic resolution to the crisis affected peoples' minds and souls, and profoundly influenced the shape of politics. The antislavery movement, for example, beginning in earnest in the 1830s, reacted with moral outrage and a mounting sense of frustration to the continued existence of slavery. With the identification of slavery as a national sin, the antislavery movement brought a new earnestness and zeal to the political process.[6] During the 1830s a strong religious fervor encouraged abolitionists to commit themselves to a variety of reform movements (especially temperance) and remain peaceful, even pacifist, in their means.[7] But after the war with Mexico and the huge land grab in 1848 seemed to open up the country to domination by a white-led South based in slavery, abolitionists felt the struggle for radical but peaceful social change was being lost. Moral persuasion was not working. The old pacifism gave way to accommodation to violence as the only way to end slavery. For example, John Brown's attack on some proslavery settlers in 1856 at Pottawatomie in Kansas reshaped attitudes and prepared the ground for his attempted raid on Harper's Ferry in 1859. That raid, said the leading African American intellectual, Frederick Douglass, "has attacked slavery with the weapons precisely adapted to bring it to the death. . . . Like Sampson, he [Brown] has laid his hands upon the pillars of this great national temple of cruelty and blood, and when he falls, that temple will speedily crumble to its final doom, burying its denizens in its ruins."[8]

An underlying dread pushed the culture to extremes. There was almost a war in 1850, especially over the return of fugitive slaves. Some, like Lincoln, reluctantly accepted the great compromise measures of that year ("I confess," he said, "I hate to see the poor creatures hunted down . . . but I bite my lip and keep quiet.") Others, however, were much more vehement in their denunciation. "Let the President drench our land of freedom in blood," said Joshua Giddings of Ohio, "but he will never make us obey *that* law."[9] Throughout the rest of the decade there was much apocalyptic rhetoric about the "irrepressible conflict" (William H. Seward), the "impending crisis" (Hinton R. Helper), more loosely of the great fight to come, and of course Lincoln's own imagery of the "House Divided" in 1858 (which resonated so widely partly because it was imagery drawn from three of the four Gospels):[10] "It will become *all* one thing, or *all* the other," Lincoln said from the floor of the House of Representatives in Springfield, prophesying a climactic end to the great issue facing the nation.[11]

As the crisis over slavery deepened in the next three years, so did the sense of inevitability, North and South, about the approaching war. For the first time in the country's history, voters faced stark presidential choices regarding secession and slavery: the southern wing of the Democratic party openly favored secession against a Republican candidate widely perceived as an active enemy of the South determined to abolish slavery. Even the centrist Stephen A. Douglas blamed the Harper's Ferry raid on the "doctrines and teachings" of the Republican party.[12] Nevertheless, as Don Fehrenbacher has recently noted, it remains surprising that the South should have taken such an apocalyptic view of the perfectly legal election of Abraham Lincoln. Somehow Southerners had come to feel that the Republican party was a "hostile, revolutionary organization bent on total destruction of the slaveholding system."[13] And so, mysteriously it seems to me, the Confederate States of America squandered whatever moral authority they might have possessed in their attempt to build a new nation and fired the first shot at Fort Sumter.

Arthur Schlesinger, Jr., has said that the end of slavery in America is a good example of the triumph of the rational in our history.[14] If true, it is an odd characterization of the rational. Slavery itself was grounded in wild fantasies on the part of Europeans about Africans;[15] the antislavery movement, from the moment of its active beginnings in the 1830s, drew its entire inspiration from biblical images of moral reform, and when it turned toward an accommodation with violence in the 1850s generated apocalyptic (and sometimes mad) leaders like John Brown, while even its moderates, like William Lloyd Garrison, thundered with Mosaic certainty: "Ardently as my soul yearns for universal peace, and greatly shocking to it as are the horrors of war, I deem this a time when the friends of peace will best subserve their holy cause to wait until the whirlwind, the fire and the earthquake are past, and then 'the still small voice' may be understandingly and improvingly heard."[16] The forces that the war set loose pushed the sluggish system toward radical change;[17] and the great jubilee of emancipation itself inspired apocalyptic rhetoric in almost all observers, including in that seemingly rational man of action whom history pushed to actually free the slaves.

The Civil War shattered the dream of infinite progress that Americans had long nourished. De Tocqueville noted, with grudging respect but more than a little irritation, that Americans possessed a complete confidence that they rode the wave of the future and that their democratic institutions would eventually triumph over the tired monarchies of Europe. Ideas about American millennial purpose reached a kind of apotheosis in the notion, first formulated in 1845, of our "manifest destiny" in the world. Such exuberance in both the North and South cloaked imperialistic (and genocidal) motives while at the same time expressing a genuine sense of chosenness. The South felt entitled to create a nation in its own image while the North felt virtuous in its condemnation of the extension of slavery and its commitment to keeping the Union intact. Perhaps clashing forms of self-righteousness were required for such a bloody civil war to result. The special forms of our mission had been taking shape since the seventeenth century, when some ministers began calling their congregations "our Israel" and culminated in the northern idea of the Civil War as "ennobling."[18] Such attitudes led a man like Matthew Simpson, a confidant of Lincoln and champion of the Union, to comment during the war that, "If the world is to be raised to its proper place, I would say it with all reverence, God cannot do without America."[19]

War also gave reality to images of apocalyptic horror. Americans before the 1860s, to a large degree, had been insulated from the violence of war. The Indians were uprooted and pushed west with relatively small contingents of regular troops and only rarely engaged in actual battles. On the edges of American life, an edge that kept pushing west, of course, there was some experience of violence and fighting. Otherwise, despite the violence of slavery, in our systematic destruction of Native American life and culture, violence in the family, in the newly emerging cities, and, one might say, in the soul of Americans,[20] Americans had been pampered in relation to war before the 1860s. We simply had no idea what it meant for hundreds of thousands of people to die in vast battles on our own soil. The Civil War prompted powerful yearnings among whites and, as far as one can tell without a written record, blacks as well, for an apocalyptic cleansing in the fires of war. War would purge the virus of rebellion and remove the blot of slavery. This idea was clearest among abolitionists, who talked of American sin in slavery with every breath and urged the battalions onward to redeem the land. Lydia Maria Child said that she abhorred war, "yet I have become so desperate with hope-deferred, that a hurra goes up from my heart, when the army rises to carry out God's laws."[21] And George Ide, a noted preacher, seemed to justify any destruction as part of the war's higher purpose: "The cause of our country and the cause of religion, the cause of humanity, the cause of eternal Right and Justice, are so intimately blended in this crisis, that you cannot separate them. The triumph of the Government will be . . . the triumph of pure Gospel."[22] Some, like Lincoln and a few of his more timid or humane generals, were appalled at the carnage, but most seemed to revel in it.

An extraordinary number of Civil War generals, most notably

Stonewall Jackson, were self-defined as Christian soldiers marching onward, and only slightly more secular types, such as William T. Sherman, often sounded like Old Testament prophets.[23] In general, as Charles Royster has noted, northern military, political, and spiritual leaders talked loosely of a policy of extermination and repopulation of the South that would have to precede any regeneration of it in a way that set no limits on the destruction necessary to accomplish such goals. Both sides descended into "visions of purgation and redemption, into anticipation and intuition and spiritual apotheosis, into bloodshed that was not only intentional pursuit of interests of state but was also sacramental, erotic, mystical, and strangely gratifying. This process of taking the war to heart, believing that it would change everyone, worked as strongly as any other influence toward making it more inclusive and more destructive."[24]

Even Robert E. Lee worked from within an apocalyptic script. Lee's misplaced sense of "honor" led him to pursue the war long past the time he was personally convinced it was lost. As Alan Nolan has thoughtfully argued, Lee despaired more than has been recognized in the summer of 1863 after the defeats at both Gettysburg and Vicksburg, though he could reasonably cling to a shred of hope in northern opposition to the war. After the siege of Petersburg began in June 1864 (a full ten months before Appomattox), Lee characterized the certainty of southern defeat as "categorical" and "unqualified." He then lost even the remotest hope for the Confederate States of America with the reelection of Lincoln in November 1864, which was still five months before the final surrender. As Nolan points out, military leadership is not just a private matter. To continue a lost cause means that thousands more must die, or be maimed, or suffer.[25] Why did Lee keep fighting when he knew it was hopeless? Certainly he was insensitive to his obligations as a general not to waste lives. But in all other ways Lee seemed to care greatly for the welfare of his soldiers, who reciprocated with a blind worship of him. The issue would appear to be a more complicated one psychologically, one that is common to leaders—military, political, business, whatever—in many situations of looming defeat, namely the enlargement of their own grandiosity so that they can no longer distinguish between their own failure and that of the world (or army, or government, or business); indeed, that if they go down to defeat the world ends in an apocalyptic sense. For those with a paranoid cast, like Hitler, suicide is the preferred route at such a final moment. Lee, being sensible, instead built a protective myth of the "Lost Cause" that shielded him and the South in general from facing the moral and political consequences of his disastrous leadership in the bloody war.

But perhaps only defeat could satisfy the South, which lacked the morale to win due to their uncertainty about their identity, the peculiar circumstances that created secession, and doubts about the validity of their cause. They were economically and militarily ill-equipped for a long war, but much more importantly they were not spiritually or ideologically ready to fight one. There was much bravado. Alexander Stephens, Vice President of the Confederate States of America, said at the outset of the war: "Lincoln may bring his 75,000 troops against us. We fight for our homes, our fathers and mothers, our wives, brothers, sisters, sons and daughters! . . . We can call out a million of peoples if need be, and when they are cut down we can call another, and still another."[26] But in fact most white Southerners "could not persuade themselves," as Kenneth Stampp has argued, "that slavery was a positive good, defensible on Christian and ethical principles." Abolitionism, as they recognized at some level, was the "echo of their own conscience." It was a $2 billion investment and white Southerners dreaded the consequences of living with four million free blacks in their region. But they also knew it was basically wrong to keep Africans enslaved. It was an impossible dilemma. Only defeat served their purposes, something they embraced, probably unconsciously, on the road to Appomattox.[27]

Lincoln, in turn, was not always helpful in taming the apocalyptic impulses in the culture. In his first inaugural address he talked loosely about secession as the "essence of anarchy," and soon after characterized the firing on Fort Sumter as an attempt to "end free government upon the earth" (July 4, 1861), which became, by the end of 1862, a war to defend our fragile democracy as the "last, best hope on earth." The apocalyptic, in fact, was everywhere in Lincoln's rhetoric: in military strategy ("I think to lose Kentucky is nearly the same as to lose the whole game");[28] in his ready embrace of unconditional surrender as the goal of the fighting;[29] in his transmutation of individual soldiers' mortality for the nation's immortality in the Gettysburg Address;[30] and in his characterization of the war as a "fiery trial" through which we must pass.[31] As David Hein has noted, Lincoln surely used this phrase in conscious knowledge of its biblical origins in 1 Peter 4:12–13, where the experience of the fiery trial is that of martyrdom, or participation in the sufferings of Christ.[32]

Americans moved easily and quickly into this imagery of a purging through violence. As James H. Moorhead has noted, for example, the Civil War was the first time (and I would add the last) in our history that there was a virtually unanimous feeling among northern ministers that the war was hastening the day of the Lord and was a "climactic test of the redeemer nation and its millennial role."[33] By the second year of the war soldiers were singing that apocalyptic favorite, "Mine eyes have seen the glory of the coming of the Lord," who is "trampling out the vintage where the grapes of wrath are stored," not to mention the implicit theme of sacrifice in their song, "We are coming Father Abraham, We are coming, We are coming." Horace Greeley spoke from within the violence of the apocalyptic when he wrote on July 7, 1864: "Our bleeding, bankrupt, almost dying country longs for peace—shudders at the prospect of fresh conscriptions, of further wholesale devastations, and of new rivers of human blood."[34]

Many thoughtful observers have been mistaken in their strenuous efforts to rationalize Abraham Lincoln and take him out of this cultural apocalyptic in which he thrived and to which he gave such powerful voice. He was himself undogmatic, cautious, forgiving, ambiguous, and always sensitive to the inscrutable ways of God. One has to be impressed by the subtle irony of someone who could call Americans the "almost chosen people."[35] Furthermore, Lincoln's avowed use of apocalyptic rhetoric is always tempered with a human touch of doubt and forgiveness. The stark choices for the country he lays out in the first inaugural address culminate in an appeal for us all to be touched by the better angels of our nature. His passionate commitment to democracy was grounded in his belief that only free government can insure justice. He talked of fiery trials but moved quickly toward compromise about reconstruction in Louisiana as early as 1862. He insisted on the defeat and surrender of southern armies in the field but strictly avoided himself using the rhetoric of unconditional surrender and never talked of purging any land with blood.

And yet Lincoln defined the policies that created the war and formulated the specific apocalyptic language that gave it meaning for a Bible-drenched culture, from the image of the "fiery trial" in 1862, to that of the sacrificial redefinition of the nation's purpose at Gettysburg in 1863,[36] to God's purposes in ending slavery about which he spoke in his second inaugural address:

> *If we shall suppose that American Slavery is one of*
> *those offences which, in the providence of God, must*
> *needs come, but which, having continued through*
> *His appointed time, he now wills to remove, and that*
> *He gives to both North and South, this terrible war,*
> *as the woe due to those by whom the offence came,*
> *shall we discern therein any departure from those*
> *divine attributes which the believers in a Living*
> *God always ascribe to Him? Fondly do we hope—*
> *fervently do we pray—that this mighty scourge of*
> *war may speedily pass away. Yet, if God wills that it*
> *continue, until all the wealth piled by the bond-man's*
> *two hundred and fifty years of unrequited toil shall*
> *be sunk, and until every drop of blood drawn with*
> *the lash, shall be paid by another drawn with the*
> *sword, as was said three thousand years ago, so still*
> *it must be said "the judgments of the Lord, are true*
> *and righteous altogether."[37]*

The most extraordinary development of the apocalyptic in the Civil War, however, occurred in connection with the death of Abraham Lincoln. Shot on Good Friday and dead the following morning, Lincoln immediately became, in those 1865 Easter Morning sermons, a modern Jesus whose blood sacrifice fulfilled prophecy.[38] This "terrible tragedy," said the Reverend C. B. Crane of Hartford, Connecticut, is the "blackest page save one" in the history of the world and is an "after-type" of the passion of Jesus. It was "meet" that Lincoln should have been shot on Good Friday. "Jesus Christ died for the world; Abraham Lincoln died for his country."[39] The Reverend Rolla Chubb, in turn, noted: "On that sacred day, made holy and consecrated to the freedom of our race, by the crucifixion of Him, who died to redeem mankind from the thraldom of Sin and the slavery of the Devil, we were called as a nation to mourn the martyrdom of the great emancipator of four millions of slaves from the vilest bondage that ever saw the sun." The parallel was not exact, he recognized. And yet the spiritual joining of Jesus and Lincoln was virtually complete: "Those who thought to crucify the spirit of Freedom, will behold it roll away the stone from the sepulchre, and visit with a pentacostical effusion its disciples, inspiring them with a faith that shall revolutionize the world."[40]

The analogy with Jesus helped explain God's purposes in the war. The "serene Providence" gave us Lincoln, said Ralph Waldo Emerson, to direct the country through the war.[41] And Henry Ward Beecher added that, "His life now is grafted upon the Infinite, and will be fruitful as no earthly life can be."[42] In the minds of at least his northern contemporaries, including some of its intellectual and moral leaders, Lincoln thus carried out divine intention. This keen sense of American mission in the immediate wake of both Lincoln's death and Lee's surrender at Appomattox was cast in millennial terms. "In blessing our Abraham," Theodore L. Cuyler said, "God blessed our regenerated country, and the whole household of humanity." And the noted historian George Bancroft opined in his sermon that, "Heaven has willed it that the United States shall live. The nations of the earth cannot spare them."[43] Through Lincoln God revealed his plan. "The great battle of Gog and Magog," said Chubb, "is being fought on the gory field of Armageddon, which is the American Republic—a contest between freedom and oppression, liberty and slavery, light and darkness—and O how that conflict has raged during the past four years!"[44]

The sanctification of the Union was essential in constructing the Lincoln/Jesus myth. On the day Lincoln was shot but without knowledge of the assassination, the Reverend George Dana Boardman, speaking at the "re-establishment of the flag at Fort Sumter," described the American Republic as not a league but a nation, not a confederacy but a people, not a congeries of states but a Union. It is a "vital, throbbing, indivisible organism" and secession is more than subtraction or amputation but a "vivisection, suicide, murder, a death." And now with peace "a millennium awaits the groaning, travailing creation" that we call this Union. The celebration at which Boardman spoke marked the return of the fort where the fighting began and, by extension, of the Union itself. At the ceremony the actual tattered flag that had been lowered in defeat four years earlier was raised to the salute of one hundred guns.[45] It was a moment of great significance for the Union; and within hours Lincoln lay dying. This eerie, almost mystical, sequence of events was hardly lost on contemporaries, which is why the Boardman sermon on April 14 got published together with his Easter Sunday sermon on the assassination two days later; why the Reverend Theodore L. Cuyler talked of the "resurrection" of the flag at Fort Sumter in his Easter sermon;[46] and why the Reverend S. S. Guthrie could say: "His [Lincoln's] soul took its flight amid the echoes of solemn praises which accompanied the raising of the old flag over Sumter. Both are significant. The nation has completed its atonement; let the New Man and the People see to it that the New Dispensation shall come."[47]

There was, of course, a good deal of variety in the sermons and many regional and denominational idiosyncrasies. The eastern as opposed to the western, and the Unitarian and Congregational as opposed to the Baptist and Methodist, sermons tended to be more literate and less likely to fall into extravagant comparisons of Lincoln with Jesus, except by allusion and context. But in the end the *common* themes in the sermons are more striking than the variations. A great American secular and religious myth took shape almost instantly in the pews that Sunday morning. The historian and minister William E. Baron noted in the 1920s that there probably had not been a Sunday in American history when as many people attended church.[48] "Certainly history," noted a Boston preacher, "furnishes no case in which death has so instantly invested its victim with the sanctity of an approval more spontaneous and universal."[49] The Reverend W. E. Guthrie noted that Lincoln's death was his "apotheosis" and that he was now "The American Martyr."[50] "These trappings of sorrow," noted a Massachusetts minister, "—this sable, fringing and shadowing the nation's flag—these wailing Misereres that rise in the place of the joyful Easter Jubilates that we thought to sing—they are but poor symbols of the grief that lies too deep for tears. What has he not been to us—this high priest of Freedom—murdered at the altar."[51]

The most hopeful version of the apocalyptic was explicitly joined to images of Lincoln's own generosity and spirit of forgiveness[52] and expressed the transformative power of the bloody sacrifices of the war. The war, said one minister, "baptized our land with blood."[53] But God caught us up short in our moment of victory and took Lincoln. God hopes that Lincoln's death will bring Americans to their knees in a pious sense of their dependence on the Almighty. We will then become, through the sacrifice of Lincoln, fully aware of God's gift.[54]

Many sermons also developed transformative images of Lincoln as Moses, leading blacks out from slavery and glimpsing the promised land but not actually inhabiting it. Lincoln's identity as the Great Emancipator made such a comparison almost inevitable. Furthermore, the rhetoric of most preachers when they did refer to Lincoln as Moses slipped almost unconsciously, and sometimes unbiblically, into images of Jesus. The Reverend Charles S. Robinson said blacks expected Lincoln, and had been waiting for him, as the Israelites did Moses. "They prayed he would come. They waited for him to come. And then he came! . . . He seemed to them and their children a second Messiah." This "world's Redeemer" became then for blacks "*their* Messiah" (though one has to wonder about the patronizing way Robinson speaks so grandly for African Americans), "the seed of the woman [Mary], appointed to bruise the head of the serpent, in whose folds so many generations of their race had been crushed." In the end Robinson adopted an explicit note of apocalyptic hope: "Over the sad pall that covers our buried hopes bloom the bright flowers of resurrection."[55]

But for all the bright and hopeful—if extravagant—images in these sermons, there was as well a violent and vindictive theme that expressed the passions of a country just emerging from four long years of civil war. The assassination itself (America's first) was darkly evil in the minds of many ministers. As the Reverend James Douglas noted: "We mourn, in our deepest humiliation, the disgrace inflicted on our national character, in the most odious crime known, not only to civilization, but to barbarism."[56] No one doubted where ultimate responsibility lay for the assassination. A relatively unknown but quite typical minister, the Reverend James DeNormandie, rhetorically asked, Who killed Lincoln? It is said a man named Booth did it, he replied to himself. But that man was only an instrument. The true cause lay in those who supported slavery for two hundred years.[57] In most cases, in fact, the sermons gloss over the person of John Wilkes Booth, who on that Sunday was still at large. All felt that Booth would surely be caught and his co-conspirators hanged. The larger issue was whether the South would somehow reassert itself and restore slavery, which, some darkly noted, was by no means fully eradicated since the Thirteenth Amendment, though passed in Congress, had not been adopted in a number of states.

This vindictive endism erupted in the sermons even though most ministers recognized it was out of character with Lincoln himself, as well as with the spirit of renewal and joy in the resurrection of Jesus on Easter Morning. Those who developed this theme searched biblical texts for a rationale that would ground the theme of retribution. The Reverend John Chester, for example, quoted 1 Samuel 15:23, which equates rebellion with witchcraft, and Exodus 22:18, which says that witches should not be allowed to live. His conclusion was that the South had a "sinful complicity with slavery," was then rebellious, and like witches must die. Now they have murdered Lincoln. In dealing with their crime, there should be no "undue leniency," especially with the leaders of the Confederacy. "If this people let this sin of rebellion go unpunished, they will repent it in sackcloth and ashes."[58] The Reverend William Chaffin emphasized as well that those who murdered Lincoln were seeking to restore slavery. "Not to punish them with memorable penalties, is to set a premium on treason and bid for a recurrence of rebellions in the future. It is but right that we should be roused to a state of terrible indignation, for our uncompromising severity will, in the end, be the greatest mercy."[59]

There are those, said Charles Robinson, who were "nurtured under the hot debasements and vile luxuries of the slave system, sojourning here on our charitable sufferance, in order meanly to escape the perils of the ruinous war they have helped to incite, who clap their hands in applause of this murder! I think, in serious self-defense, we are to see that this thing is ended. This wickedness clamors for retributive judgment, and invokes the wrath of God." Although Lincoln himself demonstrated forgiveness in much of his life, Robinson thought that forgiveness was inappropriate in light of what the nation faced at this moment. "Let it be said, in reply [to the call for forgiveness], that the tidings of this murder, going into the ranks of rebellion, will be hailed with a howl of gladness and satisfaction, equal to the yell of Pandemonium, when Satan seduced Adam, and buried a race in ruin." Ultimate issues were at stake. The very existence of the Union, indeed of humanity, seemed in the balance. We do not want revenge but retribution, he concluded: "Let judgment follow on as implacable as doom."[60]

FUNDAMENTALISM AND THE APOCALYPTIC

"Strange (is it not?)," wrote Walt Whitman, "that battles, martyrs, blood, even assassination should so condense—perhaps only really, lastingly condense—a Nationality."[61] There is no question that the war, however terrible, brought some good and perhaps had to be fought; the end of the obnoxious institution of slavery has to be judged as a positive outcome of the war. But what is the nature of that millennium for which all those people, black and white, died? And what is the meaning today of having forged, but not discarded, the apocalyptic as the core experience of our nationality?

The great disappointment of it all was the huge letdown when it was over. The American character had been "tempered in the furnaces of war"[62] without much to show for it except missing limbs and a broken heart. The expectations of freedmen were dashed in the wake of a white southern backlash and a feeble national effort to protect the gains of the war.[63] Whole cities were destroyed, families broken, social and political institutions were in chaos. The Apocalypse had not brought the millennium. The story remained unful-filled, the script only partially enacted. The Union was secure, but the war shattered the dream of infinite American progress. We could no longer fully trust a human future—and this loss of faith in the ground of our being was to find deeper resonance in the ultimate threats of the twentieth century.

The war that seemed to settle so much for the future—the secure institutions of a national government and the end of slavery—in fact left open, bleeding wounds. Out of it came a postwar culture rent by the discords of modernization. The old patterns of communal life were breaking down. Basic changes in the infrastructure (especially those fostered by the railroad) were changing the very face of America. New cities sprang up everywhere, and old ones altered beyond recognition in the wake of huge population shifts from South to North and East to West, along with the largest influx of immigrants ever in American history. A new phase in industrialization took shape by the end of the century, one that some have called a second industrial revolution grounded in the new industries of oil and electricity and fed by the systematic expansion of scientific knowledge.[64] In addition, a widespread cultural insecurity, as Elaine Showalter has argued, "was expressed in fears of regression and degeneration, and the longing for strict border controls around the definition of gender, as well as race, class, and nationality." The terms "feminism" and "homosexuality" both came into existence in the 1890s. The anxiety then, she argues, parallels our contemporary fears about AIDS and homophobia that have prompted a return to patriarchy and celibacy.[65]

The conventional view of the formative influences in the shaping of fundamentalism keeps the analysis tightly within the boundaries of religion. This religious view holds that certain doctrinal developments occurred that fed the popularity of a seductive new approach to scripture. "Fundamentalism was primarily a religious movement," says George Marsden in the very first sentence of his authoritative monograph on the origins of American fundamentalism between 1870 and 1925.[66] Even Timothy Weber, in his excellent study of premillennialism, which acknowledges the apparent relationship between it and the rise of industrialization and the disintegration of American society, asserts: "Premillennialism's rise cannot be explained on environmental or even psychological grounds." His view, on the contrary, is that it arose "as an authentic part of the conservative evangelical movement at the end of the nineteenth century that gained popularity among those conservatives who favored a rather literalistic interpretation of Scripture and who recognized in premillennialism a way to remain both biblical and evangelical under difficult circumstances."[67]

Such an approach, which passes over the Civil War as a mere backdrop, privileges the heated theological and doctrinal disputes of the era and downplays the significance of their cultural context. But the whole period from the 1830s to the 1880s was one of radical ideological change within Christianity, and the appearance of premillennialism only became a movement of any significance after the Civil War. The key ideas of this emerging theory—dispensationalism, the rapture, and the "new" premillennialism (new because it was associated with these other ideas as part of a larger theory)—all dated from the 1830s, with sources in much earlier thinking.[68] The only subsequent development at the level of theory that mattered was the notion of inerrancy that forged a long tradition of loose biblical literalism into dogma.[69]

The key figure in this process of ideological change was John Nelson Darby, who was born in London of Irish parents and had been ordained in the Church of England before he broke from it in the 1830s, first to join the Brethren, and then in the 1840s to lead a faction within that group called the Plymouth Brethren (or Darbyites).[70] Darby's theory of "premillennial dispensationalism" included the idea of the rapture as the way Jesus returns before his millennial rule, and his idea of dispensationalism, which placed us in the last days without having to predict the actual time of the end, was a substitute for the kind of end-time arithmetic of William Miller. While Darby's theory was a new mix, it is worth pointing out that many of the individual strands of his ideas had earlier sources: · his basic apocalypticism evoked that of the early Christians; the notion that Christ would return before the millennium was well established, especially in America; the essential idea of dispensationalism is at least as old as Joachim of Fiore's three Ages (the third of which, the Age of the Spirit, lies in the future) from the twelfth century; and glimmerings of the rapture doctrine can be seen in Increase Mather's thinking from the seventeenth century.[71]

Nevertheless, earlier sources are not the same as final formulation. The seven dispensations Darby worked up fit the biblical story well and are much more concrete and evocative than Joachim's amorphous Ages. The rapture in Darby's hands became a central idea in his prophetic system: it was the moment of separation of the faithful from human time, the spark that starts the end time clock ticking, rather than a mere possibility in the apocalyptic margins of Mather's thought. Darby also came up with some completely new prophetic notions, especially regarding the Jews and Israel, that had enormous consequences later. Darby, in other words, created a whole ideological system out of some existing strands of thought and some that he added. This whole was much larger than the sum of its parts, of sufficient depth and breadth and adequately enough based in scripture to ground the subsequent mass movement of fundamentalism.

It took the Civil War, however, before the culture began to be receptive to these new ideas—and even then things moved slowly. Darby himself was a tireless promoter of his ideas. He preached often outside the British Isles and was particularly influential in the United States, especially after 1859 (between then and 1877 he made at least six major tours in this country).[72] In these years Darby's ideas joined with the more homegrown theory of biblical "inerrancy" that took shape in the 1870s and 1880s. What is often lost in historical discussions of the origins of the idea of inerrancy is that from the outset the motivation for creating a systematic theology of biblical authority was apocalyptic. Spiritually and emotionally it is relatively easy to be literal about the sores on Job or Jonah's whale. It can be quite problematic, on the other hand, to take literally and theologically the complex symbols in prophecy. And that is what inerrancy was all about. What people really wanted to know was how to make sense of the seven weeks of Daniel, or the millennium of Revelation. If God loosed Satan from the bottomless pit, does that mean hell must be at the center of the earth? Where are the books of life and death that are opened at the final judgment? Are the wars and rumors of war in Matthew portents of an imminent return of Jesus?

Biblical literalists emerged out of a history of what is called Scottish Common Sense Realism and near reverence for the philosopher Francis Bacon.[73] In this value system (or discourse), the world presented itself in relatively simple, direct form, and the task of the observer was to gather evidence of its meaning. Enough carefully selected facts on a given problem yielded an answer that amounted to truth. In the spiritual realm, the search for Truth was subject to the same method. Close biblical analysis of a text thought to be without error proved the scientific validity of God's revelation to humans. Blind faith was unnecessary. One only needed to accept the validity of the scientific method. The most advanced and modern of approaches could prove the ineffable. Belief seemed ever more certain, grounded, secure.

Such literalism, of course, sometimes bordered on the absurd, as it does sometimes today, and spoke mainly to the observer's lack of sophistication, or education, or lack of psychological flexibility. But it was a comfortable academic setting that provided the crucial institutional framework for the development of a *theology* of literalism. The Princeton Seminary, founded in 1811, proved remarkable in this regard. Its most famous professor was Charles Hodge, a voluminous writer and editor. His magnum opus was his *Systematic Theology*, published in three volumes in 1872 and 1873. Hodge built something of a dynasty at Princeton (and immortalized his scheme of biblical interpretation), since two of his sons and one grandson all held chairs in the seminary. Other figures at Princeton, such as Benjamin B. Warfield, were important in the new theology, but none had the commanding influence of the Hodges. Within the ivy walls of Princeton, seemingly insulated from the outside world but in fact directly and interdependently connected to it, these Calvinist scholars pored over the Bible and its meanings in an attempt to formulate a theology relevant for the new world of postwar uncertainty.

The notion of inerrancy took concrete shape in the 1870s. Charles Hodge, in his *Systematic Theology*, argued that all of scripture, every book and every word in every book, was divinely inspired, based on his reading of Jeremiah 1:9: "Then the Lord put forth his hand, and touched my mouth. And the Lord said unto me, Behold, I have put my words in thy mouth." How God actually put his words into the mouths of humans remained inscrutable, but as Hodge once said, biblical writers "were controlled by Him in the words which they used," a formulation that has not unreasonably led to the persistent idea among literalists that God dictated the Bible to his oracles.[74] Hodge himself could easily allow for errors in biblical texts ("No sane man would deny that the Parthenon was built of marble, even if here and there a speck of sandstone should be detected in its structure"), but his son, A. A. Hodge, and colleague, Benjamin Warfield, pushed his ideas to new heights of certainty. In an 1881 article, the two argued that "all the affirmations of Scripture of all kinds whether of spiritual doctrine or duty, or of physical or historical fact, or of psychological or philosophical principle, are without any error." And Warfield wrote: "A proved error in Scripture contradicts not only our doctrine, but the Scripture claims and, therefore, its inspiration in making those claims."[75] In the theory of inerrancy, in other words, literalism became dogma.

However, one key problem in the theory that threatened to undermine the new theology needed to be solved. Careful research, especially by German scholars, was continually unearthing contradictions in the texts of the Bible. Since Charles Hodge stopped short of an absolute theory of inerrancy, he could airily dismiss such apparent errors as sandstone specks in the marble, but once his son and colleague had turned his ideas of literalism into dogma, the issue of mistakes in the biblical texts could not be avoided. So they came up with the convenient idea of "original autographs," or the notion that the only truly inerrant texts were the first ones written. Since then, with all the copying and translations, errors have inevitably crept in. It was a convenient theory, since the original texts have long since been lost, but it also created further problems of its own for which there was no easy or logical solution. What an inerrant believer has to accept in reading the Bible is that it is a surviving text that is simultaneously seriously flawed and yet perfect. Ernest Sandeen rightly sniffs with disdain at such a "scholastic" argument.[76] It is worth noting, however, that psychologically inerrancy at its core has a mystical grounding: The perfect text can only be imagined, not seen; must be believed, not read; worshipped, but never directly encountered. Perhaps any literalism, whether Christian or Marxist, requires such an intellectual and spiritual adjustment. Biblical literalism makes mystics of the whole fundamentalist movement.

In the remaining decades of the nineteenth and the early years of the twentieth centuries, the new movement gained a wide audience. It sometimes named itself premillennial but is better seen as a loose coalition of like-minded conservative evangelicals who drew loosely on Darby, the Hodges, and others. It would be an historicist fallacy to portray the movement as unified in theory, practice, or membership, but nevertheless a movement was taking shape. Regularly held "prophecy conventions" were hugely popular; the *New York Tribune* issued the 1878 sermons from one such meeting at the city's Holy Trinity Episcopal Church in a special "extra" of 50,000 copies.[77] Dwight Moody in turn created a number of institutes, the first of which was in Chicago in 1888, that trained "gapmen" to "go into the shops and meet these bareheaded infidels and skeptics" in order to appeal to them "in the name of Jesus Christ." Moody dispensed with laborious training in Greek and Hebrew in his institutes. He wanted to graduate evangelists, not exegetes, as he put it. Hundreds graduated each year from his institutes (which numbered fifty by 1900), and many more attended for brief courses of study. In a matter of a few short years and largely via this new institutional vehicle, premillennialism transformed the missions field.[78]

The waning years of the nineteenth century was a time of religious enthusiasms on a variety of fronts. Some new sects appeared (for example, Christian Scientism), while Seventh-Day Adventism, founded in 1863, gradually shed its dismaying Millerite background and became an important premillennial group. Charles Taze Russell founded the Watchtower Bible and Tract Society (Jehovah's Witnesses) in 1884, which was explicitly built on the predicted end of the world in 1914 (needless to say, it developed some new ideas about the end after that). A surge in revivalism in the early part of the twentieth century furthered these prophetic developments. The most famous was the Los Angeles revival in 1906 that led directly to

Pentecostalism and its leading denomination, the Assemblies of God, founded in 1914.[79]

The fundamentalist movement also acquired grounding in two texts that became the basis for a new canon. The first was Cyrus I. Scofield's edition of the Bible that was published in 1909 and sold as many 10 million copies by 1967 and since then 2.5 million more copies of a revised edition.[80] It had long been a convention in the Judeo-Christian tradition that notes and commentary on the Bible should be published separately from the text itself. Scofield, an ardent premillennial dispensationalist, broke that rule and incorporated both into his edition of the King James Bible. In the Scofield Bible each book is introduced with a brief essay that provides some basic background about the author and the premillennial dispensational meaning of the text. The tone of this version of the Bible is clear in the first textual note, which *precedes* the first word of Genesis: "The Bible," that note states with authority, "begins with God, not with philosophic arguments for His existence." Each of God's dispensations is explained with great care, and anything obscure or relevant to the larger theory is explained with forward and backward references. Most of all the prophetic texts are interpreted in elaborate detail. The mention of "tribulation" in Revelation 7:14, for example, calls forth a note that begins: "Although God's people may expect tribulation throughout the present age (Jn. 16:33; Acts 14:22), the word 'tribulation,' as here, is also used specifically of a future time (Mt. 24:21, 29; Mk. 13:24).

"Since our Lord links the abomination of desolation spoken of by Daniel with this time of tribulation (Mt. 24:15–21; Mk. 13:14–19), it is evident that the tribulation is to be connected with the seventieth week of Daniel (Dan. 9:27). Furthermore, the biblical references have in common an allusion to unprecedented trouble (Jer. 30:7; Dan. 9:27; 12:1; Mt. 24:21–22)." The note continues for four long and turgid paragraphs.

The Scofield Bible *is* the inerrant text of God in the minds of many unsophisticated fundamentalist believers. One man with whom I attended a Bible study class for two years had well over half of it highlighted with various brightly colored markers and never seemed to have it out of his hands. Another related a complicated story from the end of Revelation in the course of one of my interviews with him and confused a note with the text. Indeed, that is exactly the power of this edition, which for the first time incorporated a whole interpretive framework into the notes on the Bible. The notes come to assume a canonical quality. The Bible is a difficult book, written over the course of more than a millennium with many different authors in different languages and styles and even beliefs. It is more like a library than a book. Comprehending the Bible understandably raises a good deal of anxiety among mostly naive believers who have been told there is only one right way to read it—and that way is not always readily apparent. With the Scofield Bible, little is left obscure. One evidence of its amazing authority is that most popular fundamentalist books are either slightly revised versions of the Scofield notes, or adapt his theory to contemporary events.[81] It may well be that the Scofield Bible has touched the lives of more people than any other single book published in this century.

The second text, actually a series of twelve paperback pamphlets named *The Fundamentals* published between 1910 and 1915, codified the dogma of the emerging movement. A Christian philanthropist, Lyman Stewart, with some help from his brother, Milton, provided $300,000 for the dissemination of three million free copies of the pamphlets. Milton, who regularly supported the Moody Institutes and helped underwrite Cyrus Scofield's edition of the Bible, was motivated to reply to those "infidel professors at Chicago University." He selected the well-known and contentious evangelist, the Reverend A. C. Dixon, to lead the effort. Dixon in turn appointed an editorial committee that conceptualized the topics to cover and selected the numerous authors to write for the series. All the leaders of premillennialism in the country participated in the effort, including Arno Gaebelein and Cyrus Scofield, as well as leading academic figures like Benjamin Warfield from Princeton. Compared with the stridency of later battles, the authors of *The Fundamentals* took a fairly moderate position on most issues (except that of inerrancy). On Darwinism, for example, *The Fundamentals* allowed that the days of creation may have lasted a long time, allowing for some evolution during those intervals. The volumes were primarily conceived as a defense of the faith against the "higher criticism" of the Bible that dominated the seminaries of most major universities and the modernism in the culture of which it was a part. The most surprising aspect of the volumes is that their contemporary impact was far less than their historical role marking the consolidation of ideas that were to ground the fundamentalist movement. Few journals even reviewed the volumes, and certainly they failed to close the floodgates of modernism. Mostly, it seems, they were ignored, to be noted later as marking something they never did at the time.[82]

In 1920 this movement, with its diverse history, apocalyptic concerns, dogmas, emerging institutional grounding, and texts, got a name. Curtis Lee Laws, an editor of a Baptist newspaper, said a fundamentalist was someone who was willing to "do battle royal" on behalf of the fundamentals of the faith. "It was both a description and a call to action," says Nancy Ammerman, "and the name stuck."[83] Fundamentalism, however, soon faced a great test—and lost, or so it seemed, profoundly altering its history for the next half century. John Scopes, a high school biology teacher in Tennessee, decided to test the state's law against teaching evolution. He was prosecuted for breaking the law. In the dramatic trial that was the century's first true media event, two of the nation's greatest trial lawyers and orators lined up on opposite sides of the case. Henry Mencken, the caustic reporter for the *Baltimore Sun*, attended the trial and wrote of fundamentalist "boobs." The *New York Times* ran daily coverage on its front pages. The case quickly turned into a struggle of the old versus the new, of the twentieth versus the nineteenth centuries, of progress versus obscurantism. Clarence Darrow and the ACLU lost the case but won the war for public opinion. William Jennings Bryan, who won, appeared to be a beaten and humiliated man in the arguments with Darrow, something Bryan's death shortly after the trial only made more real.[84]

That at least is the official version, encrusted now with tradition. In fact, it is not so clear that the fundamentalists lost, or even felt they were defeated. Smart-aleck modernists like Mencken, who were not in the daily reading of true believers anyway, failed to change the face of emerging fundamentalism in Tennessee, or anywhere else, for that matter. The trial crystalized the lines of opposition in the country. It showed just how far apart the two worlds had gotten by 1925. But the Scopes trial hardly marked the defeat of the "boobs." For various reasons, fundamentalists after Scopes went into a period of retreat and relative quiescence. Those in the ranks who had imagined taking over the citadels of power for the faith had to plot a more modest, sober course of action. But most ordinary believers simply returned to their local concerns, churches, and institutions, unrepentant and unbowed, without shame or even a sense of having been defeated. This alternating rhythm of engagement with and withdrawal from modern culture has characterized fundamentalism for most of the twentieth century. The contrast between the fundamentalist activism of the 1980s on the national stage and its current involvement in the 1990s with local fights compares with the period before and after Scopes. Unlike then, however, no secularist of any sound judgment would now argue that fundamentalism is over with.

FUNDAMENTALISM TRIUMPHANT

In the two decades after 1925 the movement reorganized in various self-contained institutions, like the Moody Bible institutes, Wheaton College, and the Dallas Theological Seminary.[85] Somewhat later the Fuller Theological Seminary and Bob Jones University became important fundamentalist centers.[86] Various special publications emerged, and Christian schools, often directly associated with individual churches, proliferated. This subcultural network had little to do with the increasingly secular world of colleges and universities, which continued to dismiss it, unwisely, as a largely Southern, atavistic irrelevance. That is why the surprise was so great when Jerry Falwell and Ronald Reagan burst on the scene.

An important structural change, however, did occur within fundamentalism in the 1940s and 1950s: The looser, more moderate, less ideological evangelicals assumed a personal and institutional identity separate from the harsher and less numerous fundamentalists. Until the early to mid 1940s, "evangelical" and "fundamentalist" had been used interchangeably; after that they came to represent distinct styles within a larger movement. In retrospect the differences were apparent well before the 1940s, but they had little significance in the minds of believers or outside observers. Without the ideological clarity that developed in fundamentalism between 1880 and 1920, a schism was not possible because there was no moderate position to define in opposition to a more dogmatic one. But by 1942, with the founding of the National Association of Evangelicals, a breach opened up in the movement.

The evangelical/fundamentalist split was, and remains, a difference in degree, not kind. D. H. Watt has recently argued that the evangelicals sharply turned fundamentalism away from end time concerns to "private matters" of family and related issues. By the 1970s evangelicalism, Watt argues, presented quite a different picture from the 1930s. "Postwar evangelicals have not abandoned the doctrine of the Second Advent," he says, "but, on the other hand, not many evangelicals have meditated on it day and night." The family became the central concern of the Billy Graham Evangelistic Association, for example. Graham talked about it constantly from the late 1940s on, and half his mail dealt with family matters. In the late 1960s and early 1970s, as well, there were many vast evangelical congresses on the family, which Watt compares to the important prophecy conferences in the latter part of the nineteenth century that played such an important part in defining the emerging movement.[87]

Watt's distinction, however, may be more apparent than real. Conservative evangelicals, as I tried to show in earlier chapters, have much more in common with their fundamentalist brethren than with mainstream Christians. Watt also fails to incorporate into his analysis the important issue of the numbers of people involved in the competing fundamentalist styles. As far as one can judge, the most important change that occurred in the 1940s and into the 1950s is that a once marginal movement became mainstream. The evangelicals hardly "turned" fundamentalism inward. The old ideologues remained firmly in place in the Bible schools and places like Wheaton, Bob Jones, and Dallas. What happened is that a vast *new* group of believing Christians moved toward them, incorporating their essential apocalypticism without all the theoretical trappings. This much larger group of evangelicals brought with them concerns and commitments, especially about the family, that are not always in full agreement with the fundamentalists. The two groups have been fighting it out ever since. As Bob Jones and Billy Graham quarreled in the 1950s, so Jerry Falwell and Jim Bakker became rivals in the 1970s. But it is a fight within one family, more a sibling rivalry than a generational struggle or a basic disagreement over belief.

My point in this book is that the enormous enlargement of the movement, from the margins to now a quarter of the entire U.S. population, is what stands in need of explanation. In the middle of this century a powerful anti-modern group with a clear Christian end time ideology rather suddenly became a mass movement.[88] It is not surprising that differences in emphasis over issues of doctrine and practice emerged, or even that the further one moved from the ideological core of the movement the less passionate was its apocalypticism. It is more surprising that so many people choose to live their lives with a sense of the urgency of Christ's return. As late as the 1960s the significance of what was happening eluded some good observers, for example Harvey Cox, whose book *The Secular City* might have made one think humanism reigned supreme in America.

The purpose of this chapter, however, is not to rehearse the now-familiar story of the rise and demise of the Moral Majority; the great falls of people like Jimmy Swaggart; the recent and dramatic role of the Christian Coalition; the institutional rhythms of change in the fundamentalist subculture; or most of all the recent history of prophecy writing in America.[89] It is instead to understand the historical origins within the American experience of the contemporary mass movement of fundamentalism. The one piece of Darby's nineteenth-century theory that I have thus far left largely undeveloped is a set of ideas that has entered into the imagination of twentieth-century fundamentalists with a vengeance; they concern Jews and Israel, and the way both are part of a process that paves the way for the return of Jesus. These ideas, to which I turn in the next chapter, are of more than historical interest, for they continue to exert enormous influence on the minds of fundamentalists.

9

JEWS, ISRAEL,
AND THE PARADOX
OF THE INGATHERING

THE BLOOD TAINT. Beginnings matter. Matthew 27:1–26 tells us that the chief priests and the elders of the Jews took counsel against Jesus. They bound him and carried him before Pontius Pilate. Pilate, seeking escape from the dilemma of not wanting to condemn Jesus, asked the assembled multitude of Jews whether they would accept a substitute for Jesus in Barabbas. But the multitude cried out for Jesus: "Let him be crucified." Pilate, feeling guilty for condemning this righteous man, washed his hands and claimed he was innocent of Jesus' blood. To which the crowd replied, "His blood be on us and on our children." Then he released Jesus to them for crucifixion.

This blood taint has haunted relations between Jews and Christians for nearly two thousand years. The image of Jews as Christ-killers lay behind the medieval legal institutions that restricted Jews to certain professions. It was the underlying basis for enduring popular anti-Semitism and periodic pogroms, and it shaped the anti-Semitic thinking of theologians like Martin Luther, which fed into the many forms of Protestantism after the sixteenth century. Such ingrained hatred for the Jews provided the basis for the emergence, during the late nineteenth and early twentieth centuries, of "scientific" anti-Semitism, or the modern version of anti-Semitism that was grounded in evolutionary thought. This "social Darwinism" postulated a biological basis for the notion of a hierarchy of human races extending from Jews to Aryans and has had a significant global impact, particularly in the hands of Hitler.[1]

But were the Jews in fact complicit in the death of Jesus? There is no question that the Romans carried out the actual punishment. They ruled the land, Pontius Pilate was a Roman judge, and Roman authorities erected the cross and nailed Jesus to it. Haim Cohn, in an exhaustive study, even concludes that the Jews, in fact, "took no part" in the trial and death of Jesus, "but did all that they possibly and humanly could to save Jesus, whom they dearly loved and cherished as one of their own, from his tragic end at the hands of the Roman oppressor." Cohn argues that the stories of Jewish guilt for the death of Jesus were motivated by the desire to portray Jewish suffering after the destruction of the Temple as God's punishment for killing Christ,[2] and to the extent it is true is a distortion based in apocalyptic yearnings with fateful consequences.

Not all would agree. The story of the trial told in Mark (14:53–65), which is generally regarded as the oldest Gospel, and echoed in Luke (22:63–71), talks more darkly of Jewish complicity, of false witnesses, and condemnation to death by the Jewish authorities. At this late date, there is no easy way to sort out historical truth in a story so laden with conflicting meanings and passions. It would seem, though, that the conventional anti-Semitic view, now weighted with two millennia of tradition, that blames Jews for the death of Jesus and casts the blood taint on them, is inaccurate. The Romans killed Jesus, and, as Cohn emphasizes, they were the imperial power in a position to control all minorities under their rule. On the other hand, it is facile not to recognize that *some* Jewish leaders were coopted by the Romans and participated in the condemnation of Jesus, which made the trial and execution of this local, religious troublemaker much easier.[3]

For most of the last two thousand years the relationship between Jews and Christians has been at best ambivalent and often fraught with misunderstanding and violence. But in the last half century, with the widespread secularization associated with modernism, the creation of Israel as a state, and global ecumenism, relations between most Jews and Christians have been put on a new footing. Particularly in the United States, mutual acceptance is part of the social fabric. But in the florid imagination of the fundamentalists, which returns to the oldest of views of the crucifixion of Jesus,[4] a new, post-Holocaust chapter has opened.

HISTORICAL EXPERIENCE

Historically, Jews are one of America's many stable immigrant ethnic groups, though they have often had to contend with special religious antagonisms based ultimately on the blood taint. Some argue anti-Semitism has been steadily declining in America during the last forty years. Jerome Chanes, in a recent review of the relevant literature, enthusiastically concludes that anti-Semitism "is simply no longer a factor in American life." Chanes argues that there is broad acceptance of intermarriage and of Judaism as a faith (Unitarian Universalists generally rank lower in respectability in some polls), as well as a decline in stereotypical images of Jews and a decoupling of ambivalent attitudes toward Israel from feelings toward Jewish neighbors. Black anti-Semitism remains a haunting mystery, Chanes says, but he argues that it is mingled with class resentments and general anti-white sentiment.[5] Others, understandably, question such upbeat sentiments and worry that the deteriorating relations between African and Jewish Americans are basically rooted in religion and that often negative attitudes toward Israel overlap American domestic relations.[6]

Fundamentalists, for their part, feel no special guilt about the Holocaust, and treat it as something perpetrated by other people in a distant land.[7] They typically have little knowledge of what actually occurred, and what they do know is distorted by their theology. Fundamentalists' general feeling about the Holocaust is that the Nazis were agents of God's judgment against his rebellious people, and that the vast persecution and death of so many Jews could have a positive outcome in pushing Jews toward conversion. As one scholar puts it, summarizing the fundamentalist view, "God was using the Nazi horror to bring the Jews to faith in Jesus Christ and to rekindle their desire for a homeland in Palestine."[8] Furthermore, the Holocaust joins fundamentalist prophecy: It created the historical conditions necessary for the founding of the state of Israel. Hitler served God's purposes, as fundamentalists generally understand it.

Evocative Holocaust imagery, however, operates at many levels for fundamentalists, whose theology lends itself to images of shared suffering. One particularly subtle level is the opportunity the Holocaust offers fundamentalists to identify with Jewish suffering, persecution, and genocide. Otto, for example, drew his image of Christian suffering in the end times directly from the Holocaust. "Jews," he said, "as they were being brought into these cattle cars or into the concentration camps were crying out 'Messiah, Come!'" And Christians, too, whom he believed already suffer ridicule and abuse for their faith, will continue to face mounting persecution in these end times. Things are much better for Christians than for Jews, whose tragic deaths in the ovens found no fulfillment in God's intervention in human history. "So I mean," Otto said, "it's threatening, it'll be purification. But it won't necessarily be something like the Holocaust where, at least I don't think it would be, where just all Christians are put together and gassed or put in the oven, or mowed down with machine gun fire or something."

Such identification with Jewish persecution and genocide connects generally with the fundamentalist multifaceted response to Jews and Judaism. Many fundamentalists have a powerful, if somewhat abstract, respect for both Jews and Judaism. As people of the book themselves, fundamentalists revere Jews as chosen by God. Their story begins with Jews, and they feel they share a common narrative, and a common God. In this sense Jews are central to the Christian experience. As Deborah put it: "The Bible definitely tells us to pray for the peace of Jerusalem and for his people, for the Jewish people." This sentiment was warmly echoed by Isaac: "I find anti-Semitism one of the most horrible things . . . because I've read a lot of Jewish history. I pray for the country of Israel, I pray for it because they had the oracles of God given to them, our basic fundamental laws, right and wrong are based on Judeo-Christian traditions."

Jews and Christians share a common experience in the apocalyptic. Jesus was, of course, the Jewish Messiah (as understood by those Jews who accepted him), and the book of Revelation, in one sense, as the Christian prophetic story, merely updates its Jewish analogue, the book of Daniel. It may be that Jewish messianism has been more thoroughly secularized (Freud and Marx), which makes it only more apparently distant from its Christian analogue. And the affinity continues. In Jewish tradition, there are two views of what occurs just before messianic time: Either great evil and destruction occur, or things get so good that there is a natural enlargement of the human to encompass the divine. The parallel with Christian premillennialism and postmillennialism is exact. Jews and Christians mirror each other in their messianic ruminations, but differ in which messiah they await.

THEOLOGICAL ABSTRACTIONS

Below the surface, however, things are more complicated. One must begin with an examination of some important distinctions in dispensational theology that help shape the contemporary fundamentalist attitudes toward Jews and Israel. The leading theoretician of these ideas, indeed of most fundamentalist ideology, is John F. Walvoord, the former chancellor of Dallas Theological Seminary, who carries the mantle of John Nelson Darby for all literalist Christians in the late twentieth century trying to figure out the mysteries of the second advent. Walvoord's special concern has always been Jews and Israel in prophecy, which he has been writing about for some three decades.[9] Alert to nuance and well informed, Walvoord has clarified (as much as anyone can) the fundamentalist argument about Israel and the Jews and shaped a whole generation's thinking on these matters.

Walvoord argues that God's promise to the Jews covers both the natural descendants of Abraham (his "seed") and the spiritual children of God, or those Jews who followed the laws, but accepted Jesus as Christ. This crucial distinction has defined fundamentalist thinking since Darby.[10] Israel and the church move in separate directions, for it is a given that some kind of transcendence occurred with Jesus, some shifting of God's covenant. In the fundamentalist discourse, God is pursuing two distinct purposes. One purpose, with the Jews, is earthly, while the purpose with Christians is heavenly. Within certain bounds Jews can expect God's blessing, but that cannot be confused with his ultimate purposes regarding true Christian believers. "This is probably the most basic theological test of whether or not a man is a dispensationalist," says the fundamentalist writer Charles C. Ryrie. "A man who fails to distinguish Israel and the Church will inevitably not hold to dispensational distinctions; and one who does, will."[11]

Despite the potentially deadly dualism of the language in this distinction between Jews and Christians, the key fundamentalist point is to stress that Jews qua Jews (that is, unconverted ones) remain chosen and special in God's eyes. They were by no means simply discarded when Jesus came along, which is the older, simpler, and pre-Darby form of literalist prejudice against the Jews. But the question is, what are they chosen to do when and how? If God does not abandon the Jews, how will he use them? How can the explicit promises in the Old Testament be reconciled with the mission of Jesus *and* his prophetic return? What is the Jews' "future or continuance as a nation"?[12] Fundamentalists have been wrestling with this central question since Darby and others in the nineteenth century. The question as well as the answer is premised, of course, on a particular reading of the texts and assumes that Old Testament promises, interpreted literally, must be reconciled with prophetic reckonings in the book of Revelation. The creation of Israel and the ingathering of the Jews thus serve God's ultimate purposes in the second coming of Jesus.

Walvoord stresses that God promised the land to Abraham and his seed. "Get thee out of thy country," God tells Abram in Genesis 12:1, "and from thy kindred, and from thy father's house, unto a land that I will show thee." There is nothing figurative about this "land" for Walvoord. God meant the "literal land of Canaan," the proof of which leads Walvoord in a march through Genesis and Isaiah with a great leap forward into Hebrews.[13] The argument is that the covenant with the Jews is everlasting. Israel is forever theirs. And Israel, that nation of Jews, must be located in exactly the same place as promised to Abraham. Israel is not an idea in the minds of Jews. It is a sacred space with definite boundaries in the Middle East.[14] Since he takes scripture literally, Walvoord worries about the inconsistency of God, who made promises to Abraham and his seed, only to be broken once Jesus comes along. Genesis 17:7–8, for example, declares that the covenant with Israel is an everlasting one, a commitment that is repeated both to Isaac and to Jacob and is "constantly referred to throughout the Old Testament."[15] And "God never breaks his promises," as I heard often from fundamentalists.

When the modern state of Israel came into existence in 1948, fundamentalists felt it was a great confirmation of *their* prophecy. "[Revelation] required Israel to be a nation," Isaac said. "With the Jews back in Jerusalem," as Otto put it, "back in Israel, their own nation again, different things the prophecy has said about them have been fulfilled." And Frank: "God has good plans for Israel." In fact, it is fair to say that no other event of the twentieth century has had the same significance in the belief system of fundamentalists as the creation of the state of Israel.[16] The year 1948 marked—and continues to mark—"the winding down of the prophetic clock," as fundamentalists like to put it. I encountered this idea (and phrase) repeatedly in the churches. "The nation of Israel's existence is an important sign," said Mary. Otto added: "Jesus doesn't really return until the Jews are gathered back in Israel." And Elaine (Reverend Matthew's wife) noted: "Jesus says that they would be brought back to their land and that has taken place."

Otto and Elaine were referring, of course, not just to the creation of the state of Israel but also to the ingathering, or the return of the Jews to Canaan. The two are inseparable parts of the same process, which in turn marks the beginning of the end times that will culminate in the millennium and the return of Jesus. "The present regathering being witnessed by our generation," Walvoord says portentously, "is the largest movement of the people of Israel since the days of Moses."[17] The single most important text for the millennial significance of this ingathering is Isaiah 66:20 ("And they shall bring all your brethren *for* an offering unto the Lord out of all nations upon horses, and in chariots, and in litters, and upon mules, and upon swift beasts, to my holy mountain Jerusalem, saith the Lord, as the children of Israel bring an offering in a clean vessel into the house of the Lord"), but Walvoord also calls on Isaiah 11:1–12, 14:1, 27:13, 43:5–7, 60:21; Jeremiah 16:14–16, 31:21–40, 32:37–44; Ezekiel 11:17, 20:33–38 and 42, 37:21–22, 39:25–29; as well as more obscure passages from the minor prophets Joel, Amos, Obadiah, Micah, Zephaniah, and Zechariah.[18]

The ingathering moves inexorably toward Armageddon. The ingathered Jews who survive the violence of tribulation and the false peace engineered by Antichrist *must* all convert before Jesus returns to rule over his millennial kingdom. Again, since John Nelson Darby, this notion of a surviving remnant of Jews who will accept their long-rejected Messiah has been a cornerstone of fundamentalist theology.[19] The text here is the baffling reference in Revelation 7:4 to the so-called remnant of Israel: "And I heard the number of them which were sealed: *and there were* sealed an hundred *and* forty *and* four thousand of all the tribes of the children of Israel." Walvoord does some fancy footwork with this text: "Out of the total number of Israel, a representative group of 144,000 are sealed and thereby protected from destruction in this period [of the tribulation]. In Revelation 7, they are enumerated with their respective tribes. In Revelation 14, they are depicted on Mount Zion with the Lamb at the close of the tribulation, still intact and singing praises to the Lord. They form therefore the core of the godly remnant which will be awaiting Christ when he returns to set up His millennial kingdom."[20] It is an article of faith among premillennial dispensationalists, from Darby to Walvoord, that the rapture occurs before the tribulation, and removes the faithful from the suffering of that period. The remnant of converted Jews, however, who are "still intact" at the end of tribulation on Mount Zion awaiting Christ, survive because they are "sealed" before the suffering begins. Converted Jews are not raptured but survive as believers whose only purpose seems to be to make up for past sins by proclaiming the glory of Jesus' return.

It might seem that *converted* Jews would lose their death taint for fundamentalists because they affirm, rather than threaten, the fundamentalist belief system. Fundamentalist theologians try to be generous. During the millennium itself, for example, Walvoord allows for the inclusion of converted Jews. He thus argues that all are equal to participate in that kingdom, Jew and Christian alike, who are "joined by the baptism of the Spirit, placed in Christ, born again of the Spirit of God, and indwelt by the triune God."[21] But we should keep in mind that Walvoord's criteria of inclusion would exclude most Christians, let alone Jews, from "participation" in the millennium. Furthermore, premillennial dispensationalism in general, and Walvoord most especially, targets Jews for special suffering. Besides the extraordinary idea that converted Jews are not raptured, most converted Jews do not even live, for they suffer an appalling rate of destruction during the tribulation. "During the Grand Tribulation," Walvoord says, "two out of three of the Jews in the land attempting to flee their persecutor, the future world leader [Antichrist], will perish, and only one-third will escape and be waiting for Christ when He comes."[22] There is an important technical question that arises here, even a contradiction: How can a third of the Jews survive the tribulation if only 144,000 of them are "sealed"? Presumably those not "sealed" will shortly die a natural death and suffer eventual damnation (along with other nonbelievers who make it through the tribulation). In other words, of some twelve million Jews worldwide all but 144,000 will die during and shortly after the end time events, according to Christian fundamentalists.

It should be noted that many end timers—from Baptists to Jehovah's Witnesses—vigorously dispute the meaning of the figure 144,000 mentioned in Revelation 7:4. But for most fundamentalist Christians, the meaning of that sacred number centers on the notion that surviving and ingathered Jews, one way or another, *will be* converted in the end times. The ingathering is the precondition for the second coming, and in a mystically significant sense it is the massed presence of Jews that forces Jesus to return. "Jews for Jesus," interestingly, see themselves as the vanguard in this process, an evangelical idea warmly embraced by Mary. She believed the figure 144,000 in Revelation describes the horde of Jewish evangelicals who will lead the way in the conversion process. As she colorfully puts it:

"There are going to be 144,000 [Jewish] Billy Grahams running around the world."

JEWISH INSTRUMENTALITY

Jews, in other words, are instruments of fate in the minds of fundamentalists. The only historical role for Jews is to prepare for the arrival of Jesus. It is, needless to say, not a role most Jews accept. Most feel it is demeaning, even infuriating, to be fitted into a theological system to which they do not ascribe. Irving Kristol, a neo-conservative Jewish writer and editor, however, gives some pragmatic reasons for accepting fundamentalist attitudes: "This real world is rife with conflict and savagery. . . . We are constrained to take our allies where and how we can find them."[23] In regard to fundamentalist support for Israel, Kristol writes: "Why should Jews care about the theology of a fundamentalist preacher when they do not for a moment believe that he speaks with any authority on the question of God's attentiveness to human prayer? And what do such theological abstractions matter as against the mundane fact that this same preacher is vigorously pro-Israel." And he adds: "It is their theology, but it is our Israel."[24]

There are costs to this friendship. At the very least, the instrumentality of Jews in the minds of fundamentalists can mean that Jews are the object of intense scrutiny and evangelizing. New York City fundamentalists are fascinated with the large number of Orthodox and Hasidic Jews in the city. Monroe, for example, told me earnestly of his near success in "bringing in" a Jewish owner of a clothes factory in the city that would have meant his three hundred employees would be open to conversion as well. Mary conducted a series of special services for Jews at her church, which often featured guest speakers who minister and witness to Jews. One fundamentalist radio station in the city directs its broadcasts at the Hasidim in the Williamsburg section of Brooklyn. The station director made an emotional appeal to Mary's congregation, prior to a special collection, for their support in the effort to "save" even one Jew. The Jews "are all going to come back [to] Israel," Mary said.

At Abiding Light, largely as a result of Mary's initiative, there were a number of special outreach activities for Jews whom she felt were approachable because they were only "partially hardened" (Romans 9:18 and 10:14–21). At the beginning of Hanukkah one year, for example, she devised a skit to be performed for various groups in the city. With the menorah lit up, Mary began singing, "O, Holy Night." She had donned a dark wig and covered it with a black head scarf. A mock dialogue between two neighbors, a Mrs. Finklestein and a Mrs. Jones, followed the song. Mary played the role of Mrs. Finklestein. Using a Yiddish accent, she related how the two women met at the grocery store and became friends. The fictional Mrs. Finklestein talked about how impressed she was with Mrs. Jones. She said something had been missing in her life, and how gradually she began to understand that Mrs. Jones's peace and stability came from Jesus. The monologue was carried on with folksy humor, meant to convey how strange Christians must seem to a Jewish housewife. The presentation also included several songs, which seemed to represent the stories and feelings of diverse biblical women. For each song and each character, Mary changed head scarves.

The instrumentality of the Jews for fundamentalists is, in general, based on a lack of understanding or concern for the other and can carry within it the potential for violence. For most fundamentalists I talked with (as with theologians like Walvoord), the specific instrument of the violence against the Jews will be Antichrist, who will "strike at" the Jews first, said Reverend Matthew. Reverend Matthew's verb "strike at" is ambiguous in terms of the intentions of Antichrist toward the Jews. The verb could mean attack with intent to kill, but it could also simply suggest "get to and act upon" or, in other words, convert. But Reverend Matthew's latent meaning is clearer in a later statement: "The Antichrist will seek to make peace with the nation that needed most to be destroyed." Reverend Lester added his own twist about Antichrist to these violent images of destruction of the Jews. For him Antichrist will appear in the world as a "powerful orator and leader out of Europe." He will deceive people into thinking he is the Messiah, the ultimate savior. The certain proof of his secret deception is that Israel in fact will sign a treaty with him, but then three and a half years into the treaty they are going to realize their mistake. Then there will be a tremendous judgment.

But why does Israel need to be destroyed? The easy answer, that biblical prophecy foretells its destruction, fails to satisfy even the fundamentalists themselves, who uneasily combine abstruse points of theology with old-fashioned prejudice. Otto, for example, is fascinated by what he perceives as the warp and woof of Jews' relationship with God: "Someone has said that the biggest proof that there is a God [is that] the Jews are God's chosen people. There has never been a people that time and time again someone has tried to destroy and been unsuccessful in doing so. . . . I believe . . . they have been in rebellion against God. God protected them to the degree they sinned. God hasn't [forsaken] them, but punishes them." And yet, as Frank (a "Jew for Jesus") said, Assyria's invasion of Israel was an "instrument of judgment against Israel" for their "horrible abuses" against one another, their "inhumanity" toward each other, their "idolatry," and their "forsaking" of God. Elaine was more mundane: "Israel disobeyed God . . . they didn't follow his teachings . . . and they were scattered." "Problem is Jews have a set image of the Messiah as political," said Nigel. "They were wrong." Otto added: "Jews had these problems because of their idolatry in the past. . . . They would sacrifice their children to these altars." But the ultimate mark against Jews is, as Nigel said, "[because of their] refusal to accept Jesus."

Even fairly moderate evangelicals can be surprisingly severe in their attitudes about Jewish conversion. A group of fifteen evangelical Protestant theologians in 1989 issued a statement warning that creating a dialogue with Jews cannot substitute for converting them. The theologians noted that the only historical purpose of the Jews was to prepare for Jesus, and that after the resurrection God had broken his covenant with them. The Jews, the statement said, are "branches of God's olive tree" that have "broken off" (a reference to Romans 11:17–20). Contemporary Judaism in no way "contains within itself true knowledge of God's salvation." At the same time, the group of evangelical theologians condemned anti-Semitism and stressed the need for Israel to secure its existence and borders. There should be no "coercive or deceptive proselytizing."

But Christians must not compromise on God's purpose in relation to the Jews. As the chairman of the group put it, "We are under a New Testament mandate to carry the Gospel to all people, including Jews."[25]

This evangelical statement epitomizes the ambiguities of the more fervent Christian image of the Jews. Jews are abandoned children of God, fallen branches from his olive tree. They may find salvation *only* through the good evangelical efforts of Christians. Once exalted and chosen, Jews now are relegated to the margins of God's purpose in history. They sinned against God once too often. They continue to exist as a people and to retain a measure of his divine providence, but only because God does not go back on his promises. The new Israel is created, not the Israel of old, but an Israel in desiccated political fragments. The Jewish state, which fulfills the ancient promise, exists only as a sacred arena for the ingathering of Jews and the site from which Jesus will rule during the millennium. During the end times, which again it must be stressed we are *in*, Jews must be vigorously converted. God has given a great sign of his purpose in the creation of the state of Israel; now Christians must obediently fulfill his evangelical commandments, while Jews themselves await the worst kinds of suffering. Generally, then, fundamentalism is theologically pro-Jewish and at the same time anti-Semitic. Jews are special targets, something that is clear in the theology, as well as in the minds of ordinary believers, and their suffering rounds out a history of God's wrath from the Exodus to the Holocaust. Theologically, one might say, God saves Israel for Jesus while at the same time he destroys the Jews. At the end, Mary said, there will be a "showdown in the OK Corral in Israel."

Fundamentalists, in the end, have little empathy for Jews. They talk about "them" in the abstract and move quickly from discussing the seed of Abraham to Antichrist. It is important in this context to distinguish blatant anti-Semitism from the more subtle and pervasive forms of ambivalence and confusion about Jews that exist in the theology and in the minds of ordinary Christian believers. Fundamentalist writers themselves often react with sarcasm to the charge of anti-Semitism, stressing that they are "ardent supporters" of Israel and the Jewish heritage. They "chuckle inwardly" at the way Jewish intellectuals court liberal Protestants, who are in fact the enemies of both fundamentalists and Jews.[26] But as we have seen, the fundamentalist support for Jews and the state of Israel is much more complicated. For nearly all fundamentalists, instrumental images of the Jewish contribution to the end times make them and their state of Israel worth support only to fulfill apocalyptic visions. In the last analysis, fundamentalists find little of spiritual merit in contemporary Judaism, and most have in their minds a notably derogatory and devalued view of Jews as people. Ancient Christian prejudices find renewed life in this context.

The lack of genuine empathy that fundamentalists have for Jews has many consequences. Jews tend to be either idealized or debased but seldom perceived as people. Mary weeps when she sees the flag of Israel, a rather peculiar response for a thirty-year-old woman born in Georgia and raised a Baptist. For her it is important *only* that the flag waves over the land where she believes the resurrected Jesus will soon rule. Such pieces of Jewish experience have no authenticity in and of themselves. Mary's odd weeping at the sight of the Israeli flag is rooted in the basic Christian principle that God extended his promise from the Jews to Christians after Jesus. In the last analysis, for fundamentalists, "There is no kingdom for Israel apart from the suffering Saviour as well as the reigning King."[27] Even if muted, as it is in mainstream Christianity, it is clear that if one believes Jesus is the Messiah then some kind of transcendence of God's promises to the Jews has occurred in history.[28] That notion changed the cultural history of the west. It introduced the idea that Jews have been superseded by divine intervention in history, or abandoned by God altogether, depending on the theological interpretation. This notion of God's abandonment of the Jews, taken together with the taint of their assumed role in killing Christ, has resulted in the profound victimization of Jews for centuries. Even in a liberal democracy like the United States and in an age of secular humanism, the free-floating idea that Jews are somehow bad is not easily abandoned.

Clearly, in the extreme case of Nazism, the potential for violence in the western encounter between Jews and Christians was cruelly realized. Nor can one be entirely sanguine about the future. Despite a century and a half of writing, and much tragic history, it is fair to say that premillennial dispensational theology as well as most fundamentalists themselves are still confused about the Jews. Yet there are reasons to hope fundamentalists could in time soften and humanize their views of Jews. At the very least, it is worth noting that in all my work in New York I never once heard a fundamentalist say anything that would suggest images of actually rounding up surviving Jews on the Temple Mount and forcing conversion (or in any way threatening death to those who refused). But healthier images might also evolve out of the more ambivalent ones that currently prevail. Fundamentalists are part of the larger American society that many feel is moving toward a postmodern reconciliation of cultural and ethnic tensions. More specifically, fundamentalists may be saved eventually by the very confusion of their own ideas about Jews, Israel, and the ingathering. Their theology is quite inconsistent about basic issues such as whether Jews can be truly saved (as noted, converted Jews cannot be raptured), and ordinary believers often seem almost unconscious of their contradictions as they espouse a great love for Jews while talking numbly of their annihilation in the end times. More self-critical participants in the movement, especially younger people, might find it difficult to live with such tensions.[29] There is some room for cautious hope in these very contradictions about Jews and Israel.

10

THE HOPI WAY

━━━━━━━━━━

THE HOPI APOCALYPTIC. It would be difficult to imagine a people more unlike Christian fundamentalists than the Hopi. The Christians are literalists, dogmatic, oriented to suffering and guilt, focused on ultimate violence, and often deeply dissociated in their personalities. The Hopi, on the other hand, are peaceful, gentle, non-dogmatic and non-literalistic (their language is not even written), and they purposely blur the line between the sacred and the profane. One is alienated from the world, from nature, from themselves. The other is at one with the universe, and their sense of the sacred infuses the most mundane of daily acts. The Hopi are even deeply psychological. Dreams, especially bad ones, must be recounted at breakfast or the spirits will be disturbed and the dream will come true.[1] And yet both Christian fundamentalists and the Hopi are apocalyptic. The Hopi live quietly on the three mesas overlooking the Painted Desert in what is now Arizona as they have for nearly a thousand years.[2] They plant their maize in the traditional way and perform the remarkable cycle of ceremonial kachina dances. Despite "Anglos" invading their world in RVs, they cling to their sacred Hopi way and ancient traditions. They also await the end of this, the Fourth World, when Pahana, the true white redeemer from the east, will appear with the broken piece of the tablet.

All Hopi prophecy concerns the coming of the "true white brother," Pahana, the redeemer, at which time all evil will be purified and the world remade. There are many versions of this story. In one Maasaw, the ruler over the Fourth World, just before he became invisible, gave the Fire Clan a tablet with instructions to migrate to their permanent home where, after a time, they would be conquered by a strange people. But he instructed them to remain faithful, for he assured them they would be delivered by Pahana, their lost white brother, who would return with a piece of the tablet that Maasaw had broken off before giving it to them.[3] In another version, the prophesied white man catches up with the Hopi and tests whether they have been true to tradition. If not, he will shake a Hopi by the ear and they will become like whites. But if the Hopi have been true, Pahana will go to an ash heap and kick an old shoe, after which whites will become Hopi.[4] And in yet another version the true white brother will return and slay all Hopi Two-Hearts (or false Hopi) and the races will unite.[5]

Perhaps such stories that center around deliverance by a good white man are simply apocalyptic accretions. But some evidence suggests the autonomy of the Hopi myth. One reason Cortés and the Spanish soldiers so easily defeated Montezuma's advanced Aztec civilization after they arrived in 1519 was the Aztec belief that they were descendants of their complex god, Quetzalcoatl. This beneficent deity with many mystical meanings had disappeared to the east some years earlier. It happened that the culture was actively waiting for the return of Quetzalcoatl when the Spanish arrived from the east. By the time Montezuma and his councillors awoke to their mistake it was too late.[6]

The Hopi by legend are direct descendants of the Aztecs. It may be that the Hopi were a special religious community at the northern edges of Pueblo civilization. Quetzalcoatl is not in the Hopi pantheon, but it is quite possible that the Hopi theme of waiting for the redeemer from the east was spiritually informed by connection with Aztec belief. Their subsequent experience with the Spanish dispelled Hopi faith in white-faced redeemers and also made them permanently hostile to Christianity. For a time in the first decade of the twentieth century, Americans required Hopi attendance at Christian churches, though the reaction was so negative the rule was eventually lifted. Although only about 2 percent of Hopi are Christians,[7] the impact of white Christian culture is far greater than such a statistic suggests. Schools that purport to be secular, for example, are outposts of a largely Christian culture and carry its assumptions and values. Hopi language, the carrier of religious traditions, has thus never been taught in the schools. And needless to say modern texts treating science, history, and literature that children on the reservation are required to read directly contradict and undermine the Hopi way. But it seems the Hopi have never given up on their prophetic assumption that the "true white brother" will be the instrument of the remaking of this world.

The Hopi have also incorporated into their end time discourse many apparently Christian elements. They talk of a "remnant" that has survived each of the previous worlds and will presumably make it through to the next, which is a familiar and important concept in Judeo-Christian apocalypticism.[8] The Hopi have an appointed "Last Day," called Nuutungk Talongvaqa, which is hauntingly like its Christian counterpart ("Last Days").[9] Their kachina dances, as well, which connect past and future, have been profoundly influenced by white and Christian themes.[10] The Hopi even talk about "signs" of the end. One informant told the researcher John Loftin, who has written an excellent book about the Hopi, that "by taking note of prophecy and recognizing the signs of its fulfillment, people can adjust their lives in accordance with the ways of the universe, and by doing so, prolong the existence of this world."[11] Another white researcher shared additional recent information on Hopi attitudes about the "signs" of the end. These include: various weather reversals; the blooming of certain yellow flowers in the winter of 1991; and further back in time, the dropping of the atomic bombs and the assassination of John F. Kennedy.[12] Unlike the Christian apocalypse, what is suggested in these signs for the Hopi, indeed in the end itself, only repeats something that occurred much earlier. That is why the most spiritual among the Hopi, those who still know the myths and legends of the past, also embody the greatest knowledge of the future.

In one sense, there are two primordia in Hopi conception that correspond to what we might consider mythic and historical time, though the Hopi themselves would never think of it in these terms. In the first is the creation, destruction, and recreation of the world through three stages of mythic imagination. Historical time occurs only in the Fourth World—our own—when myth approaches the remembered past. All Hopi images of the future are built, in large part, on the stories of the past, for apocalyptic endings and new beginnings are an essential element in Hopi cosmography. It is therefore worth outlining the story of creation in some detail.

All of the first three worlds were underground. The Creator, Taiowa, or *a'ni himu*,[13] who embodies the infinite, conceived of the finite. First he created a nephew, Sotuknang, that is, a kind of incarnated presence of the ineffable, to carry out his wishes. Sotuknang shaped the earth. But then he said he needed a companion, a mother of the world to come, a web to unite it all. And so the Creator made Spider Woman. Taiowa also created two spirit twins, who were to look after, protect, and inhabit the world. All four—Sotuknang, Spider Woman, and the twins—were to participate in the creation of humankind, but they had to have a song to do it. The younger twin wrote the song:

> *From the four corners of the universe:*
>   *From the East, for red is its color;*
>   *From the North, for white is its color;*
>   *From the West, for yellow is its color;*
>   *And from the South, for blue is its color;*
> *In the counterclockwise motion of* Tawa Taka, *the Sun Father.*
>
> *Come the four colors of the races of humankind,*
>   *each with its leaders,*

each with its destiny.
Soon they will fight, as it is prophesied,
but someday they shall unite.
  Then they will remember
  that Taiowa is their Spirit Father;
  that Sotuknang is their adoptive one;
  and the Spider Woman is the web
  which unites them all.[14]

Out of the power of the song people of all races and colors were created. Their one responsibility was to sing the Song of Creation, a song they were never to forget or they would lose the way. At first things went well and there was harmony everywhere. There was no sickness, no evil, and the people multiplied. They enjoyed the world and their bodies. But in time most forgot to sing the Song of Creation. Only a few remembered, and this "remnant" gathered into the home of the ant people while Sotuknang destroyed the world by fire. After that Sotuknang hesitated in his disappointment to create the world again but finally overcame his reluctance. But before letting the survivors come forth from the ant people he told them to remember their pledge to sing the Song, not to be greedy, and to respect themselves and Spider Woman.[15]

The world this second time around was even more plentiful. The plants were lush and strange new animals roamed about. People were happy. They built villages and sang the Song of Creation. But, alas, some of the men got greedy and fought each other for more possessions and for the women. In one version of the myth, Lavai-hoya, or the Talker, came among people as a mockingbird and convinced them of all the artificial racial and social and economic differences among them, leading to jealousies and alienation from the animals and from nature. Again, Sotuknang was furious. He gathered together the few who still lived by the laws of creation and remembered the Song. To them he gave safe haven once more with the ant people. Then he froze the earth solid from pole to pole, and even stopped it from spinning for a while.[16]

The story of the Third World repeats the pattern of the first two worlds but also introduces some important variations in its apocalyptic ending. People at first emerged from the anthills and prospered all over the earth. They built large cities, even civilizations and boxes (or shields in another myth) that flew in the sky. But they became so powerful that they tried to dominate each other, waging war and annihilating each other with their advanced weapons. Spider Woman, who at this point in the creation story begins to assume greater significance, was distraught. She went to Sotuknang and asked how she could save all the wayward people. He told her to gather the few holy ones and seal them in the reeds, or hollow stems of tall plants, while he destroyed the earth by flood. After the flood, however, the survivors did not come out from their sealed reeds into a new world but entered the same old one flooded over.[17]

At this point the myths proliferate and become complex, for in fact the Hopi are more interested in the emergence into the Fourth World than they are in the details of the creation of life and the story of the first three worlds. Harry James, for example, who spent fifty years in close contact with the Hopi, does not even mention the first three worlds in his account of their creation myths. He concerns himself instead with the story of the emergence into the Fourth World through the *sipapu*, the point of entry into the Fourth World.[18] As Loftin points out, the emergence through the *sipapu* marks the separation for the Hopi between myth and history, life and death, the here and now, and the world and the underworld, though at the same time everything in Hopi religion dissolves these dualities and contradictions.[19]

For my purposes, what is most interesting is that the apocalypse at the end of the Third World is not complete. When the survivors come out from their reeds the world is still there, just flooded over. In various accounts, they wander in boats searching for access to the new creation of Sotuknang, and go first north then south before hearing Maasaw's footsteps on the ceiling of their world. That ceiling turns out to be the crust of the earth as we now know it. The survivors summon various birds to try to locate the entrance into that world. In time the hole is found, but it is almost impossible to reach. Finally, a chipmunk is summoned who urges the people to say their prayers as he plants a special reed and then encourages it to grow up to the hole.[20] The people crawl through that reed and emerge through the *sipapu* into the Fourth World; this event is recreated in the emergence of each baby from a darkened hut after twenty days, in countless prayers during the ceremonies in the kivas, and is sacralized in reverse at the death of each Hopi.

The first being the people encounter is Maasaw, whom the Creator had put in charge of the Fourth World, since as master of the Under, or Third, World he had gotten arrogant but had been given a second chance. Maasaw tells them they may stay, but if they go back to their evil ways he will take the earth from them. In one account he says:

> *I am going to delegate some of my responsibilities to you,*
> *I am going to leave the Earth and all living things on it*
> *in your care. I appoint you guardians of this new world.*
> *Take care of it, protect it from pollution. It is your home.*
> *If you watch over it, it will feed you, clothe you,*
> *and keep your children and grandchildren healthy and happy.*
> *There will be hard times, when you will doubt.*
> *But never lose faith that what I told you today is the truth.*[21]

In other stories, both Sotuknang and Spider Woman also implore the people to avoid evil and sing praises to the Creator. Spider Woman especially assures them she will protect and nurture them from conflict. She also assigns different tasks to men and women to encourage harmony and prevent dissension.[22] With such blessings, the people undertake their new life. They begin, of course, with a vast store of knowledge, for memory of the achievements of people in their previous world is necessarily the beginning point in the minds of the remnant that survives. That knowledge, however, is of evil as well as of good. And the pattern is clear: Each time "the paradisaic situation is destroyed through disobedience, evil magic and sexual immorality."[23] The Creator destroys the world and creates a new one for the surviving few who have not strayed from holiness.

A crucial part of the creation myth, and one often talked about in Hopi legends and ceremonies, concerns the migrations that followed the emergence. Maasaw told the people they must first wander over the earth until they found the right place to settle. Maasaw detailed the elaborate pattern of their migration in a number of sacred tablets he gave different clans of the Hopi.[24] Interestingly, this sequence of legend merging into history corresponds with archaeological data that suggest the Pueblo people wandered for thousands of years, began to concentrate roughly in what is now Arizona after A.D. 700, and then, due to various droughts and other crises, began to congregate in larger communities and settle on the three mesas after the twelfth century.[25]

In the Hopi myths describing the making and unmaking of the four worlds, our own imaginable earth retains its ecological integrity. Fire, ice, and flood wipe out most living creatures (except for the ant people at the end of the first two worlds and then those tightly sealed in reeds at the end of the Third World). But in each case, the earth itself remains and is then repopulated with survivors from the previous world in another effort by the Creator to have a decent and holy people inhabit his creation. Indeed, the first three worlds as experienced by their inhabitants continue in a topographic and symbolic sense as the underworld; the earth as we know it now is simply an overlay, joined with these previous worlds through the *sipapu*. Just as life and death are a continuous process for the Hopi, the earth itself endures, while human culture goes through three waves of destruction. Those genocides, however, turn back on themselves in a cyclical pattern of recreation. Many die at the point of an old world's end, but life itself continues, and the earth's potential to nourish the fondest hopes of the Creator always remains in place. One might say the Hopi imagine an apocalypse of hope.

THE LITTLE PEOPLE OF PEACE

I came to the Hopi relatively late in my work on fundamentalism. I was finished with my fieldwork among the Christian fundamentalists and writing this book. But I kept coming back to the Hopi. I could not get the image of this peaceful group of Indians who were waiting for the end out of my mind. My interest increased as I read everything I could get my hands on and talked with people familiar with their culture and beliefs. But the Hopi baffled me. Who were these people who numbered less than ten thousand but whose culture and religion seemed of world-historical significance?[26] Who were these *Hopitu-Shinumu*, the Hopi self-designation as the "little people of peace"?[27] Were they really as mystical as they seemed? How did their sense of the apocalyptic fit into their culture? What did they believe comes after the end? These and many other questions seemed worth investigating.

Besides reading, I needed to undertake a brief period of additional fieldwork with the Hopi and discover my own sense of these unusual people. If I could have done so, I would have gone to Hopiland for six months. As it was, I gathered whatever insights I could manage in an intensive week of observation in the summer of 1992. I thought of it more as a pilgrimage than fieldwork, though I was in short pants and kept elaborate notes and a personal log. I had no specific agenda and no illusions that I would have the time to develop contacts to conduct formal interviews. I camped by myself on the Second Mesa and wandered the various villages throughout the reservation. I talked with everyone I could, though always informally, given the Hopi dread of tape recorders and cameras, and was even allowed to observe one of the major kachina dances, which are almost always closed to outsiders.

The Hopi have become highly suspicious of whites, who refuse to honor their sense of privacy and the sacred. Everything that matters is secret for the Hopi. The large sign at the entrance to Kykotsmovi speaks for all the villages. It says please take no pictures, don't use any kind of recording device, and don't pick up anything up from the ground to take with you. At Old Oraibi you are handed a piece of paper in the gift shop with a similar message, only it adds that you are not to walk on the roofs of the kivas, the underground ceremonial rooms with a distinctive ladder sticking up out of the entrance. At the back of Old Oraibi I strayed too far afield by accident, when a mean black dog lurched out at me from under a pick-up truck and chased one terrified white researcher back toward the Arts and Crafts shop at the entrance to the village. I felt properly chastened.

Most kachina dances, which go back some seven centuries, have been closed in recent years.[28] The First Mesa tribal chief published a statement in December 1990, closing off all dances on First Mesa to outsiders and had it posted throughout the reservation. On the other mesas, the ban seems to be more informal but equally universal. Sometimes individual dances are open, because the sponsor, or the

village, wants it that way. Yet some ceremonies, like the Shalako
dance that was going on while I was in Hopiland, even exclude
other uninitiated Hopi. In part this extreme trend toward self-
containment and separation from whites, however understandable,
is something of a contradiction for those who embrace all people of
peace into their spiritual world. But, sadly, outsiders too often secretly photograph or tape the dances. To reveal Hopi ceremonial secrets, including the preparatory prayers that go on in the kivas for
days before the dances, is a sacrilege.[29] Nothing less than cosmic order is at stake. Secrecy is even built into the meaning of the dances. If
a kachina takes off his mask, for example, the whole dance is compromised and the consequences for the Hopi can be enormous. And
according to one story the end of the Fourth World itself will occur
when the clown acts in a certain way in the plaza during the dance.[30]

The ultimate sense of the sacred infuses Hopi life at all levels. They
live apart from modern, materialistic, urban, media-drenched
America. In their self-contained rituals and communion with nature
they express the belief that God and the world are one. Seeds are not
future plants but spirits that, properly nurtured, bring forth sustenance. Seeds, in other words, are not "responsible" for the growth of
plants. "Rather," John Loftin says, "seeds tell May'ingwa, the underworld god or manifestation of germination, which kind of plant
is desired."[31] The cycle of dances from December to July harmonizes
humans and nature. Then the spirits are sent off to the San Francisco
Mountains to rest. If there is concordance between the spiritual and
earthly, the rains and crops follow. At death the Hopi's breath re-
joins *a'ni himu.*

The Hopi world is full of paradox and humor. It is an axiom
among the Hopi that all humans are clowns.[32] The clown was the
first Hopi to emerge from the underworld through the giant reed
that led to the opening called *sipapu.*[33] Clown Youth and Clown
Maiden were furthermore the direct ancestors of all humankind.
When the sun failed to people the earth during the Third World, the
task was given to the clowns. They wanted to escape the immorality
and decadence of the Third World and heard the complex and mysterious god Maasaw "up there" walking around.[34]

Clowns play a particularly important role in Hopi rituals. In the Home Dance I saw, for example, some thirty kachinas danced for hours with great solemnity to the beat of drums and their haunting music. At the end of each sequence, however, fifteen or so clowns would rush into the plaza where the dance was being held, mock the kachinas and sometimes goose them, pull women from the audience, try to kiss them, and pour water on their heads. They also acted out scatological skits among themselves. As Louis Hieb notes, clowns usually speak English purposely to mock the religious seriousness of Hopi, and in their play might loudly note that they had no time for preparation for the dance in the kiva ceremonies.[35] One function clowns always play is to distribute food to the people watching the dance. These days, this is as likely to be loaves of Wonder Bread as stalks of maize, a substitution which is itself ironic.

Hopi cultural and religious ideas themselves are also full of contradiction and paradox. For example, Maasaw, who owns the Hopi lands, is the god of both death and fertility. In death one returns to the underworld, which is also the spiritual source of life. What endures is the breath and moisture, for the underworld is the source of rain. The Hopi petition their dead ancestors to bless them with rain. The Hopi word *gatungwu* means both human corpse and a harvested corn plant. In one legend, at the harvest Maasaw appears to farmers just as they finish stacking corn in heaps. He dresses paradoxically in an old woman's dress put on backwards and wears a mask of bloodied rabbit skin. He chases the men away from the corn. They run in terror, for if hit with his club they will die since he is the god of death. Yet his most important act at this moment is to touch the corn to mark his ownership. That provides a blessing of fertility.[36]

Hopi love to tell stories about Maasaw. He brings together the apocalyptic with life and sex. An unusually ugly and frightening looking god, he is the guardian of Old Oraibi. Each night he circles the village four times to protect it from danger, even though he himself is the embodiment of ultimate danger. Maasaw frequently changes into human form in order to court some beautiful maiden. In one such story Maasaw forgot about his disguise as he broke into song—and in the lyrics mentioned his festering and bony shins. The maiden fainted away dead. Maasaw then waited by her grave on the fourth day when, according to custom, she emerged from the grave. At that point Maasaw told her how much he loved her and how he wanted her to die so that she could marry him. She responded to his entreaties, and they "lived" happily ever after.[37] In another tale, Maasaw took on the skin of an old woman so that he could get close to her granddaughter. He then seduced the girl by telling her that old women always grow a penis; it is their appointed task to copulate with young maidens. Later, when Maasaw gives back his skin to the old lady and the grandmother returns, a funny scene occurs when the maiden turns to her expecting sex. The grandmother realizes in horror what has happened, though at the end one has a sense that the switch is laughed off as a joke, and certainly there is no regret on the part of the maiden.[38]

Hopi attitudes toward sex in general have always been tolerant. The best source on these issues is Mischa Titiev, whose work describes Hopi life in the 1930s. Lacking an authoritative update on Titiev's research, one has to assume the customs and attitudes he describes remain more or less in place. Parents and often many children sleep together in tiny rooms, and no taboo restricts parental intercourse, except during ceremonial preparation when the husband sleeps in his kiva. Children encounter sexual issues early. It is common to soothe babies by stroking their genitals. In clown skits little boys are taught racy behavior, and it is not uncommon during skits for adult women to simulate copulation with pre-adolescent boys. Sexual topics are discussed openly. Courtship is particularly unencumbered by restriction. Soon after puberty girls move into a separate room from their parents, while boys sleep together in the kivas and roam about at night as they please. Covering their faces with their blankets, they call on girls who decide whether to receive them. If a girl takes the boy in, they spend the rest of the night together. The custom is called *dumaiya* and is only interfered with by parents if a girl gets attached to a boy whom they feel is unworthy of her attentions. But in most cases girls and boys have multiple partners and parents stay out of the courtship ritual. Eventually, of course, the girl gets pregnant, though often without knowing the identity of the father. It is her prerogative, however, to choose her husband from among her suitors (though she may be rejected), irrespective of who the actual father of her child is.[39]

Hopi sexual customs, at least traditionally, even seem to include an easy acceptance of homosexuality. Mischa Titiev, the most reliable scholar on the Hopi, is somewhat hesitant about dealing with this subject. In his monograph he merely mentions that there was once widespread homosexuality among the Hopi, but that it appears to be less prevalent now. That "now" was the 1930s, and Titiev's point is supported by the later ethnographic work of Armin Geertz in the late 1970s, who says there is a strong Hopi taboo against homosexuality.[40] In his diary, however, Titiev is much clearer about the way the kachina dancers, and especially the clowns, explicitly embody and express themes of bisexuality.[41] The white historian Martin Duberman (himself an acknowledged homosexual) has unearthed references to some clown skits portraying men sucking penises and a general attitude of acceptance by the Hopi toward homosexuality. Duberman's work, perhaps not surprisingly, occasioned the loud protests of some white researchers, but the scholarship on which he relies seems beyond reproach.[42]

The Hopi, in terms of future directions, are granted a degree of latitude in choosing their own path.[43] They seem to have, in other words, a degree of conscious choice in relating to prophecy. The Hopi live in intimate communication with their gods, even though *a'ni himu* is ineffable. One would expect this godly people to direct their path toward mysterious communication with divine forms in a way that rediscovers the past. Such a vision is the antithesis of Christian end time theology, which envisions a return of Jesus and the creation of an altogether new world in the millennium, a final judgment, and eternal bliss for believers in heaven that bears no relation to anything before it. The Christian image of the end is directional, or teleological, awash in warlike and patriarchal symbols (for example, the appearance of Jesus with a suggestive sword coming out of his mouth).[44]

The Hopi, on the other hand, whose sense of future narrative is not at all clear, seem to envision in prophecy a future world that would either be something we have already known, or an extension of the Fourth World into a Fifth, or Sixth, or whatever. The pattern of creation, destruction, and re-creation is fairly well established in their myths and legends. There is no need to speculate on what might await us. One lives with the sacred as its meanings unfold. On the one hand, as Loftin points out, Third Mesa Hopi believe that the kachina dances will be the last to die, which is why they struggle to keep them going, while, on the other hand, "at the level of mythic continuity" these Hopi have no doubt that "the sacred essence of the ceremonies remains unchanged and always will."[45]

I talked with a man selling kachina dolls who bemoaned the frustrations that Hopi face. They are poor and only a few jobs exist on the reservation, though he himself chooses a marginal economic life in his village, rather than moving to Flagstaff or Phoenix where he might work in construction but would have to stay in the city. But the major dances are dying out, the young are not learning the ceremonies, and fewer and fewer are properly initiated into the culture. "People now fuck it up," he said. "Then they get sick or disappear." Still, he had not lost his hope. There was no question in his mind his people will endure. Things simply change. He was even baffled at my question whether he thought the Hopi would survive into the future. My question, it seems, ran counter to an apocalyptic mind-set that recycles future cultural forms from past experience. His view was echoed by the woman who guided me through Walpi. She had two years of college in Phoenix but got lonely and returned home, as she says 90 percent of all Hopi do who leave the reservation. She also saw many intrusions into the traditional way of doing things. She objected to the ugly public housing project in Polacca that we could look down on from the mesa heights of Walpi. She strongly felt that Hopi language and culture should be taught in school. And she quietly took swipes at the progressive tribal leadership, which would abandon the old for assimilation. But she remained hopeful. "Our people," she said, "will make it."

11

THE AGE
OF AQUARIUS

There is little doubt that "New Age" is a slippery concept. Most would agree that *A Course in Miracles* is New Age, but others would question how to connect Sun Bear's *Black Dawn, Bright Day, Path of Power*, or *Bear Tribe's Self Reliance Book* with Budd Hopkins's interest in UFOs (*Missing Time, Intruders*). Native American traditions have been a crucial influence on most New Agers, especially in their emphasis on the sacredness of the earth, though many Native Americans themselves, along with those more intimately familiar with their culture, feel trendy New Agers corrupt traditions that go back hundreds, if not thousands, of years. Christopher Lasch argues that the New Age seeks to "restore the illusion of symbiosis, a feeling of absolute oneness with the world," and is to Gnosticism what fundamentalism is to Christianity, "a literal re-statement of ideas whose original value lay in their imaginative understanding of human life and the psychology of religious experience."[1] Not all New Agers would buy into notions like the harmonic convergence (August 16–17, 1987, when, according to Jose Arguelles, the New Age dawned) or astral projection (the experience of viewing the world from outside one's physical body). Some believe in only specific ideas or aspects adopted by the New Age (like holistic medicine), while others seek to define whole new theologies and life-styles from within its spirit, as Starhawk does in her popular books on Witchcraft (which she capitalizes): *The Spiral Dance*, *Dreaming the Dark*, and *Truth or Dare*. The number of New Agers is also impossible to measure. It appears that one in five Americans believe in reincarnation, while the figure for British is 30 to 35 percent.[2] Some, tongue in cheek, might include all Californians in the New Age count; in any event, it is certainly a movement of great cultural significance.

New Age is a decidedly middle-class and white movement. There are few African Americans and hardly any Hispanics. As a religious movement it is open to everything except people who are genuinely different.[3] Many disgruntled professionals are in its ranks, along with the full range of white-collar workers (and what used to be called the housewife). Some read *A Course in Miracles*, while others are more likely to pick up the *National Enquirer*, but neither extends the discourse to accommodate minorities who are outside of mainstream cultural assumptions. This class and racial focus gives New Age an identity often lacking in the murky waters of the multicultural world of Catholic and Protestant churches; it also puts constraints on its potential for future development.

New Age is easy to mock. Prediction of the future in palm reading or Tarot cards runs counter to western traditions of scientific rationality. Middle-class and middle-aged women and men in white robes on mountain tops chanting pagan tunes strike many as ludicrous. The absence of ideas of evil, the devil, or hell, along with a conflict-free psychology, can make much of New Age seem mushy and cloying.[4] Some aspects of the New Age movement have also gotten highly commercialized, absorbed into the American tendency to turn the new into the chic. Well-known figures such as Marianne Williamson, Shirley MacLaine, or Sun Bear before his death lead workshops at which people pay hundreds of dollars for a few hours of instruction in reincarnation, the mysteries of *Miracles*, astral projection, survivalist techniques, meditation. You can make big bucks off the spirit.[5]

The specifically religious ideas of New Age can seem outlandish. Take astral projection. This idea assumes the division of the cosmos into etheric, astral, and physical dimensions. It is an old idea, given new meanings in current thinking.[6] We live in the physical world, while ghosts and other spirits dwell in the astral plane. The highest level of existence (the analogue of heaven) is the etheric plane that extends infinitely into space. Our beings, it is believed, can depart this body and life through the proper meditation and either inhabit our double (a "parasomatic" experience), or travel without a body, just "be" (an "asomatic" experience). Several levels of proof are offered for such out of body experiences, often referred to simply as "OBE." The most frequently cited are near-death experiences,[7] though many would also say we actually travel while asleep. Freud's psychologizing of such events into "mere" dreams, it is argued, obscures the reality of psychic and spiritual life.

But many religious ideas, if deconstructed, can seem odd. In the mainstream Judeo-Christian world, God speaks to Hebrew prophets out of burning bushes, while Jesus raises the dead and heals the sick, before he himself is resurrected. It is at least ungenerous for someone who ascribes to such a belief system to label as laughable the New Age belief in reincarnation, especially given its significance in eastern religions. In the fundamentalist world, furthermore, God and the devil speak to the tormented believer in separate ears. As we've seen, the details of the end time scenario almost defy rational observers to take it in. Between torrents of violence pouring out of heaven, there appear disguised forms of Satan, confusing images of the Lord with a sharp two-edged sword coming out of his mouth, and Jesus rapturing believers into the clouds before touching back to earth.

In addition, the New Age has a general integrity that warrants more than cursory attention. In certain areas, it has had a profound impact. The environmental concerns of recent years draw much energy from New Age people and ideas. Holistic medicine, which has been virtually taken over by New Age, is altering the way we think about our bodies and how to heal its forms of illness. The self-help movement, including Alcoholics Anonymous and the plethora of 12-step programs, which fed into the creation of New Age and is now almost synonymous with it, has proven a durable and often remarkably effective alternative to some of the deadening abuses of medical psychiatry. New Age thought, which in many ways is making it up as it goes along, is at least trying to figure out some new beliefs about our understanding of ourselves, our world, and the cosmos. It may be, as Erikson once suggested, that our world-images have become corrupt because they have been left to ecclesiastic bureaucracies.[8] "The New Age must begin in fantasy," says Michael Grosso, "for the old age is dying of reality."[9]

In New Age there are no dogmas, no set texts, and certainly no orthodoxies. Unlike the Hopi, there are not even agreed-upon stories that define certain parameters of faith. The *Course in Miracles* inspires some (and in the hands of Marianne Williamson has enjoyed a renaissance of late), but others are put off by its earnest Christianity.[10] Some do, and some don't, believe in UFOs. The more theoretical New Age adherents read Carl Jung and his disciples. He is their source for myths and legends, and their philosopher of the psyche who opens up the ego to transcendental experience. Jung was open to the parapsychological and, in religion, to the mystical. He spent many years investigating alchemy, not to figure out how to make gold but to understand the secrets of mystical researchers. His interpretation of dreams connects the individual unconscious experience of desire with collective memory. It is not an anti-rational psychology but neither is it rationalistic in the tradition of Freud. God enters into the Jungian world of interpretation and healing.

New Age discourse has a Jungian cast to it. People talk of "living archetypes" and the "collective unconscious" with a breezy familiarity. Any New Age bookstore worth its name includes some, often many, books by Jung, as well as his more important contemporary interpreters, James Hillman and Robbie Bosnak. Jung, as well, grounds New Age practice. Clarissa Pinkola Estes, a Jungian analyst, has written a best-selling book, *Women Who Run with the Wolves,* that advises women to get in touch with their "wild woman archetype" by sipping jasmine tea, taking long baths, and dancing at night on bare earth.[11] A therapist advertising "Wholeness Meditation" explains that, through deep breathing and "staying the moment," one can "make the Deep Self connection."[12] *New Age Magazine's* 1992 "Sourcebook" included an article on all the current New Age books, cassettes, and workshops that treat "Meeting your dark side." The article mentions Robert Bly's *A Little Book on the Human Shadow* (1988), along with his two-cassette program, "Meeting Your Dark Side," as well as W. Brugh Joy's *Avalanche: Heretical Reflections on the Dark and the Light* (1990) and his 12-Day Workshop, "The Dark Side: Death, Demons, and Difficult Dreams." Many, in fact, deride New Age exactly because it relies so heavily in its philosophical foundations on the work of Jung, a psychoanalytic renegade. But the effort to connect the exploration of deep spirituality with the writings of Jung adds a measure of continuity with western thought in this radical psychological and religious movement.

New Age terrain is constantly changing, as writers introduce new ideas and approaches that gain appeal, then rapidly fade away. One year Tarot reading is in, the next it's UFOs. Things are loose, ambiguous, unsystematic, even disorganized, but they are also creative. I would suggest an ad hoc, purely phenomenological definition of New Age: whatever books you find in a good New Age bookstore mark the contours of the field of inquiry. This is a definition from the bottom up. New Age ideas do not quite constitute an ideology and certainly are not yet a complete religion. It tends to reject tradition rather uncritically and is certainly murky about its myth of origins or its ethic. But New Age, if nothing else, has one thing about it that is utterly clear: it has an apocalyptic.

NEW AGE APOCALYPTICS

The New Age apocalyptic works in many unsettled modes that have yet to converge around a common story. There is a modified Christian version, a variant for witches, one that draws inspiration from Native Americans and connects with the environmental movement, another rooted in astrology, and the wildest of all in recent work on UFOs. A movement in search of religious grounding requires an apocalyptic, but in something as diverse as New Age there is no simple revelation we await, no one disclosure that can be easily predicted. The diversity of stories, however, is the key. As in so many other areas, New Age holds everything as possible. No white male, even a mystical one on Patmos, can dictate a vision of endings to control our cultural strivings.

The apocalyptic holds center stage in the spiritual imaginations of New Agers. The very term *New Age* has an apocalyptic flavor to it and implies a transformation of the world that is not necessarily conveyed in some of its component activities or sub-groups (like holistic medicine). The movement is larger than the sum of its parts.[13] If William McLoughlin is correct, it may presage a move into a "Fourth Great Awakening."[14] J. Gordon Melton stresses the transformative character of New Age ideas. "The New Age Movement can be defined by its primal experience of transformation. New Agers have either experienced or are diligently seeking a profound personal transformation from an old, unacceptable life to a new, exciting future. . . . Having experienced a personal transformation, New Agers project the possibility of the transformation not of just a number of additional individuals, but of the culture and of humanity itself."[15]

In a very general way, three forms of the apocalyptic compete in New Age discourse. These forms overlap in the minds of many people, and in typically open New Age fashion many take in all three without worrying about being consistent. But for heuristic purposes it helps to define the field by getting a clear sense of how *different* each approach is to the revelation of New Age. The three apocalyptic styles can be generally characterized as catastrophic, magical, and efficacious.

Catastrophe

Many believe the New Age will dawn in violence and destruction. Ruth Montgomery, for example, who dominated the New Age scene in the 1970s and into the early 1980s, may be the best-known prophet of doom. Once a journalist and columnist, Montgomery found her true voice as a guru in some ten books that describe channeling, walk-ins (where a historical figure, often of great renown, actively inhabits one's body), and the dawning of the New Age. Her writing is highly accessible to a mass audience. She takes esoteric topics and turns them into understandable, if still mystical, themes for the committed to ponder.

Montgomery's model (and that of many others) is that the coming of Jesus Christ marked the beginning of the Piscean age that has now reached its culmination. We await the age of Aquarius, which will realize the millennium spoken of in the Bible (at least as Montgomery conceives of it). That millennium will be a time of love and brotherhood. Schools will be unnecessary, for our expanded consciousness will allow us to tap directly into the minds of others and vastly expand our knowledge. We will be able to read books at a glance. Souls will be able to reach perfection, and not have to keep returning to human bodies to confront the same temptations of avarice, greed, and lust. Walk-ins bring messages of the end, and other "signs" that foretell the future millennium. With the environmental movement, for example, Montgomery sees a tremendous surge of collective empowerment in people simply refusing any longer to let big government control their lives and destroy the planet by moving back to the wilderness, using herbal remedies, and growing their own food. "The emphasis is on individual effort, rather than mass society, and on freedom of choice," she writes.[16]

The way into this millennium, however, is full of violence. The great change into the Aquarian age has begun to take place, she argues, but will not be "fully recognized" until the "shift of the axis has eradicated some of the evils of the present age." Such phrasing avoids naming exactly how many die in the transformation. Montgomery, however, leaves no doubt that the greedy and lusting are among those to be "eradicated" in the New Age. The next two decades will be a "strenuous" time for "Mother Earth," and many souls will wish "they had not chosen this particular time for rebirth into the flesh." We face the certainty of World War III, which she hints will be nuclear and will certainly generate famine and riots. Montgomery even suggests an ethic for the New Age: it will be "fraught with peril" for those not adequately prepared in spirit. In a directly fundamentalist way, Montgomery also argues in several books that Antichrist is now in college in an eastern seaboard state and will reveal himself at the end of the century as the final shift of the axis occurs.[17]

The active presence of and role for Antichrist in the minds of some New Agers, not to mention images of the millennium and "signs" of the "end times," suggest some of the many ways Christian fundamentalist imagery has worked its way into New Age ideas of catastrophe. One UFO abductee reported that her experience left her with one strong thought: "By the year 2000 the world would be totally different than we know it, but it would be only for the young and strong."[18] David Solomon, as many others, uses the idea of the "end times" to refer to the end of this present age of Pisces.[19] Others, like Nada-Yolanda, make the notion of living in the end times concrete. For her the period 1960 to the year 2000 is the most important span of time in the history of the solar system, or at least of the last 26,000 years. In this period, all of history must be "reexperienced, renewed, reevaluated and discarded." To be cleansed in this period, one must demonstrate the "I Am Consciousness," which will make us more self-reliant. The "sixth-phase rending of the seventh veil" ran from 1988 until the end of 1992. A "severe" cleansing period ended in 1988 but much more is to come. It will be painful but eventually beneficial. And we must learn about it and how to move the changes forward creatively by encounter with the cosmic law. All else, especially our "erroneous theories," are entirely misleading and confusing.[20]

In general, both among fundamentalists and New Agers, one consequence of any concrete dating of the end is that it tends to be associated with more violent images of destruction. There is something about naming catastrophe that brings it closer to hand, rather like the difference between those who talk generally about suicide and those who give details of their planned death. As therapists learn from bitter experience, the latter has far more dangerous meanings. Fundamentalists, of course, have only one date to be concerned about, the return of Jesus. Their question is how specifically one can locate that mystical event in time and space. New Agers, on the other hand, have a looser set of images that control their sense of renewal. The transformations leading to the creation of the New Age of Aquarius come in stages, in a kind of serial apocalypse.[21] Phases of it may already have dawned and the rest will unfold in steps. But the transformations are also potentials within us, which we can influence and shape; indeed, we have an obligation (though to whom or to what is not always clear) to get ahead of the apocalyptic and direct it.

That obligation, however, is fraught with danger. The "11:11 Doorway" movement claims that we are now in a twenty-year period of opportunity to end the earth's period of duality and conflict between dark and light. In this interval, there must be a "cleansing," after which we will find ourselves on a new earth. The "doorway" of opportunity opened on January 12, 1992, and will close on December 31, 2011. Opening the doorway could open a "major planetary activation" and the participation of (the Revelation-inspired number) 144,000 "Activated Star-Borne [united] together in conscious Oneness world-wide" to bring about "our mass ascension into new realms of consciousness." The 11:11 symbol itself, according to a self-appointed seer, Solara, was "pre-encoded within our cellular memory banks, long, long ago, prior to our descent into matter, under a time release mechanism, which when activated signified that our time of completion is near." This knowledge of the symbol somehow came to Solara looking at digital clocks. The 11:11 Doorway is, for its adherents, much more important than the "harmonic convergence" that Jose Arguelles identified. As Solara puts it: "It's moving onto a patterning of octaves, not dimensions anymore, under a template of oneness, aligned with a great central sun system. This signifies our graduation into mastery and freedom."[22]

As with fundamentalists, however, the issue of failed prophecy for those who name a date, even a vague one, lurks in the background for anyone working with the apocalyptic. New Agers have so far handled this problem by talking only very generally of being in a still-unfolding period of transformation, or with a vague retreat into the mysteries of astrological understanding. The "11:11 Doorway" movement, for example, since 1986 has mentioned five major and three minor periods of potential planetary alignments that could usher in a transformation of human evolution.[23] The potential for change is not quite a prediction on the order of William Miller (and others before and since) predicting the return of Jesus on a certain day, but it pushes up against concrete prediction, as does most of such discussion in New Age.

If Ruth Montgomery and others combine Christian apocalyptic imagery with astrology, Sun Bear brings his sense of the approaching catastrophe together (loosely, as always in New Age) with Hopi and other Native American traditions. This controversial figure was the son of a Chippewa father and a mother of German-Norwegian descent. He grew up on the White Earth Indian Reservation in northern Minnesota and received an eighth-grade education. After being drafted into the Korean War, he became a deserter for reasons of conscience. For many years he was an activist in Indian causes. He also founded the Bear Tribe Medicine Society, which has a national following and sponsors "medicine wheel gatherings." At such gatherings, Sun Bear evolved a variety of rituals that connect New Age with Native Americanism, including sweat lodge purifications and crystal healing ceremonies.[24]

Sun Bear's message is the conviction that Earth Mother is a living being now in the midst of what he calls a "deep cleansing." Earth is in tribulation. She is sick from all the poisons she has absorbed from humans. "It's plain to see," he said in 1983, "with the volcanoes, the earthquakes, the changes in weather patterns." His medicine wheels are a vehicle for getting people to connect with the earth. Hug a tree, he advocates, to begin your healing. "Trees are conductors of energy between the heavens and earth. When you hold and hug a tree, you feel the energy and it can be like a blood transfusion."[25]

Sun Bear notes the significance of prophecy in human history from the Hopi through the books of Matthew and Revelation in the Bible. He argues that we need to listen to those who can hear the future. He offers himself up as such a person, a shaman to be listened to. Sun Bear says he has had dreams of things that happened and those that will come to pass. He has organized his Bear-tribe as a rural-based community because he foresees major destruction in the cities. Those in the greatest danger are the ones near nuclear and chemical plants. He sees piles of garbage, breakdown of services, race riots, wars, and destruction on a vast scale.[26]

Sun Bear's image of change involves great violence and destruction. "The planet will survive, even though perhaps millions of people will perish."[27] (Or, in a more folksy apocalyptic image, he says the Earth is like a big shaggy dog full of testy fleas. When the dog gets sufficiently annoyed he scratches and shakes at the creatures. "Well," Sun Bear concludes, "there is going to be a lot of shaking and a lot of frightened humans during the Earth changes."[28]) The only human survivors he sees are "small bands of people living very close to the earth."[29] What will end is the Fourth World, which specifically evokes the Hopi tradition, and one fourth of the world's population will survive, which is one way of calculating the destruction in the Book of Revelation.[30] The outcome of all this violence, however, is regenerative and hopeful: "All those who do survive will come through with a higher level of consciousness." There will be great spiritual leaders. "So this is a time of cleansing."[31] There are many bad things going on, things on "many levels" that will no longer be around when the cleansing is completed.

The "period of change," furthermore, is upon us. "Between now and the year 2000 is the time span in which most of the major changes are going to be happening," Sun Bear says.[32] Everything is accelerating and happening "so rapidly" that he has to update his examples weekly, even daily. These examples are changes in the earth (quakes and other natural disasters), as well as the effects of destructive pollution. It is this rending of the earth that most tore at his soul. *Black Dawn, Bright Day*, in a sense, is a great lament for the earth, which for him is a "living, intelligent being."

Sun Bear is ambivalent on the question of human efficacy. The earth changes cannot be reversed; they have gone too far. He asked Spirit that once and learned that, "No, the changes are sealed."[33] But Sun Bear also stresses that humans are not powerless in "beginning to bring about a solution." You can, he says, "help heal the Earth and yourself."[34] Much of *Black Dawn, Bright Day*, in fact, consists of detailed and pragmatic advice on survival during this period of change. Be prepared for unexpected weather changes, for example, and take both extra layers and a sun hat and umbrella when you travel; support education about birth control as well as pro-choice politicians; try bathing and washing your hair in five gallons of water you heat on a wood stove; move away from the coasts, especially California.[35] His sacred world on what he calls "Vision Mountain" seeks to create just such a safe refuge.

The *only* survivors will be those who make a conscious decision to change "in the way they look at life, in the way they understand things, and in their actions toward all creation."[36] You must be awakened to "true reality," which is the spirit within and in the earth. They can only be healed together. Humans and the earth must be in harmony.

Magic

New Age is a world of ghosts and spirits, not entirely explained but also not ignored. In a chapter on "A Typology of Helping Apparitions," Michael Grosso, for example, in *The Final Choice*, discusses much material from paganism, Christianity, and popular culture about the world of spirits. In one typical story a woman reported stopping at an intersection. As she started up, she looked down briefly at the cigarette lighter. When she glanced up the long-dead figure of her mother stood directly in front of her car. The woman slammed on her brakes, just in time to avoid a semi truck running a red light in front of her. Was the figure a projection of the woman's unconscious? asks Grosso. Or was it the saving act of the ghost of her mother? In fact, Grosso finds something of a middle ground: "Let us just say that these phenomena are signs of the Extended Self—the total or subliminal Self, the 'higher' or 'true' Self."[37] The Cartesian notion of a limited and rational self will not work, argues Grosso. There is just too much that happens to make such claims to rationalism false. The New Age conclusions to such ideas are not always clear, but all would agree that we can only begin to improve, indeed to save, our world by getting in touch with these dimensions of self experience. It could well be that these areas of the unknown extend to communication with aliens from space, which is not that far removed from the notion of ghosts and spirits returning to save the living from car wrecks and our own souls reincarnating in another body after a period of transformation in the astral realm.[38]

Grosso analyzes the significance of nuclear threat to human existence and concludes that "only a radical spirituality, a new metaphysics strong enough to command a new kind of courage and solidarity, will overturn the system of the nuclear warriors."[39] He finds some hints of the possibilities of such "radical spirituality" in the near-death experiences, and notes with encouragement that many have such transformative imagery even apart from actual death. "By analogy," he concludes, "the vivid premonition of catastrophe [in the collective psyche] might activate the reordering mechanisms of the deep psyche; we might then escape our bad fate and buy a lesson in enlightenment cheaply."[40] Grosso talks of the collective uncon-scious as being in a "state of unrest" as "The Bomb" stirs "Mind at Large" into action. The mechanism for that transformation, Grosso says in a chapter titled "The Morphology of the Apocalypse" is through the "archetype of death and enlightenment" and its adap-tive capabilities, revealed, it seems, in UFO contacts and visions of the Blessed Virgin Mary.[41] "There must be light at the end of the tun-nel," Grosso asserts. The prophetic visions, whether Marian or UFO, signal the end of an age and the dawning of something new, something beyond the smoke and rubble.[42]

The Marian visions represent for Grosso the "general awaken-ing" to the "energies, the qualities, the sensibility, associated with the multiplex archetype of the feminine." Specifically, "the Marian experience resuscitates the earth goddesses of antiquity; the Marian age reconnects modern spiritual sensibilities with the age of Eleu-sis—the ancient mysteries, a world in which the divine was experi-enced in relation to certain collective feminine realities."[43] Put more succinctly: "The process of empowering the feminine archetype, if carried out authentically, would exert a powerful influence on plan-etary life."[44] Similar factors are at work with UFOs. In near-death visions, Grosso says, the soul sends up messages of guidance and consolation. The information addresses the transpersonal, or the collective, which is both response and warning at the level of arche-type. UFO sightings, for example, vastly increased after 1947, which for Grosso is part of the response to the threat of nuclear war. Sightings "register perturbations in the collective psyche."[45]

The whole UFO phenomenon has become almost trendy of late in America. Frequent sightings are reported, and it is estimated by those in the field that some 700,000 to 3.5 million people have been abducted.[46] The pioneering and zealous, almost evangelical, work of people like Budd Hopkins has convinced large numbers of people that something real might be happening to which serious attention should be directed. On the five-hundredth anniversary of the birth of Christopher Columbus, the United States government recently turned a huge, 100-million-dollar dish to the heavens to receive messages. A noted Harvard psychiatrist, John Mack, leads UFO support groups, interviews abductees, and is writing a scholarly book on the subject.

The most famous observer of UFOs, however, is undoubtedly Budd Hopkins. In the clear, dispassionate prose of his two books (*Missing Time* and *Intruders*), Hopkins has described his astounding findings over the last several decades. A hallmark of his work is that he stays close to the available, if not quite empirical, evidence. He is scrupulous about not tainting his respondents with information from what he hears from others, about using witnesses, about taping interviews, about not jumping to explanations too quickly. He readily admits his findings are remarkable, indeed "unbelievable." He talks about the BB-like implants in the abducted, and attempts several possible explanations, but backs off from them quickly. "I do not wish to dwell on any of these paranoia-inducing theories. Perhaps these BB-like objects have some other, as yet unimagined purpose or purposes. Whenever we consider these large, theoretical questions about the ultimate nature, source and intention of the UFO phenomenon, we must admit that we still have no final answers."[47]

Hopkins takes his respondents seriously. He gets to know them, hypnotizes them, and talks for seemingly endless hours with them on the phone. He pays attention to details, like the reports of abductees being cold as they enter the UFO crafts or the exact nature of the scars people report (which he also photographs). He also studies the phenomenon with the care of a scientist, and includes in his book long transcripts (and excerpts where relevant) from his taped interviews. Without question Hopkins is a believer in UFOs, but he tries to maintain the distance of the serious scientific investigator, albeit a committed one. Hopkins may well be wrong but he should not be dismissed.

In the historical literature on abuse in the beginning of psycho-analysis, most now feel that Freud had it right the first time, and that psychoanalysis took a decided turn for the worse when Freud decided his early hysterical patients had only fantasized the seductions by their fathers that they remembered as real when adults.[48] In the same vein, the evidence Hopkins and others have assembled about UFO abductions is quite impressive about something, though it is not entirely clear what. He has uncovered all kinds of remembered traumas in otherwise relatively normal people, physical evidence, and converging stories.[49] Some kind of apocalyptic vision is at work (which could have some common roots in various forms of abuse).

The question, of course, is what the aliens want from us and why they would bother conducting their research on so many individuals over such a relatively long period of time, not to mention implanting things that mark abductees (or extracting semen from men and sexually abusing women). Some report a simple plot to conquer and destroy us. But other abductees report far more complicated and interesting communications from the aliens. The sexual experimentation, for example, they say appears to be in the interest of creating hybrids in breeding pools, which the aliens see as one way of saving something on earth before the final destruction. Indeed, that destruction appears to be the central concern of the aliens, and from what they tell some abductees the aliens cannot understand why we would be so earnestly trying to destroy earth. The purpose of their interventions, in this view, is to offset the destruction of the planet by humans, to save us from ourselves, in other words, or at least become part of a process of co-creation in a transformed new age.[50]

Among other New Age thinkers the magical apocalypse takes some extraordinary twists and turns. Augusta Almeida brought together UFOs, Jesus, and the rapture.[51] She claimed that Jesus was an extraterrestrial and the commander of a large force he has already brought with him to earth, many of whom still remain. Almeida claims that the earth is to be "evacuated" between 1993 and 1997 so it can be repaired; then Jesus will return. She names this process of repair the "Grand Lift" and says it will begin in the Philippines; in fact, she recommends some specific churches where those wanting to be saved should go for that purpose. After the "repairs" the earth will be a paradise again. People will then be returned to live in peace on it for a thousand years.

For her part Virginia Essene reports (from a channel) that we might be uncomfortable enduring the transition to the coming age, which is millennial in tone and feeling. That discomfort will be due to our interdependence with cosmic forces. As Essene puts it, we are each a "cosmic pattern, a template of celestial potential," and we are all precursors of a "new human species." The change itself is thought of as "waves of energy and light" that will "shower earth."[52]

This kind of idea has influenced New Agers to develop an evolving network of rituals that is gradually defining its own spirituality. From a loose and individualistic beginning that included massage, palm readings, and crystal wearing, and progressed into more organized and communal forms with workshops, lectures, and rebirthing weekends in hot tubs,[53] New Age has begun to formalize things. Some meet in nonconventional but organized ways to share and worship as they understand that concept. Witches regularly gather in covens and occasionally meet for special ceremonies for which they have become famous. New Age conventions are held frequently in large cities in central hotels and can draw thousands. Some groups strive at least to draw in huge audiences for their rituals. Solara, for example, instructs participants in 11:11 Doorway events to gather in the largest groups they can manage and perform prescribed movements in synchrony. Worldwide, these rituals must involve at least 144,000 people and are to be performed at 11:11 A.M. and P.M. local time.[54] In the spring of 1992 DaVid announced his presidential candidacy of the Human Ecology Party at a New York nightclub. DaVid timed the announcement to coincide with an 11:11 event. He was surrounded by followers with raised hands (a symbolic way of stopping time) greeting each other with a chant: "I offer you peace. I offer you friendship. I offer you love. I hear your needs. I see your beauty. I feel your feelings. All wisdom flows from a higher source. I salute that source. Let us work together."[55]

Channeling (which emerged in 1952 among UFO contactee groups to describe the nature of the communications they were receiving from the inhabitants of the alien spacecrafts) is central to the magical apocalypse.[56] The underlying concepts of channeling are often left vague, though the basic idea is that "cosmic awareness" is a force that has revealed itself through Jesus, Buddha, Krishna, Muhammad, and Edgar Cayce, and is now speaking through other, anonymous channels helping to guide us through the change to the Age of Aquarius.[57] William H. Kautz and Melanie Branon, in *Channeling: The Intuitive Connection*, tell us that "Ye who merge the mind, the body and the spirit shall experience greater longevity," that in fact by the year 3000, "Ye shall have fulfilled the thousand years of brotherhood—physical immortality."[58] A figure like Nada-Yolanda describes in detail her communications with Sanada/Jesus and how she has helped reinforce "the special new shield around the United States, with its dome at the top." She has broken through to new levels of consciousness and come to accept her responsibility as a cosmic relay from the "Hierarchical Board." She has had the sound "Om" implanted in her which has activated her light body. Her meditations on Easter, 1992, included "a loud, crunching crack. A boulder, the size of my forehead, tore across the front of my head. And I realized that my brain was . . . the inside of a cave or tomb." It might be said that this meditation is a kind of New Age form of the Resurrection, as the Christ-self is realized in each of us.[59]

The question of agency in channeling is a fascinating one. In a preface written in 1977 for the second edition of *A Course in Miracles*, Helen Schucman notes how she received the material in the *Course* from the Holy Spirit. A "little willingness" is sufficient, she says, "to enable Him to use any situation for His purposes and provide it with His power." Sometimes it is vaguer who is actually sending the information and why it is being sent, as in automatic writing. The key thing is to be in the grip of a higher power who communicates through you in some way that defies rational explanation. For Helen Schucman, who was a professor of medical psychology at Columbia University's College of Physicians and Surgeons in New York City, she heard "the Voice." As she put it: "It made no sound, but seemed to be giving me a kind of rapid, inner dictation which I took down in a shorthand notebook." You never quite know why you are being contacted, but clearly spiritual forces for good are at-tempting to transform the earth's evil ways by communicating mes-sages of change, uplift, and hope.[60]

Personal Efficacy

For many New Agers neither catastrophic nor magical images of revelation dominate their thinking. Instead, they place the creative and efficacious role of human action at the center of any possibility for transformation in a New Age. In this view, the New Age is com-ing, perhaps inevitably, but in fits and starts, and without our push it may descend on us with tragic consequences.

A Course in Miracles urges personal responsibility to liberate the spirit from the guilt and sense of badness in the Judeo-Christian tra-dition. For some, the Course is too specifically Christian, in its feel-ing almost like a Bible (with the breakdown of chapters and the numbered sentences or verses), and in its use of Holy Spirit, of Christ, of God and His Son. The language is curiously old-fashioned and sexist, since the Course was published in 1973, just before the language change brought on by feminism. But its essential message is that we must be free to be human, and to be in God's eyes: "The veil across the face of Christ, the fear of God and of salvation, and the love of guilt and death, they all are different names for just one error; that there is a space between you and your brother, kept apart by an illusion of yourself that holds him off from you, and you away from him." And a little later: "To everyone has God entrusted all, be-cause a partial savior would be one who is but partly saved."[61]

Douglas Grant works such Course ideas into his own writings about channeling and rituals of prayer. Grant argues that we are all to fulfill our own second comings by "reviving" our "inner Christ-selves" in preparation for the return of Christ. Only our own nega-tivity and low self-esteem prevent this realization. We must become channels and take responsibility for what we receive. We must speak and live for God, and filter out our own desires and interpretations. Prayer thus precedes channeling, and we must be prepared for years of study and personal preparation. What we receive is prophecy, which prepares people in times like these of cosmic change. We are not helpless, however, in the face of approaching disaster. All events are influenced by human thought and desire. We become aware of disaster in order to enable us to avoid or forestall it. Just as we attempt to channel Christly energies we will "attract energies and entities of the same Christ level of vibration and beingness" and repel "lesser energies in our force field . . . caus[ing] new levels of purification to be achieved." This process multiplied raises the planet to a "new level of spiritual expression."[62]

Environmentalism draws New Agers into the world of politics. The basic idea in New Age thought is that we are somehow already in the process of transformation, and that an awareness of the environment is essential to the process. What is involved is a recognition of the "Oneness of Life." We are "kin" not only to all the animals on the earth but to stars and subatomic particles. And consciousness always evolves to higher levels and a "more inclusive integration."[63] There is seldom the kind of joining of prophecy and current events that one finds in the work of someone like Hal Lindsey. But the end of the cold war, perhaps because of its magnitude, contradicts the political insularity of New Age. It lends itself easily to the vision of transformation so central to New Age apocalyptic yearnings. Capitalism is dying of its own polluted weight, and communism clearly has proven to be a worthless form of social engineering. What is left is the "progressive transformation of human culture" in an "evolution toward divinity."[64]

Like many fundamentalists, many New Agers are apolitical and withdrawn from the mainstream political process in America (though there has been no study of this fascinating phenomenon), except for the active involvement of New Agers in the environmental movement. Aside from widespread individual action, some take part in the Human Ecology Party, which proposes a 15 percent across-the-board tax that can be itemized by the citizen. They foresee that the result would be a vast downsizing of government, especially the military. They would create a huge corporation to invest the funds taken from the military that would develop energy in harmony with the laws of nature, introducing the solar age. They would build a global peace center on Alcatraz Island in the shape of a hexagram to broadcast Artainment video to the global family.[65] Although there is no devil or hell in New Age, those who despoil the earth, those polluters who have subjected Mother Earth to sacrilege, may suffer.[66]

One suspects that the neo-pagan leader Starhawk would agree, as would Sun Bear and those interested in Native American beliefs, who tend to talk about our personal responsibility for the earth's destruction. The ethics in such a message are collective and communal. The individual must survive (and Sun Bear provides quite detailed information on how to live out the period of change we are in), but our ethical obligation is to the planet, to the human race, and to all living creatures.

Witches in turn, Starhawk argues, are bound to serve the life force. Some killing must occur for survival (for "life feeds on life"), but the wanton destruction of the environment contradicts all ethics. The Goddess may be immanent, "but she needs human help to realize her fullest beauty," as Starhawk puts it. Meditation is a spiritual act in Witchcraft but not as much as cleaning up garbage or marching on a nuclear test site. We are all interdependent, and both need one another and have responsibilities toward one another. To harm one is to harm everyone.[67] "What you send, returns three times over," say witches, which Starhawk sees as an "amplified version" of "Do unto others as you would have them do unto you." Our growing awareness of ecology, the impending environmental apocalypse, has forced on us a realization of our interconnectedness with all forms of life, which is one of the bases of Goddess religion.

Our changing cultural attitudes toward sexuality are influencing New Age spirituality as well.[68] In this regard, Starhawk asks a "hard-headed, critical question" about eastern religions: Are they not also hierarchical, denying sexuality, and demeaning women in many of the same ways as western religions? Eastern religions seem good for men. They open them up to cooperative, interdependent ways. For women, however, they seem only to offer further passivity and are "playing the same old song." We do not need messiahs, martyrs, or saints, she says. Instead, we need to find our own reality, inner and outer, to become fully human, "fully alive with all the human passions and desires," and the "infinite possibilities." Sexuality is a powerful and wonderful force for Starhawk. It is the "expression of the creative life force of the universe," and in orgasm "we share in the force that moves the stars" (though Starhawk adds that one has to be aware that the sexual revolution has generally meant the easy marketing of women's bodies).[69] Xaviere Gauthier supports this connection between witchcraft and sexuality. Why witches? she asks: "*Because witches dance.* They dance in the moonlight. Lunar, lunatic women, stricken, they say, with periodic madness. Swollen with lightninglike revile, bursting with anger, with desire, they dance wild dances on the wild moors. Wildwomen, uncivilized, as the white man says of other races; wildcats, as the government and the unions say of some strikes; as they say of some of our schemes. The witches dance, wild and unjustifiable, like desire."[70]

Witchcraft is a powerful affirmation of efficacy for women. The Goddess, Starhawk says, is manifest in humans and thus it is contrary to the spirit to deny the human. The task of "feminist religion" is to learn the simple things. It is easier to be celibate, for example, than fully alive sexually, to withdraw than to be in the world, to be a hermit than to raise a child, to repress feelings than to feel them, to meditate than to communicate, to submit to authority than to trust oneself. "In order to truly transform our culture," she concludes, "we need that orientation toward life, toward the body, toward sexuality, ego, will, toward all the muckiness and adventure of being human."[71]

The three "core principles" of Goddess religion are immanence, interconnection, and community. Immanence means that we are the "manifestation of the living being of earth," and that all forms of life in its diversity are sacred.[72] Starhawk does not *believe* in *the* Goddess; "We connect with Her," she says, "through the moon, the stars, the ocean, the earth, through trees, animals, through other human beings, through ourselves. She is the full circle: earth, air, fire, water, and essence—body, mind, spirit, emotions, change."[73] Interconnection expresses our link with "all of the cosmos as parts of one living organism." And this Starhawk interprets both ecologically (the felling of tropical forests affects our weather) and politically (the crying of a homeless child upsets our well-being).[74] Community, finally, speaks to the collective dimension. The goal is not individual salvation or enlightenment. "Community" also includes animals and plants, and is both personal and global.[75]

New Age images of transformation operate in their most salient form at the personal level. Self-help and empowerment govern its ethics, its style of spirituality, and its apocalyptic. This dimension of New Age lends it a cultural and healing power that a trendier movement like that of the Jesus People entirely lacked.[76] The sense of sacred healing gives New Age a remarkable potency. In this regard nothing has been more significant among the sources of inspiration for New Age than Alcoholics Anonymous, and the related 12-step programs for a variety of addictions in a troubled age that have sprung from AA's original principles. AA's astonishingly successful self-help program for alcoholics has shaped New Age ideas of empowerment and its commitment to leaderless groups.

AA was founded in 1935 by Bill W. in Akron, Ohio.[77] Bill had been a successful trader on Wall Street and a gregarious, friendly man. For years he drank to excess and could never find a way of curing his addiction as he watched his life and work crumble before his eyes. At the depths of his despair he was visited by an old drinking buddy who was now straight, well groomed, and sober. The friend, named Ebby, was a member of a zealous religious sect called the Oxford Group that had helped him overcome his drinking problem. The Oxford Group encouraged open confession from its members and guided its followers in assembled groups. Ten of AA's twelve "steps" were carried over directly from the Oxford Group.[78] Bill's first ally was a Dr. Bob, who was also a recovered alcoholic. The organization expanded rapidly, and now is worldwide with 58,576 chapters in over ninety countries and over a million members as of 1985.[79]

The genius of AA's organizational structure is its completely democratic character in what Marc Galanter has called, after Max Weber, a "routinization of charismatic leadership."[80] The crucial first step in membership is the entirely free selection of a sponsor (who can also be changed at will) who takes the inductee through the twelve steps and provides help in "working the program." A series of rituals govern AA attendance, such as always introducing oneself as "My name is _____, and I am an alcoholic" to mark the end of denial, along with expectations such as daily attendance at meetings for the first three months ("ninety meetings in ninety days"). Nevertheless, the actual membership of any given AA chapter is in constant flux, there are any number of possible meetings one can attend, and nothing prevents a member from withdrawing from the organization altogether and possibly returning later. Each chapter is autonomous and decides on its own format and rules. There are no dues, and funds for chapters to cover the cost of rental space (if not free) and pay for the ever-present coffee come from small contributions of those attending any given meeting. No money is ever taken as a gift from nonalcoholics. The name of AA can never be used for any kind of endorsement, commercial or political. The movement keeps itself focused on only one purpose and never gets involved in other causes, though individual members may do what they want politically with the rest of their lives.[81] The skeletal AA national office is run by volunteers.[82]

Galanter argues that AA healing has a cult-like quality with its public confessions, tight cohesion, shared beliefs, and behavior strongly influenced by the group.[83] It is a given in AA, for example, that "personal recovery depends on AA unity" and that members must "adjust, temper, and discipline" their own freedom to protect AA itself.[84] Galanter grants that AA, because of its effective structure, has avoided the faults of groups like Synanon but nevertheless heals its members of their alcoholism through their abject submission, public confessions, strict attendance, and subtle control of dissenting opinions (such as controlled drinking, which is gaining favor among some researchers but is denied as even possible by AA). Most AA members end up socializing with others in the organization, which can put stress on some marriages and old friendships, and fill their language with AA buzzwords that reflect the enthusiasm of a new member of a religious cult.

Certainly, AA rituals and ideals are strongly influenced by evangelical Christianity. The first step in AA is an affirmation of one's utter helplessness before alcohol that parallels the depravity of one's unsaved self before conversion. The second step accepts the existence of a "Higher Power," an ecumenical (though euphemistic) denotation that makes clear its Christian origins in the revelatory experiences that make up AA literature, in the way all AA participants talk about it, and in the famous prayer of Reinhold Niebuhr that is invoked at the beginning of every meeting: "God grant me the serenity to accept the things I cannot change, courage to change the things I can, and wisdom to know the difference." In the third step you are to turn over your will to God as you understand him. Other steps require various forms of self-surrender, personal improvement, public confessional, and prayer. The final step returns to the fundamentalist, evangelical model in requiring those who have had a "spiritual awakening" and healing through following the previous eleven steps to now take their message to other alcoholics. Faith without works is dead, says Bill W. in the "Big Book."[85] From rebirth and conversion to personal transformation to sharing the word, AA adapts Christian forms to its secular task of healing alcoholism.

AA traditions of self-surrender, confession, deep spirituality, mutual support and empowerment, nurturing relationships (especially in the tradition of the sponsor), equality of members, and the structure of leaderless groups have profoundly influenced the values and life-styles of many New Agers. It is difficult to imagine feminist consciousness-raising groups, or most communes, or witches' covens, or UFO support groups except in an age of the self-help movement shaped by AA. New Age spurns medical psychiatry and Freudian psychotherapy as highly suspect in their rational scientism and embedded patriarchy, though they are drawn to less conventional forms of talk therapies. They believe we must recognize and submit to a "Higher Power." Healing in the New Age comes from a spiritual process of personal transformation. We need to be nurtured and touched, often literally as in massage.

The transformative character of the 12-step/New Age healing process reveals its apocalyptic subtext. In Bill W.'s famous and now archetypal story, he describes his conversion as "the fourth dimension of experience."[86] From a long tradition of mystics to New Age, the "fourth dimension" has become a buzzword to evoke the ground of spirituality that transcends the self. The revelation according to Bill W. is script for AA, built as it is on stories of sin and redemption that reveal inner truths. Martha Morrison, for example, was a talented and hopelessly addicted doctor in Arkansas in the 1970s who shot up vast quantities of hard drugs besides consuming whole bottles of Southern Comfort. After reaching bottom, Morrison had a religious experience on the banks of the Chattahoochee River in Georgia. At that point she "came to understand and to concede that I had to stop trying to dominate other people and situations. Then, and only then, did I begin to grow."[87] And grow she did into a successful doctor once again, this time helping other addicts, while marrying the son of her mentor and founder of Talbott Recovery Systems, G. Douglas Talbott. Her new self reveals the power of God, and her well-written book, *White Rabbit*, is one way of "witnessing" to others.

The apocalyptic is at the center of New Age. Not as a movement of mystics and fellow travelers; nor as an eclectic blending of Carl Jung and Native Americanism; nor as a therapeutics that rivals scientific medicine; nor least of all as a religion in formation can New Age begin to make sense or cohere without understanding its images of personal and collective transformation.

Clearly, the New Age apocalyptic evokes fundamentalist notions of the end times. Specific images from fundamentalist end time theory—like that of Antichrist, tribulation, even the rapture—creep into New Age thinking. More generally, Catherine Albanese has argued that New Age as a movement has some striking similarities with Christian fundamentalism. Both seek a personal transformation that must find its reflection in the transformation of society; both hear voices rather than see visions and clothe their mysticism as ongoing revelation; both stress healing and what the Puritans once called the "outer signs of inner goodness," or the spiritual benefits of material prosperity; both are literalists (one in terms of biblical scripture, the other in terms of reincarnation); and both espouse a democratized spirituality that looks forward into visions of the millennium.[88]

Perhaps both New Age and fundamentalism are plowing the same apocalyptic ground. We are in it, and it is in us. It cannot be escaped, though there is much uncertainty about our responsibilities toward it, and the role of violence in the move from the old into the new. But what opens up at the other end for New Agers is quite a different picture of the millennium from that of the fundamentalists. In the *inclusive* utopian images of the New Age, global justice and equitable distribution of resources prevail. The sacredness of "Mother Earth" is respected. There are neither executioners nor victims in a world of peace. And instead of a present God or resurrected Jesus leading the faithful, each individual is an empowered and fully realized human being.

CONCLUSION

There is no easy way to conclude a book like this. There are too many stories, and my interpretive points are imbedded in them. I can only underline some ideas that seem particularly significant, and look toward the future of endism and fundamentalism in American culture.

First, endism is a part of all our lives at some level, and has always been woven into religious imaginings at least since culture emerged. But until the last half century endism has been mostly a marginal phenomenon, as best we can tell, and the important task of imagining the end has been assigned to the deeply spiritual, the artistic or creative, and the psychotic. Endism has ebbed and flowed in significance within the self and culture, depending on historical circumstance. Now, however, in our postmodern age when it is a scientifically real possibility that human history could end in a bang of nuclear destruction or a whimper of environmental degradation, it takes an act of imagination *not* to ponder end time issues. The true craziness we live with is the way life itself has been transformed by the continuing presence of absurd threats to the human experiment, which could only make a "pointless apocalypse,"[1] not the varied and sometimes confused human responses to those threats. Fundamentalists speak in a rhetoric that is out of sync with contemporary secular culture; they also touch the real, and give voice to our underlying dread. It was something of a historical accident that Christian apocalypticism emerged in clear ideological form in the nineteenth century out of the crisis of war and as a response to the stirrings of modernism. But once clearly articulated in dogma by 1920, fundamentalism (which even then was at the edges of society), was uniquely well positioned to become a mass movement later in the century. End time theology and the scientific reality of prospective human endings were made for each other.[2] But those ultimate threats affect all of us, not just the fundamentalists. As we have seen, many others besides Christian fundamentalists in our culture have found ways to imagine the end. The Hopi Indians locate elements of hope in their notions of cultural transformations that manage to preserve the ecological integrity of the earth, while New Agers struggle in a variety of secular modes to explain the changes that they believe are upon us. In this broader sense, then, this book is both an interpretation of Christian fundamentalism and a comment on modern life.

Endism in our culture embraces many forms, and partially touches everyone's life in its connection with death. Endism is an attitude as much as a myth, a sense of foreboding as much as a given story, an orientation to ultimate concerns as much as a commitment to a specific end time narrative. Endism describes the future location and deepest yearnings of the self. Endism is process and vision. It cuts against all logic, is usually mystical, and may become magical. Endism stirs hope, which can inspire the dispossessed but can also come to serve as yet another instrument of control for the rich: consider, for example, the involvement of Mrs. Grady in right-wing causes. Endism surely has roots in trauma in the self, but that individual, psychological perspective must be broadened to locate the self in the historical crises of the twentieth century. As a result, there is a paradoxical, or dialectic, relationship between endism and our human future. Something is broken, and it is not even clear God is the glue. To be alive and even reasonably aware at the end of the millennium requires us to ask of ourselves, of our families, of our leaders: Will the human experiment continue?

The most troubling dimension of endism is its relationship to violence. In the endist imagination, transformation out of our present misery—however differently that is understood by people—occupies a central place. The result of the change is inevitably a new age, whether millennial or Aquarian, one that is radically and profoundly different from the present. Fundamentalists generally believe that this transformation can only be accomplished violently, and that the move from our time into the next requires mass death and destruction. Yet it is possible to be future-oriented and nonviolent. Much religious thinking about ultimate issues, from Jesus to Gandhi, purposely rejects violence in constructing images of future redemption, and it is important to take firmer hold of these traditions as we struggle to build utopias that continue a human future. But the more passionate forms of endism I encountered in this study seem to require violence to produce the transformation that will end what is experienced as the tormenting ambiguity and pain of human existence, indeed of time itself, and re-make history. That is the point of the biblical genocide described in the book of Revelation.

But ordinary people do not take in ultimate threats or absorb the grand or violent myths in their culture or religions in simple ways. In its Christian fundamentalist form, which occupies most of my attention in this book, endism (or the apocalyptic) varies enormously with different individuals. There are certain key ideas people take from the theory—like the idea of the rapture or the general notion of tribulation—but most fundamentalists bring their own concerns into their end time reflections and reveal in their apocalypticism projections of the self. Such a process of exchange always occurs in the transaction between the individual and his or her forms of faith. But fundamentalist theory is especially well suited for such end time projections; it is much more immediate in this regard than the impossibly far-off notions of heaven in traditional Christianity.

The immediacy that fundamentalism brings to the traditional Christian message, however, has its potential costs. The apocalyptic tends to undermine personal efficacy and a commitment to human purposes. That can raise ethical and political concerns. The reborn self can isolate the fundamentalist individual from complex social interactions. The intimate communion with the divine (and the devil) realigns moral responsibility in the fundamentalist mind, and can result in a withdrawal from participation in solving social problems. Moreover, the faith commitments of fundamentalists are thoroughly dogmatic; they believe *that* something is true, rather than *in* a transcendent God whom one can only know as immanent in our lives.[3] Something important is lost as fundamentalists shift the Christian emphasis from the Sermon on the Mount to the book of Revelation. Their ideology, to rephrase Diana Trilling, is the sterner face of the Christian myth.[4] The effects of such religious attitudes are readily apparent in the political realm, for certainty about ultimate issues lends ideological clarity to proximate concerns like gender equality, free speech, sexual choice, and curriculum change. For opponents, the certainty of fundamentalists can be vexing and seems to run counter to the dynamics of compromise in a democracy.

Pervasive dualisms and exclusivism are central to fundamentalism. Otto said of the end that, "He [God] is coming back for his people first." God has "his" people, those who have accepted him and believe in him. At the end they will be rewarded in their faith, for he will come back for them first. But such a notion of a chosen people excludes everybody else, especially given the suffering outlined for these "others" in fundamentalist theology. As Erik Erikson observes:

> *While man is obviously one species, he appears and continues on the scene split up into groups (from tribes to nations, from castes to classes, from religions to ideologies) which provide their members with a firm sense of distinct and superior identity—*

and immortality. This demands, however, that each
group must invent for itself a place and a moment in
the very center of the universe where and when an
especially provident deity caused it to be created
superior to all others, the mere mortals.[5]

Part of the power of Erikson's insight is his recognition that destruction between groups can only make sense with a spiritual grounding. We cannot value ourselves and degrade and ultimately kill the other unless we call God onto our side in the struggle. In the same way, the genocidal impulse is grounded in perverse forms of idealism and deep yearnings for spiritual purification.[6] Individuals kill others for many reasons, including greed and malice. But mass death, or genocide, though it may embody many motivations, must aim primarily at renewal and transformation of a particular group.

That is the danger. America is an affluent land with a stable political system and a long tradition of absorbing radical social movements into its vast middle. But fundamentalism, largely because it so directly touches ultimate issues, may resist any taming, and remain positioned to expand rapidly in the face of crisis. And it would be foolish to believe that we will always remain immune to crisis. The apocalyptic sense that thrived in and found renewal from the Civil War is enough part of American identity to prompt risky undertakings (like Bush's Gulf War). Protracted fighting abroad or racial war at home, large-scale terrorism, environmental disaster, or whatever, could easily prompt the eruption of the apocalyptic within fundamentalism.

Much, however, works against these dangers. James Davison Hunter, in careful survey work accompanied by interviews, has shown that the younger generation of fundamentalists are generally more moderate in their beliefs and more open in their life-styles than their parents. They think only loosely about the rapture or tribulation, which makes them open to other, modifying influences. Younger fundamentalists are much less likely to be creationists, for example, than older ones. They also seem to feel little compunction about sex before marriage (with someone you love and intend to marry), and have a much more complicated interaction with the media and mass culture than their parents. It may be that Hunter has merely uncovered a blip in the demographic sequence from the 1970s to the 1990s, but he may also have documented a more profound transformation in the making.[7]

There is also hope in the very diversity, even the confusions, of fundamentalists, which end time theory attempts to suffocate. Such a powerful system, with its own boundless sense of immortality, *requires* the search to eliminate all hints of alternative images. But alternative images lurk beneath the surface and demand expression, which in turn calls forth the invocation of Satan to explain them and the difficult work of overcoming them. The fundamentalist psychological process never fully succeeds in carrying out its agenda of purification.[8] The best evidence of these complex tensions is the way fundamentalists make up or bend theory as they go along to fit their own experience. Deborah, who taught a Bible class in her church, rewrote rapture theory to allow for open-ended salvation up to the moment of the final judgment, and God for Arlene was an old black woman.

At a different level, the Christian apocalyptic, even in its most rigid ideological form, provides renewal and hope in the lives of the socially, economically, and spiritually disadvantaged. That is why Reverend Charles and Calvary Church in general were so important in my study. This congregation, which toed the premillennial dispensational line as strictly as any white fundamentalist church, combined their fundamentalism with a significant degree of social activism. They also drew hope from the apocalyptic, into which they stared as deeply as anyone. Reverend Charles, as Jonah in the Bible, knew Nineveh would eventually be destroyed. In the meanwhile, he drew psychological sustenance for himself and his parishioners from the increased sensitivity to ultimate threats to human existence. Apocalyptic hope is cautious at best, but it can be real.

Many complex social, political, and religious factors are drawing fundamentalists into mainstream culture, which may also be a reason for hope. They are themselves masters of media and increasingly attend secular schools at all levels. They are also joining the political mainstream. Jerry Falwell, for example, to the chagrin of many fellow fundamentalists, struck elaborate deals in forging powerful political alliances on key issues during his years of leadership of the Moral Majority. Falwell eventually disbanded the Moral Majority but hardly abandoned his dreams of influencing American politics; he just changed the venue. He now takes the long view and plans to work through education, especially his own Liberty University in Lynchburg, Virginia. "As far as I'm concerned," Falwell has said, "Liberty University is one of the best ways that I can [have an] impact [upon] the course of the country. I foresee creating for political conservatism what Harvard has done for political liberalism."[9] One suspects Falwell, in his grandiosity, may be failing to appreciate that education often works in mysterious ways. Pat Robertson's Christian Coalition, which had some striking political successes in the 1992 elections,[10] is perhaps more doctrinaire but, like the Moral Majority, will almost certainly be forced to compromise with secular humanists as it attempts to take over school boards and other local centers of power throughout the country.[11] What may matter most in the long run is that Falwell and Robertson have brought fundamentalists into the process of compromise that makes up American politics.

Finally, the separatism of fundamentalism can be exaggerated. At times their world can move toward totalism, but in general fundamentalism is basically a variant of Christianity that pushes up against all aspects of American life. Whatever their images of redemption, New York fundamentalists still have to take the D train in from Brooklyn.

NOTES

INTRODUCTION

1. Martin Buber, "Prophecy, Apocalyptic, and the Historical Hour," in *Pointing the Way*, ed. Maurice Friedman (New York: Books for Libraries, 1957 [1954]), pp. 192–207. Note also Harvey Cox, "Christianity and the Apocalypse," presentation at the second conference on the Apocalypse in Providence, Rhode Island, organized by Robbie Bosnak, June 14–17, 1990, comments summarized by Michael Perlman; and Paul D. Hanson, *The Dawn of the Apocalyptic: The Historical and Sociological Roots of Jewish Apocalyptic Eschatology* (Philadelphia: Fortress Press, 1979).

2. Frank Kermode, *The Sense of Ending: Studies in the Theories of Fiction* (New York: Oxford University Press, 1967), p. 27.

3. Paul Boyer, *When Time Shall Be No More: Prophetic Belief in Modern American Culture* (Cambridge, Mass.: Belknap Press of Harvard University Press, 1992), p. 2.

4. Garry Wills, *Under God: Religion and American Politics* (New York: Simon and Schuster, 1990), p. 15. The most recent Gallup data is found in George Gallup and Jim Castelli, *The People's Religion: American Faith in the 90s* (New York: Macmillan, 1989), pp. 56, 58, 61, 63, and 75. The figure about the rapture is from Marlene Tufts, "Snatched Away before the Bomb: Rapture Believers in the 1980s" (Ph.D. diss., University of Hawaii, 1986), p. vi.

5. It should, however, be noted that the conventional scholarly view would not consider conservative evangelicals as fundamentalists. Note Nancy T. Ammerman, "North American Protestant Fundamentalism," in *Fundamentalisms Observed*, ed. Martin Marty and R. Scott Appleby (Chicago: University of Chicago Press, 1991), p. 4. Other scholars see conservative evangelicalism and fundamentalists as part of a continuum. See Douglas Sweeney, "Fundamentalism and the Neo-Evangelicals," *Fides et Historia* 24, no. 1 (Winter/Spring 1991), pp. 81–96.

6. David Harrington Watt, "The Private Hopes of American Fundamentalists and Evangelicals, 1925–1975," *Religion and American Culture* 1 (1991), p. 155. See also David Harrington Watt, *A Transforming Faith: Explorations of Twentieth-Century American Evangelicalism* (New Brunswick: Rutgers University Press, 1991); and the work of Erling Jorstad, especially *Holding Fast, Pressing On: Religion in America in the 1980's* (New York: Praeger, 1990).

7. Grady House was the epitome of the modern transformation of millenarianism, as noted by political scientist Michael Barkun (*Disaster and the Millennium* [New Haven: Yale University Press, 1974], p. 211), from a rural movement historically rooted in disaster and crisis to an urban one that has become "the creature of those who seek power and dominion." The apocalyptic, or, as Barkun calls it, "the idea of the millennium," taken from those who most require it, "now animates those who need it least." This phenomenon was also reported by Nancy T. Ammerman in *Baptist Battles: Social Change and Religious Conflict in the Southern Baptist Convention* (New Brunswick: Rutgers University Press, 1990), esp. pp. 146–49. An earlier treatment of the urbanization of sectarian fundamental-

ism can be found in John B. Holt, "Holiness Religion: Cultural Shock and Social Reorganization," *American Sociological Review* 5 (October 1940), pp. 740–47. I also want to thank Dana Fenton, who is writing her Ph.D. dissertation on Grady House under my direction, for confirming my suspicion about the systematic use of the Social Register by Grady House staff for culling names to invite to the dinners. The parent organization of Grady House, it is worth noting, has also sponsored the Christian Embassy in Washington.

8. Martin Marty, *Religion and the Republic: The American Circumstance* (Boston: Beacon Press, 1989 [1987]), p. 297.

9. The best book on Jim Bakker is by Charles E. Shepard, *Forgiven: The Rise and Fall of Jim Bakker and the PTL Ministry* (New York: Atlantic Monthly Press, 1989).

10. One can see African American fundamentalism on television in the person of Frederick Price. The congregations of the white televangelists can be observed to have many African Americans in them. David Edwin Harrell's classic work *White Sects and Black Man in the Recent South* (Nashville: Vanderbilt University Press, 1971) documents the presence of African Americans in many churches that are considered fundamentalist. See also Thomas Byrne Edsall, "Political Changes in the South: Black Majority, White Men and Fundamentalists," *Dissent* 34 (Winter 1987); and Samuel D. Procter, "The Black Community and the New Religious Right," *Foundations* 25 (1982), pp. 180–87. A minority view is that African Americans, because of their "distinctive style" of worship and their "relationship to society," cannot be considered within the family of fundamentalists. Note Ammerman, "North American Protestant Fundamentalism," p. 3.

11. Erik Erikson, *Insight and Responsibility* (New York: W. W. Norton, 1964), pp. 159–215.

12. Sigmund Freud's first reference to what James Strachey translates as the "narcissism of minor differences" is in "The Taboo of Virginity" (1918), in *The Standard Edition of the Psychological Works of Sigmund Freud*, ed. James Strachey et. al., 23 vols. (London: Hogarth Press, 1955–1962), vol. 11, p. 199. He later returned to the idea in *Group Psychology and the Analysis of the Ego* (1921),

Standard Edition, vol. 18, p. 101, and in *Civilization and Its Discontents* (1930), *Standard Edition*, vol. 21, p. 114.

13. James Aho, *The Politics of Righteousness: Idaho Christian Patriotism* (Seattle: University of Washington Press, 1990).

14. Martin Marty regularly used this phrase in his fundamentalism project at the University of Chicago (in which I participated for a while as a consultant). It is a useful way to capture the aspects of Christianity at the edges of what might not fit into a stricter definition of fundamentalism.

15. Nancy Ammerman also documented this in *Bible Believers: Fundamentalists in the Modern World* (New Brunswick and London: Rutgers University Press, 1987), pp. 147–67. Jehovah's Witnesses believe that only 144,000 Christians will be saved in the end, and they are judged partly on the basis of their evangelical successes, which explains their unusual intensity in their efforts to convert non-Christians. As usual in these matters, however, such pieces of harsh theology frequently get softened in actual experience.

16. Nan made the comment to Laura Simich, who was also working in the church then and trying to convince Nan (unsuccessfully) to grant her a formal interview. It is worth noting that Nan and the woman I call Mary were close friends and lived near each other. Mary granted me two useful interviews but refused a third. I think Nan probably influenced her decision.

17. Erikson says it well: "One can study the nature of things by doing something *to* them [human beings], but one can really learn something about the essential nature of living beings only by doing something *with* them or *for* them" (*Insight and Responsibility*, p. 229). For a more detailed discussion of method, see the article I wrote with Michael Flynn, "Lifton's Method," *The Psychohistory Review* 20 (1992), pp. 131–44.

I. THE BROKEN NARRATIVE

I borrow the term "broken narrative" from B. J. Lifton, my friend and Ph.D. student, who uses it in her forthcoming book, *The Adopted Self* (New York: Basic Books).

1. Michael Franz Basch, "The Perception of Reality and the Dis-

avowal of Meaning," *Annual of Psychoanalysis* 11 (1982), pp. 125–53. The first use of the term "disavowal," however, was by Sigmund Freud in his short paper, "Fetishism": see *The Standard Edition of the Psychological Works of Sigmund Freud*, ed. James Strachey et al., 23 vols. (London: Hogarth Press, 1955–1962), vol. 21, p. 153.

2. The most interesting empirical discussion of these issues is by a former student in a dissertation I supervised: Jennifer Manlowe, *The Grains of Loss: Psychological and Theological Reflections on Eating Disorders and Incest*, unpublished Ph.D. diss., 1993, Drew University. Nicholas Humphrey and Daniel Dennett also wrote a relevant paper, "Speaking for Our Selves," *Occasional Paper*, Center on Violence and Human Survival, New York, 1990. Diane Lunt, a psychoanalyst at the Training and Research Institute in Self Psychology (where I am on the faculty), also shared with me her as-yet-unpublished case of a multiple personality she has been treating for many years. A good recent discussion in general of these issues is Judith Herman, *Trauma and Recovery: The Aftermath of Violence—From Domestic Abuse to Political Terror* (New York: Basic Books, 1992).

3. There are many ways, other than biography, of understanding history psychologically. The issue has often been debated intelligently in the pages of *The Psychohistory Review* (of which I was the founding editor in 1972). I also wrote, with Dan Offer, a history of psychohistory that addresses this issue: *The Leader: Psychohistorical Essays* (New York: Plenum Press, 1986). Robert Jay Lifton has noted the evolving and overlapping psychohistorical styles (including his own) since Freud in *The Life of the Self: Toward a New Psychology* (New York: Simon and Schuster, 1976).

4. Karen McCarthy Brown, personal communication, March 3, 1989.

5. Robert Jay Lifton, in collaboration with Charles B. Strozier, "Psychology and History," in *Psychology and the Social Sciences*, vol. 2 of *Psychology and Its Allied Disciplines*, ed. Marc H. Bornstein, 3 vols. (Hillsdale, N.J.: Lawrence Erlbaum, 1984), pp. 164–84, esp. pp. 171–75.

6. I use "mystical" in this book, following Webster, to describe

spiritual meanings that are neither apparent to the senses nor obvious to the intelligence and that involve a direct subjective communion with God.

2. ULTIMATE THREATS

1. Daniel Yankelovich, the head of the Public Agenda Foundation, in collaboration with The Center for Foreign Policy Development at Brown University, found that 39 percent of the adult population in America believed that "when the Bible predicts that the earth will be destroyed by fire, it's telling us about a nuclear war" (*Voter Options on Nuclear Arms Policy: A Briefing Book for the 1984 Elections* [New York: Public Agenda Foundation, 1984], p. 40).

2. This discovery was by no means mine alone, but part of my own John Jay College Center on Violence and Human Survival research group's collective awareness in analyzing interview material from many different groups. It will be carefully documented in a volume in preparation by myself, Michael Perlman, and Robert Jay Lifton, *Nuclear Threat and the American Self*.

3. The idea of Israel as the "fuse" in the Middle East is a conventional one in fundamentalist thinking. See John F. Walvoord, the eighty-year-old dean of premillennial dispensationalism, who in December 1990 (that is, in the middle of the Persian Gulf crisis) cranked out an updated version of his 1974 book *Armageddon, Oil, and the Middle East Crisis* (Grand Rapids: Zondervan, 1990 [1974]). In 1991, a year with a Middle East war, the book sold 713,827 copies; see *Publishers Weekly*, April 6, 1992.

4. Robert Jay Lifton and I jointly came up with this term and first used it in "Waiting for Armageddon," *New York Times Book Review*, August 12, 1990.

5. A. G. Mojtabai, *Blessed Assurance: At Home with the Bomb in Amarillo, Texas* (Albuquerque, N.M.: University of New Mexico Press, 1986), pp. 142–83, esp. pp. 148, 178–79. Mojtabai is actually quite cautious on this issue. Other journalists, arguing more out of the logic of the theology than actual contact, charge fundamentalists with some extraordinary positions.

3. THE NEW SELF

1. Augustine, *The City of God*, trans. Marcus Dods (New York: Modern Library, 1950), p. 865.

2. Otto Rank, *The Double: A Psychoanalytic Study* (Chapel Hill: University of North Carolina Press, 1971 [1925]). Note also Rank, *Beyond Psychology* (New York: Dover, 1958 [1941]), pp. 62–101.

3. Robert Jay Lifton, *The Nazi Doctors: Medical Killing and the Psychology of Genocide* (New York: Basic Books, 1986), p. 418.

4. The significance of "dissociation" and "splitting" was quite clear to the early, especially French, workers on hysteria from the 1880s well into this century, especially Pierre Janet. Even Sigmund Freud and Joseph Breuer grant the importance of splitting (*Studies on Hysteria* [1895], in *The Standard Edition of the Psychological Works of Sigmund Freud*, ed. James Strachey et al., 23 vols. [London: Hogarth Press, 1955–1962], vol. 2, pp. 227, 230ff). A good recent discussion of this early history is Bessel A. Van Der Kolk and Onno Van Der Hart, "The Intrusive Past: The Flexibility of Memory and the Engraving of Trauma," *American Imago*, special two-volume issue, "Psychoanalysis, Culture and Trauma," ed. Cathy Caruth, 48 (1991), pp. 425–54. For much of the twentieth century, however, Freud's stress on repression came to crowd out these early insights. The first thinker to begin actively recovering their meanings for the self was Heinz Kohut, especially his first book, *The Analysis of the Self: A Systematic Approach to the Psychoanalytic Treatment of Narcissistic Personality Disorders* (New York: International Universities Press, 1971). Kohut's favored term was "splitting," which was most clearly articulated in his model of the self in 1963: with Philip F. D. Seitz, "Concepts and Theories of Psychoanalysis" in *The Search for the Self: Selected Writings of Heinz Kohut*, ed. Paul H. Ornstein, 4 vols. (New York: International Universities Press, 1978 [1963]), vol. 1, pp. 337–74.

5. Heinz Kohut, *The Restoration of the Self* (Madison, N.J.: International Universities Press, 1977), p. 287.

6. James Barr, *Fundamentalism* (London: SCM, 1977), p. 51.

7. Ibid., p. 52.

4. DIVINE COMMUNION

1. Wilma used this image from Revelation but also said firmly how much she detested and never read the book itself. Such use of apocalyptic language by a woman who disavows the key text of the movement reflects how deeply such imagery has worked its way into the discourse.

2. A latent violence nevertheless seemed to haunt Nigel. He told me two chilling driving stories during his "wild period." In one he was driving on Highway 95 from Boston to New York in his sports car. Someone pulled in front of him and deliberately braked for whatever reason. Nigel moved at high speed into the passing lane, chased the car down, and purposely forced it off the road. Luckily, no one was killed. In the second story Nigel was blocked by a car and he pushed into it and forced it into the median where it crashed. He drove off into the night at high speed. "These are things that I would never do today," he said, "because I'm a different person."

5. THE END AT HAND

1. Hal Lindsey, with C. C. Carlson, *The Late Great Planet Earth* (Grand Rapids: Zondervan, 1970); John F. Walvoord, *Armageddon, Oil, and the Middle East Crisis* (Grand Rapids: Zondervan, 1990 [1974]). I also gave a paper, "Christian Fundamentalism, Nuclear Threat, and the Middle East War," Uppsala, Sweden, February 25, 1991, that was later published in *The End in Sight? Images of the End and Threats to Human Survival*, ed. Roger Williamson (Uppsala: Life and Peace Institute, 1993), pp. 49–58.

2. John F. Walvoord, *Prophecy Knowledge Handbook: All the Prophecies of Scripture Explained in One Volume* (Wheaton, Ill.: Victor Books, 1990). Note also Dwight J. Pentecost, *Things to Come: A Study in Biblical Eschatology* (Grand Rapids: Zondervan, 1958).

3. Paul Boyer, *When Time Shall Be No More: Prophetic Belief in Modern American Culture* (Cambridge, Mass.: Belknap Press of Harvard University Press, 1992), esp. pp. 1–79 and 190 on date setting.

4. Otto is a "post-tribulationist," for he believes that Christ only returns *after* the period of tribulation. What that means concretely

for Otto is that Christians first have to experience the horrors of God's destruction before being redeemed in the returned Christ.

5. Walvoord, for example, in *Prophecy Knowledge Handbook*, in his twenty references to the rapture, weaves it into the background of all sorts of crucial Gospel stories that touch on prophecy and the return of Jesus. Compare Hal Lindsey's breezy book *The Rapture* (New York: Doubleday, 1983). A study that puts the rapture in historical perspective is Timothy P. Weber, *Living in the Shadow of the Second Coming: American Premillennialism, 1875–1982* (Chicago: University of Chicago Press, 1983).

6. The question of the timing of the rapture before or after tribulation was also one of the first major sources of serious fragmentation in the evangelical movement at the turn of the century, and led to the disintegration of the Niagara Bible Conference in 1901 and the cessation of the prophetic conferences of the next decade. Note George Marsden, *Fundamentalism and American Culture: The Shaping of Twentieth-Century Evangelicalism, 1870–1925* (New York: Oxford University Press, 1980), p. 93.

7. A man at Calvary, a Brother Heflin, who runs an end time camp, went a step further in explicitness. He thought the headline was already printed and it said, "Millions Missing" in the largest type the *Times* has ever used.

8. Among the excellent studies of women in Protestant fundamentalism of all varieties are: Margaret Bendroth, "The Search for Woman's Role in American Evangelicalism, 1930–1980," in *Evangelicalism in Modern America*, ed. George Marsden (Grand Rapids: William B. Eerdman's Publishing Company, 1984), pp. 122–34; Kathleen M. Blee, *Women of the Klan: Racism and Gender in the 1920s* (Berkeley and Los Angeles: University of California Press, 1991); Virginia Lieson Brereton, *Training God's Army: The American Bible School, 1880–1940* (Bloomington and Indianapolis: Indiana University Press, 1990); Betty A. DeBerg, *Ungodly Women: Gender and the First Wave of American Fundamentalism* (Minneapolis: Fortress Press, 1990); James Davison Hunter and Helen V. L. Stehlin, "Family: Toward Androgyny" in James Davison Hunter, *Evangelicalism: The Coming Generation* (Chicago: University of Chicago Press, 1987); Rebecca Klatch, *Women of the New Right*

(Philadelphia: Temple University Press, 1987); Susan Rose, "Women Warriors: The Negotiation of Gender Roles in an Evangelical Community," *Sociological Analysis* 48 (1987), pp. 244–58; Susan Rose, *Keeping Them Out of the Hands of Satan: Evangelical Schooling in America* (New York and London: Routledge and Kegan Paul, 1988); Susan Rose, "Gender, Education, and the New Christian Right," in *In Gods We Trust: New Patterns of Religious Pluralism in America*, 2d ed., ed. Thomas Robbins and Dick Anthony (New Brunswick and London: Transaction Publishers, 1990); and Judith Stacey, *Brave New Families: Stories of Domestic Upheaval in Twentieth-Century America* (New York: Basic Books, 1990).

6. THE WORLD AND ITS EVILS

1. Catherine Keller, personal communication, January 27, 1993.

2. Robert Jay Lifton, *Death in Life: Survivors of Hiroshima* (New York: Vintage Books, 1967), p. 224.

3. Otto's memory was pretty good. 2 Timothy 3:1–5: "This know also, that in the last days perilous times shall come. / For men shall be lovers of their own selves, covetous, boasters, proud, blasphemers, disobedient to parents, unthankful, unholy, / Without natural affection, truce-breakers, false accusers, incontinent, fierce, despisers of those that are good, / Traitors, heady, high-minded, lovers of pleasures more than lovers of God, / Having a form of godliness, but denying the power thereof: from such turn away."

4. *Religion Watch* (September 1992, p. 6) reports on a study at the Center for Survey Research at the University of Virginia showing that evangelicals and fundamentalists have a strong concern for poverty and other social issues and that they are among the most generous segment of the population. In the survey, "helping the poor in America" was the number-one concern of this group, and on the average they gave 10 percent or more of their income to such issues (though the article noted, without comment, that their giving to "such issues" included gifts to the church). The more fundamentalist the respondent, however, the more likely he or she was to rate converting people as the more significant goal of a Christian.

5. Carl G. Jung, *Aion: Researches into the Phenomenology of the*

Self, trans. R. F. C. Hull, in *The Collected Works of C. G. Jung*, vol. 9, pt. II, ed. Sir Herbert Read, Michael Fordham, Gerhard Adler, and William McGuire (Princeton: Princeton University Press, 1959 [1951]), pp. 42–45, 61.

7. THE PROBLEM OF ENDISM

1. Arthur M. Schlesinger, Jr., "The Turn of the Cycle," *New Yorker*, November 11, 1992.

2. John Singleton in an interview with Bryant Gumbel on "Today," May 1, 1992.

3. Martin Gottlieb, "Police in Crown Heights: A Holding Approach," *New York Times*, November 19, 1992.

4. Henri Focillon, *The Year 1000* (New York: Frederick Ungar, 1969), p. 53.

5. Ibid., p. 40.

6. Ibid.

7. Ibid., p. 50.

8. Ibid., p. 47.

9. Sigmund Freud, *The Interpretation of Dreams* (1900 [1899]), ed. James Strachey, 1-vol. paperback edition (New York: Basic Books, 1965), p. 660. Compare Freud's other comment on this issue, ibid., p. 278: "Paradise itself is no more than a group phantasy of the childhood of the individual. That is why mankind were naked in Paradise and were without shame in one another's presence; till a moment arrived when shame and anxiety awoke, expulsion followed, and sexual life and the tasks of cultural activity began." The specifically "Edenic" idea is a personal communication from Catherine Keller.

10. Frank Kermode, *The Sense of Ending: Studies in the Theory of Fiction* (New York: Oxford University Press, 1967), p. 16. Compare, however, Paul Boyer, *When Time Shall Be No More: Prophetic Belief in Modern American Culture* (Cambridge, Mass.: Belknap Press of Harvard University Press, 1992), pp. ix and 337. Boyer by no means mocks the contemporary popular concern with prophecy (as does Kermode) but tends to stress that its current emphasis blends "age-old themes" that will keep prophecy belief alive well into the next century. I generally agree with Boyer and would only

stress the relative historical newness of fundamentalist ideas in a mass movement that is grounded, somehow, in ultimate threats to human existence.

11. Kermode, *Sense of Ending*, pp. 95–96.

12. Don DeLillo, *Mao II* (New York: Viking, 1991), p. 80.

13. Kermode, *Sense of Ending*, p. 28.

14. Lincoln Burr, "The Year 1000 and the Antecedents of the Crusades," *American Historical Review* 6 (1900), pp. 429–44, argues that the "panic of terror" in the latter part of the tenth century actually originated in the mind of the fifteenth-century abbot Johannes Trithemius, is entirely legendary, and now exists only as a "nightmare" of modern scholars. The evidence Burr rightly discounts, however, is of a popular panic that some nineteenth-century historians used to explain the crusades. He does not address the more interesting evidence that Focillon used from the monasteries. Burr, of course, wrote a half century before Focillon.

15. Norman Cohn, *The Pursuit of the Millennium* (New York: Oxford University Press, 1957).

16. See the ninety-nine-page pamphlet of the Mission that was handed out on New York City streets during the summer of 1992.

17. Elaine Showalter, *Sexual Anarchy: Gender and Culture at the Fin-de-Siècle* (New York: Viking, 1990).

18. Susan Sontag, *AIDS and Its Metaphors* (New York: Farrar, Straus, and Giroux, 1988).

19. A number of empirical studies over the years have studied the effect of nuclear threat on people. See T. R. Tyler and K. M. McGraw, "The Threat of Nuclear War: Risk Interpretation and Behavioral Response," *Journal of Social Issues* 39 (1983), p. 186; Thomas A. Knox, William G. Keilin, Ernest L. Chavez, and Scott B. Hamilton, "Thinking about the Unthinkable: The Relationship between Death Anxiety and Cognitive/Emotional Responses to the Threat of Nuclear War," *Omega* 18 (1987–88), pp. 53–61; Raymond L. Schmitt, "Symbolic Immortality in Ordinary Contexts: Impediments to the Nuclear Era," *Omega* 13 (1982–83), pp. 95–116; Scott B. Hamilton, Thomas A. Knox, William G. Keilin, and Ernest L. Chavez, "In the Eye of the Beholder: Accounting for Variability in Attitudes and Cognitive/Affective Reactions toward the Threat of

Nuclear War," *Journal of Applied Social Psychology* 17 (1987), pp. 927–52; and Jerome Rabow, Anthony C. R. Hernandez, and Michael D. Newcomb, "Nuclear Fears and Concerns among College Students: A Cross-National Study of Attitudes," *Political Psychology* 11 (1990), pp. 681–98. See also the collection of essays in Lester Grinspoon, ed., *The Long Darkness: Psychological and Moral Perspectives on Nuclear Winter* (New Haven: Yale University Press, 1986); this volume includes a scientific essay by Carl Sagan on nuclear winter and an essay reflecting on that image by Lifton. Another interesting—and controversial—area of research on nuclear threat in the 1980s was done on children. See Sybil K. Escalona, "Children and the Threat of Nuclear War," in Milton Schwebel, ed., *Behavioral Science and Human Survival* (Palo Alto, Calif.: Science and Behavior Books, 1965), pp. 201–9. See also Milton Schwebel, "Nuclear Cold War: Student Opinion and Nuclear War Responsibility," in Milton Schwebel, ed., *Behavioral Science and Human Survival*, pp. 210–40. But the most important work on children and nuclear threat, much of which was conceptual and clinical, was done by John Mack, William Beardslee, and their colleagues at Harvard: John Mack and William Beardslee, "The Impact on Children and Adolescents of Nuclear Developments," in R. Rogers, ed., *Psychosocial Aspects of Nuclear Developments*, Task Force Report No. 20 (Washington, D.C.: American Psychiatric Association, 1982); J. Mack, W. R. Beardslee, R. M. Snow, and L. A. Goodman, "The Threat of Nuclear War and the Nuclear Arms Race: Adolescent Experiences and Perceptions," *Political Psychology* 4 (1983), pp. 501–30; William R. Beardslee, "Perceptions of the Threat of Nuclear War: Research and Professional Implications," *International Journal of Mental Health* 15 (1986), pp. 242–52; and John E. Mack, "Resistances to Knowing in the Nuclear Age," *Harvard Educational Review* 54 (1984), pp. 260–70. The most bitter (and polemical) criticism of this work was C. E. Finn and Joseph Adelson, "Terrorizing Children," *Commentary* 79 (1985), pp. 29–36. Note also F. Butterfield, "Experts Disagree on Children's Worries about Nuclear War," *New York Times*, October 16, 1983.

20. Charles B. Strozier and Robert Jay Lifton, "The End of Nuclear Fear?" *New York Newsday*, November 13, 1991.

21. Randall Balmer describes the annual trade show of the Christian Booksellers Association as "one of the largest trade shows in the nation, with more than 350 exhibitors consuming more than 275,000 square feet of space." See Randall Balmer, *Mine Eyes Have Seen the Glory: A Journey into the Evangelical Subculture in America* (New York: Oxford University Press, 1989), p. 72.

22. Ammerman notes that active members of Southside Church were involved in at least Sunday morning and Wednesday night services as well as Bible studies set up for various age and gender groups, Sunday School, choirs, and various committees; Ammerman, *Bible Believers*, pp. 34–37.

23. Robert Jay Lifton, *Thought Reform and the Psychology of Totalism: A Study of "Brainwashing" in China* (New York: W. W. Norton, 1961), pp. 419–37.

24. Rick Branch, research director, "Watchmen Fellowship," Arlington, Texas, personal communication, August 8, 1993; and Ted Daniels, "Millennium Watch Institute," personal communication, August 8, 1993. Branch noted, however, that from an "evangelical" point of view (that is, from within a fundamentalist perspective that would include New Age channeling groups, as well as the Mormon Church, for example) there are easily six to seven thousand cults in America.

25. James Aho, *The Politics of Righteousness: Idaho Christian Patriotism* (Seattle: University of Washington Press, 1990).

26. It should be noted, of course, that I worked in New York City. I have had some distinctly different reactions to some churches I have visited in Georgia (where I have relatives), and, perhaps ironically, one fundamentalist church I visited three times in Sweden.

27. Philip Greven, *Spare the Child: The Religious Roots of Punishment and the Psychological Impact of Physical Abuse* (New York: Knopf, 1991). I discuss Greven's book in more detail in a forthcoming essay, "Suffer the Children," *Psychohistory Review*.

8. A HISTORY OF AMERICAN ENDISM

1. The most interesting discussion of the underlying psychological tensions in seventeenth-century America is John Demos, *Entertaining Satan: Witchcraft and the Culture of Early New England*

(New York: Oxford University Press, 1982). Note also Richard Slotkin, *Regeneration through Violence: The Mythology of the American Frontier, 1600–1860* (Middletown, Conn.: Wesleyan University Press, 1973).

2. Gordon Wood, *The Radicalism of the American Revolution* (New York: Alfred A. Knopf, 1992).

3. Catherine Keller, "De-Colon-izing Paradise: A Quincentennial Passage," unpublished paper, quoted with permission of the author.

4. Edward Pessen, *Jacksonian America: Society, Personality, and Politics* (Homewood, Ill.: Dorsey Press, 1969), chap. 1.

5. Ronald L. Numbers and Jonathan M. Butler, eds., *The Disappointed: Millerism and Millenarianism in the Nineteenth Century* (Bloomington: Indiana University Press, 1987). Note also Malcolm Bull and Keith Lockhard, *Seeking a Sanctuary: Seventh-Day Adventism and the American Dream* (New York: Harper and Row, 1989); and Paul Boyer, *When Time Shall Be No More: Prophetic Belief in Modern American Culture* (Cambridge, Mass.: Belknap Press of Harvard University Press, 1992), pp. 80–86.

6. Hazel Catherine Wolf, *On Freedom's Altar: The Martyr Complex in the Abolition Movement* (Madison, Wis.: University of Wisconsin Press, 1952), p. ix.

7. Lawrence Friedman, however, persuasively argues that the degree of genuine pacifism that infused the abolitionists in the 1830s is open to some question. See Lawrence Friedman, "Antebellum American Abolitionism and the Problem of Violent Means," *Psychohistory Review* 9 (1980), pp. 26–32. The basic question the abolitionists failed to grapple with was whether violence was acceptable if used defensively. The test case was the shooting of Elijah Lovejoy in Alton, Illinois. See Charles B. Strozier, *Lincoln's Quest for Union: Public and Private Meanings* (New York: Basic Books, 1982), p. 188.

8. Frederick Douglass, *Life and Writings of Frederick Douglass*, ed. Philip Foner, 5 vols. (New York: International Publishers, 1950), vol. 2, pp. 460–63.

9. Quotations from Geoffrey C. Ward with Rick Burns and Ken Burns, *The Civil War* (New York: Knopf, 1990), p. 19.

10. Matthew 12:22–28; Mark 3:22–26; and Luke 11:14–20.

11. Strozier, *Lincoln's Quest for Union*, pp. 182–87; compare Don Fehrenbacher, *Prelude to Greatness: Lincoln in the 1850s* (Stanford: Stanford University Press, 1962).

12. Stephen B. Oates, *To Purge This Land with Blood: A Biography of John Brown* (New York: Harper and Row, 1970), p. 310.

13. Don Fehrenbacher in Ward, *The Civil War*, p. 84.

14. Arthur Schlesinger, Jr., "The Opening of the American Mind," *New York Times Book Review*, July 23, 1989.

15. Some of the large number of studies that have dealt with this issue are: Joel Kovel, *White Racism: A Psychohistory* (New York: Pantheon Books, 1970); Robert Jay Lifton, *Death in Life: Survivors of Hiroshima* (New York: Vintage Books, 1967); and idem, *The Broken Connection: On Death and the Continuity of Life* (New York: Basic Books, 1979).

16. Peter J. Parrish, "The Instruments of Providence: Slavery, Civil War and the American Churches," *Studies in Church History* 20 (1983), p. 299.

17. Barbara Jeanne Fields, *Slavery and Freedom on the Middle Ground: Maryland During the Nineteenth Century* (New Haven: Yale University Press, 1985). Note also Fields's short and provocative essay in Ward, *The Civil War*.

18. Ernest Lee Tuveson, *Redeemer Nation: The Idea of America's Millennial Role* (Chicago: University of Chicago Press, 1968), pp. 195, 208.

19. Parrish, "The Instruments of Providence," p. 294.

20. Richard Slotkin, *Regeneration through Violence*; ibid., *The Fatal Environment: The Myth of the Frontier in the Age of Industrialization, 1880–1890* (Middletown, Conn.: Wesleyan University Press, 1986); and idem, *Gunfighter Nation: The Frontier Myth in Twentieth-Century America* (New York: Macmillan, 1992). One could also note the famous President's Commission, *Violence in America: Historical and Comparative Perspectives: A Report to the National Commission on the Causes and Prevention of Violence, June, 1969*, Hugh Davis Graham and Ted Robert Gurr for the President's Commission, eds. (New York: Signet Books, 1969).

21. Parrish, "The Instruments of Providence," p. 299.

22. Ibid., p. 304.

23. Sherman said it was all hell as he and Grant crossed some perilous lines that have led others to make total war in the twentieth century. Note Charles B. Strozier, "Unconditional Surrender and the Rhetoric of Total War: From Truman to Lincoln," Occasional Paper of the Center on Violence and Human Survival, John Jay College, City University of New York, 1987 (republished in *Military History Quarterly* 2 [1990], pp. 8–15). Compare William Tecumseh Sherman, *Memoirs of General W. T. Sherman*, ed. Charles Royster (New York: Library of America, 1990); Ulysses Grant, *Personal Memoirs of U. S. Grant and Selected Letters*, ed. Mary Drake McFeely and William S. McFeely (New York: Library of America, 1990). Two recent books on Sherman are quite useful in terms of these issues: John F. Marshalek, *Sherman: A Soldier's Passion for Order* (New York: The Free Press, 1993); and the extraordinarily interesting study by Charles Royster, *The Destructive War: William Tecumseh Sherman, Stonewall Jackson, and the Americans* (New York: Alfred A. Knopf, 1991).

24. Royster, *Destructive War*, pp. 82, 241.

25. Alan T. Nolan, *Lee Considered: General Robert E. Lee and Civil War History* (Chapel Hill: University of North Carolina Press, 1991), pp. 112–33, especially pp. 119 and 126.

26. Ward, *The Civil War*, p. 55.

27. Kenneth Stampp, "The Southern Road to Appomattox," in *The Imperiled Union: Essays on the Background of the Civil War* (New York: Oxford University Press, 1980), pp. 246–69, quotes from pp. 252, 260–61 respectively. Note also two recent books edited by Gabor S. Boritt that deal with the question of Lincoln's wartime leadership and why the South lost: *Lincoln, the War President* (New York: Oxford University Press, 1992), and *Why the Confederacy Lost* (New York: Oxford University Press, 1992).

28. Don Fehrenbacher, ed., *Lincoln*, 2 vols. (New York: The Library of America, 1989), quotes from vol. 1, pp. 220, 250, 415, and 269 respectively.

29. Note Strozier, "Unconditional Surrender." Cf. James M. McPherson, "Lincoln and the Strategy of Unconditional Surrender," in *Lincoln, the War President*, ed. Gabor S. Boritt, pp. 29–62; this

paper was first published in pamphlet form at almost the same time as my own. McPherson and I have overlapping but also quite different perspectives on the issue of unconditional surrender during the Civil War.

30. Royster, *Destructive War*, p. 151.

31. "The fiery trial through which we pass, will light us down, in honor or dishonor, to the latest generation." Fehrenbacher, *Lincoln*, vol. 1, p. 415.

32. Hans J. Morgenthau and David Hein, *Essays on Lincoln's Faith and Politics*, ed. Kenneth W. Thompson, 4 vols. (New York: Lanham, 1983), vol. 4, p. 145.

33. James H. Moorhead, *American Apocalypse: Yankee Protestants and the Civil War, 1860–1869* (New Haven: Yale University Press, 1978), p. x.

34. James M. McPherson, "American Victory, American Defeat," in *Why the Confederacy Lost*, ed. Gabor S. Boritt (New York: Oxford University Press, 1992), p. 40.

35. Fehrenbacher, *Lincoln*, vol. 2, p. 209.

36. See Garry Wills, *Lincoln at Gettysburg: The Words that Remade America* (New York: Simon and Schuster, 1992).

37. Fehrenbacher, *Lincoln*, vol. 2, p. 687.

38. Moorhead, *American Apocalypse*, pp. 174–75. I speak of "Easter Morning sermons" rather loosely in this analysis. I am particularly interested in those given that Sunday morning, April 16. In some cases, however, I draw on sermons from Lincoln's Washington funeral on April 19 and even from those of Sunday, April 23, when some ministers, such as Henry Ward Beecher and Theodore L. Cuyler, gave their sermons because they had been at a ceremony at Fort Sumter on Friday, April 14, and had been unable to return to their churches for Easter by April 16. In the larger body of "assassination sermons"—though I avoid quoting from them—there were also many sermons on May 4, the date of the Lincoln funeral in Springfield, and June 1, the national day of mourning proclaimed by President Johnson. The further one gets from the actual death of Lincoln, the more conventional and "canned" become the sermons.

39. C. B. Crane, *Sermon on the Occasion of the Death of Presi-*

dent Lincoln (Hartford: Press of Case, Lockwood and Co., 1865). Unless otherwise indicated, i.e., as separately published in a book, the sermons I read were from the collection in the Illinois State Historical Library. I used as a key to the collection Jay Monaghan's *Collections of the Illinois State Historical Library: Bibliographical Series, Volume IV: Lincoln Bibliography, 1839–1939*, vol. 1 (Springfield: Illinois State Historical Library, 1943). I also benefited from the assistance of Thomas Schwartz, the curator of the Lincoln collection of the Library, and Mark Johnson, a research historian with the Illinois Preservation Agency. As far as I can tell, some three hundred sermons survive in various collections around the country (though the Illinois State Historical Library has by far the greatest number of the sermons). I read about one hundred of them.

40. Rolla H. Chubb, *A Discourse upon the Death of President Lincoln Delivered at Greenwich M. E. Church*, June 1, 1865, p. 3.

41. Ralph Waldo Emerson, "A Plain Man of the People," in *Building the Myth: Selected Speeches Memorializing Abraham Lincoln*, ed. Waldo W. Braden (Urbana: University of Illinois Press, 1990), pp. 33–34.

42. Henry Ward Beecher, "A New Impulse of Patriotism for His Sake," in Braden, *Building the Myth*, pp. 37–46.

43. Theodore L. Cuyler, "And the Lord blessed Abraham in all things. Gen. 29:1," and George Bancroft, "Oration," in *Our Martyr President, Abraham Lincoln. Voices from the Pulpit of New York and Brooklyn* (New York: Tibbals and Whiting, 1865), p. 389.

44. Chubb, *A Discourse*, p. 7 (Illinois State Historical Library).

45. Abraham Lincoln, *The Collected Works of Abraham Lincoln*, Roy P. Basler et al., eds., 8 vols. plus appendix and supplement (New Brunswick, N.J.: Rutgers University Press, 1953), vol. 8, p. 375 n. and pp. 375–76. There was some confusion in the hectic weeks toward the end of March about the actual date Fort Sumter had fallen. On March 27 Secretary of War Edwin Stanton telegraphed Lincoln at City Point detailing the problem, namely that the surrender had been agreed to on April 13, 1861, but that the northern troops had only filed out of the fort the next day. Lincoln replied that he thought there was "little or no difference" which day was se-

lected on which to hold the ceremony. Stanton obviously chose April 14, which came to have much more meaning than he ever could have imagined.

46. Cuyler, "And the Lord blessed Abraham in all things. Gen. 29:1," in *Our Martyr President*, p. 159.

47. S. S. Guthrie, *In Memoriam: Abraham Lincoln* (Buffalo: Matthews & Warren, 1865).

48. William E. Baron, "The American Pulpit on the Death of Lincoln," *The Open Court* 37 (October 1923), p. 514.

49. A. A. Littlejohn, "Know ye not there is a prince and a great man fallen this day in Israel. 2 Sam. 3:38," in *Our Martyr President*.

50. W. E. Guthrie, *Oration on the Death of Abraham Lincoln* (Philadelphia: John Pennington & Sons, 1865), p. 9.

51. E. S. Atwood, *Discourses in Commemoration of Abraham Lincoln*, April 16 and June 1, 1865 (Salem: The Salem Gazette, 1865).

52. Lincoln was noted for his pardons of deserters who had been condemned to death by his harsher Secretary of War, Edwin Stanton. Lincoln also did things like moving quickly to prevent retaliation after the southern massacre at Fort Pillow on April 12 and 13, 1864, with the comment that "blood can not restore blood." Lincoln, *Collected Works*, vol. 7, p. 345.

53. Chubb, *A Discourse*, p. 9.

54. Henry W. Bellows, "Sorrow hath filled your heart. Nevertheless, I will tell the truth. It is expedient for you that I go away; for if I do not go away, the Comforter will not come unto you; but if I depart I will send him unto you. John 16:6, 7," in *Our Martyr President*, pp. 59–60, 62.

55. Charles H. Robinson, "He was a good man, and a just. Luke 23:50," in *Our Martyr President*, pp. 91–92.

56. James Douglas, *Funeral Discourse on the Occasion of the Obsequies of President Lincoln*, April 19, 1865 (Pulaski, N.Y.: Democrat Job Press, 1865).

57. James DeNormandie, *The Lord Reigneth: A Few Words on Sunday Morning, April 16, 1865, after the Assassination of Abraham Lincoln* (Illinois State Historical Library). See also Isaac E. Carey, *Discourse on the Death of Abraham Lincoln, April 19, 1865*

(Illinois State Historical Library); and John Chester, *The Lessons of the Hour. Justice as Well as Mercy. A Discourse Preached on the Sabbath Following the Assassination of the President* (Washington, D.C.: Washington Chronicle Print, 1865).

58. Chester, *The Lessons of the Hour*, pp. 11, 13.

59. William L. Chaffin, *A Discourse on Sunday Morning, April 23d, 1865* (Philadelphia: King & Baird, 1865).

60. Robinson, "He was a good man, and a just. Luke 23:50," in *Our Martyr President*, pp. 97, 99, 100.

61. Ward, *The Civil War*, p. 393.

62. Parrish, "The Instruments of Providence," p. 318.

63. Eric Foner, *Reconstruction: America's Unfinished Revolution, 1863–1877* (New York: Harper and Row, 1988). Note also Albion W. Tourgee, *A Fool's Errand, By One of the Fools* (New York: Fords, Howard, and Hulbert, 1879).

64. See Geoffrey Barraclough, *European Unity in Thought and Action* (Oxford: B. Blackwell, 1963).

65. Elaine Showalter, *Sexual Anarchy: Gender and Culture at the Fin-de-Siècle* (New York: Viking, 1990), pp. 3–4.

66. George Marsden, *Fundamentalism and American Culture: The Shaping of Twentieth-Century Evangelicalism, 1870–1925* (New York: Oxford University Press, 1980), p. 3.

67. Timothy P. Weber, *Living in the Shadow of the Second Coming: American Premillennialism, 1875–1982* (Chicago: University of Chicago Press, 1983), pp. 41–42.

68. Boyer, *When Time Shall Be No More*, pp. 80–112.

69. Note especially Weber, *Living in the Shadow*. Compare Ernest Sandeen, *The Roots of Fundamentalism: British and American Millenarianism, 1800–1930* (Chicago: University of Chicago Press, 1970).

70. Note especially Boyer, *When Time Shall Be No More*. Compare Marsden, *Fundamentalism and American Culture*; and Weber, *Living in the Shadow*.

71. Boyer, *When Time Shall Be No More*, p. 88.

72. Ibid., p. 90.

73. Marsden, *Fundamentalism and American Culture*, pp. 55ff; Nancy T. Ammerman, "North American Protestant Fundamental-

ism," in *Fundamentalisms Observed*, ed. Martin Marty and R. Scott Appleby (Chicago: University of Chicago Press, 1991), pp. 11ff.

74. Sandeen, *Roots of Fundamentalism*, p. 125.

75. Ibid., p. 126.

76. Ibid., p. 128.

77. Boyer, *When Time Shall Be No More*, p. 92.

78. Weber, *Living in the Shadow*, pp. 33–35.

79. Boyer, *When Time Shall Be No More*, pp. 92–93; Weber, *Living in the Shadow*; Marsden, *Fundamentalism and American Culture*; and Ammerman, "North American Protestant Fundamentalism," pp. 3–4, 13–14, 53.

80. Boyer, *When Time Shall Be No More*, pp. 95–96.

81. This can certainly be said of much of Hal Lindsey's *The Late Great Planet Earth* (Grand Rapids: Zondervan, 1970), but equally and more subtly of John F. Walvoord's *Armageddon, Oil, and the Middle East Crisis* (Grand Rapids: Zondervan, 1990 [1974]).

82. Marsden, *Fundamentalism and American Culture*, pp. 118–23; Sandeen, *Roots of Fundamentalism*, pp. 188–207.

83. Ammerman, "North American Protestant Fundamentalism," p. 2.

84. Garry Wills, *Under God: Religion and American Politics* (New York: Simon and Schuster, 1990), pp. 108–14.

85. Ammerman, "North American Protestant Fundamentalism," pp. 18–22, 27–34. See also Joel Carpenter, "Fundamentalist Institutions and the Rise of Conservative Protestantism, 1929–42," *Church History* 49 (March 1980), pp. 62–75.

86. George Marsden, *Reforming Fundamentalism: Fuller Seminary and the New Evangelicalism* (Grand Rapids: Eerdman's, 1987).

87. David Harrington Watt, "The Private Hopes of American Fundamentalists and Evangelicals, 1925–1975," *Religion and American Culture* 1 (1991), pp. 162–65.

88. Robert Wuthnow, asking a different question, comes to a surprisingly similar conclusion; Robert Wuthnow, *The Restructuring of American Religion: Society and Faith Since World War II* (Princeton: Princeton University Press, 1988).

89. The latter especially has been masterfully traced by Boyer in *When Time Shall Be No More* (1992), and continues to be updated by Ted Daniels in his encyclopedic newsletter out of what he calls his "Millennial Watch Institute." Interesting historical perspectives on fundamentalism have also been provided by Wills, *Under God* (1990). The evangelical subculture has in turn been well described by Balmer in *Mine Eyes Have Seen the Glory* (1989). Finally, Christian fundamentalism in global and comparative contexts, along with massive bibliographies, has been richly developed in The Fundamentalism Project at the University of Chicago under the direction of Martin Marty.

9. JEWS, ISRAEL, AND THE PARADOX OF THE INGATHERING

1. Note Lifton, *The Nazi Doctors: Medical Killing and the Psychology of Genocide* (New York: Basic Books, 1986). See also Benno Mueller-Hill, *Murderous Science: Elimination by Scientific Selection of Jews, Gypsies and Others, Germany, 1933–1945,* trans. George R. Fraser (New York: Oxford University Press, 1988).

2. Haim H. Cohn, *The Trial and Death of Jesus* (New York: Harper and Row, 1967). The quote is from page 331.

3. The early sources for what later became full-fledged anti-Semitism are explored in Richard Rubinstein, "Religion and the Origins of the Death Camps: A Psychoanalytic Interpretation," in *Thinking the Unthinkable: Meanings of the Holocaust,* ed. R. S. Gottlieb (New York: Paulist Press, 1990), pp. 46–63. Note also Richard Rubinstein and J. K. Roth, *Approaches to Auschwitz* (London: SCM, 1987). C. H. Dodd takes a balanced view of the matter: Jesus' claim to be the Messiah, which translated into "King of the Jews," could not be taken lightly by the authorities. See C. H. Dodd, *The Founder of Christianity* (London: Collins, 1971), p. 159. Other scholars follow this argument: see S. Neill and T. Wright, *The Interpretation of the New Testament, 1861–1986,* 2d expanded ed. (Oxford: Oxford University Press, 1988), p. 393; David J. Goldberg and John D. Rayner, *The Jewish People: Their History and Their Religion* (New York: Viking, 1987), pp. 76–77; Pinchas Lapide, *Warum kommt er nicht: Judische Evangelienauslegung* (Gutersloh:

Gutersloher Verlagshaus, Gern Mohn, 1988), p. 82; Humphrey Carpenter, *Jesus* (Oxford: Oxford University Press, 1980), pp. 87–88; William M. Thompson, *The Jesus Debate: A Survey and Synthesis* (New York: Paulist Press, 1985), pp. 206–9; E. P. Sanders, *Jesus and Judaism* (London: SCM, 1985), pp. 317–18; and F. F. Bruce, *Jesus and Christian Origins Outside the New Testament* (London: Hodden & Storighton, 1974), pp. 32–41. Note also Marc H. Tannenbaum, Marvin R. Wilson, and A. James Rudin, eds., *Evangelicals and Jews in an Age of Pluralism* (Lanham: University Press of America, 1984), pp. 257–67.

4. Joel B. Green, *The Death of Jesus: Tradition and Interpretation in the Passion Narrative* (New York: Coronet Books, 1988).

5. Jerome Chanes, "Antisemitism in the United States, 1992: Why Are the Jews Worried?" *Jerusalem Letter/Viewpoints* 255 (May 15, 1992), pp. 1–6.

6. Arthur Herzberg, "Is Anti-Semitism Dying Out?" *New York Review of Books* 40 (1993), pp. 51–57.

7. Richard John Neuhaus, "What the Fundamentalists Want," in *Piety and Politics: Evangelicals and Fundamentalists Confront the World*, ed. Richard John Neuhaus and M. Cromartie (Washington, D.C.: Ethics and Public Policy Center, 1987), p. 15.

8. Timothy P. Weber, *Living in the Shadow of the Second Coming: American Premillennialism, 1875–1982* (Chicago: University of Chicago Press, 1983), p. 199.

9. Three of John F. Walvoord's books relating to Israel and Jews have been brought together in one paperback edition, *The Nations, Israel, and the Church in Prophecy* (Grand Rapids: Academie Books, 1988 [1967, 1962, 1964]). In 1974 Walvoord published *Armageddon, Oil, and the Middle East Crisis* (Grand Rapids: Zondervan), which was brought up to date in 1990 for the Gulf War (and in the course of seven months sold nearly eight hundred thousand copies), with the suggestive subtitle: "What the Bible Says about the Future of the Middle East and the End of Western Civilization." The new edition of the book included a small picture on the cover of an F-15 landing on a suggestive desert landscape. Besides books on *The Holy Spirit*, *The Thessalonian Epistles*, *The Blessed Hope and Tribulation*, *The Millennial Kingdom*, and *The Rapture Question*, Wal-

voord's magnum opus is *Prophecy Knowledge Handbook: All the Prophecies of Scripture Explained in One Volume* (Wheaton, Ill.: Victor Books, 1990).

10. Weber, *Living in the Shadow*, pp. 17–18.

11. Charles C. Ryrie, *Dispensationalism Today* (Chicago: Moody Institute, 1965), p. 45.

12. Walvoord, *Israel*, p. 58 (see note 9 above).

13. Ibid., pp. 64–66.

14. Needless to say, this attitude has had, and continues to have, important political ramifications for Middle East politics. See, for example, Bernard Lewis, "Muslims, Christians, and Jews: The Dream of Coexistence," *New York Review of Books*, March 26, 1992, pp. 48–52.

15. Walvoord, *Israel*, p. 48 (see note 9 above).

16. Note Weber, *Living in the Shadow*, pp. 204–26. Compare Paul Boyer, *When Time Shall Be No More: Prophetic Belief in Modern American Culture* (Cambridge, Mass.: Belknap Press of Harvard University Press, 1992), p. 187.

17. Walvoord, *Israel*, p. 73 (see note 9 above).

18. Ibid., pp. 66–71.

19. Boyer, *When Time Shall Be No More*, p. 89.

20. Walvoord, *Israel*, p. 112 (see note 9 above).

21. Ibid., pp. 36–48.

22. Ibid., p. 332.

23. Irving Kristol, "The Political Dilemma of American Jews," *Commentary* 18 (1984), pp. 23–29.

24. Kristol, "The Political Dilemma," p. 25.

25. Peter Steinfels, "Evangelical Group Urges Conversion of the Jews," *New York Times*, May 21, 1989.

26. David A. Rausch, "Paranoia About Fundamentalists?" *Judaism: A Quarterly Journal of Jewish Life and Thought* 28 (1979), p. 304.

27. Ryrie, *Dispensationalism Today*, p. 163.

28. Needless to say, there are many intelligent, liberal theological answers to this quandary of apparent totalistic separation between Jews and Christians (or Christians and those of any faith, for that matter). Most of these answers revolve around reminding Christians

of John 4:22: "Ye worship ye know not what: we know what we worship: for salvation is of the Jews."

29. James Davison Hunter in *Evangelicalism: The Coming Generation* (Chicago: University of Chicago Press, 1987) notes the anti-Semitism of evangelicals in the past (pp. 124, 129), but anticipates a general softening of boundaries as evangelicals move up socioeconomically (pp. 203–13).

10. THE HOPI WAY

1. Ernest and Pearl Beaglehole, "A Note on Hopi Dreams," *Hopi of the Second Mesa, Memoirs of the American Anthropological Association*, no. 44 (Menasha, Wis.: American Anthropological Association, 1935), pp. 15–16.

2. The Hopi are one of the Pueblo people who have been living in the southwest for thousands of years. See E. Charles Adams, "Synthesis of Hopi Prehistory and History," National Park Service, July 31, 1978; and his book, *The Origins and Development of the Pueblo Katsina Cult* (Tucson: University of Arizona Press, 1991).

3. Frank Waters, *The Book of the Hopi, with Drawings and Source Material by Oswald White Bear Fredericks* (New York: Penguin Books, 1963), p. 31.

4. John D. Loftin, *Religion and Hopi Life in the Twentieth Century* (Bloomington: Indiana University Press, 1991), p. 116.

5. Don Talayesva, *Sun Chief: The Autobiography of a Hopi Indian*, ed. Leo W. Simmons (New Haven: Yale University Press, 1942), p. 379.

6. Harry C. James, *Pages from Hopi History* (Tucson: University of Arizona Press, 1990), pp. 34–35.

7. Armin Geertz, "Book of the Hopi: The Hopi Book?" *Anthropos* 78 (1983), p. 551.

8. The term occurs ten times in the King James translation of the Bible. One reference fundamentalists often quote is Ezekiel 6:8: "Yet will I leave a remnant, that ye may have *some* that shall escape the sword among the nations, when ye shall be scattered through the countries." Compare Revelation 19:21.

9. Armin Geertz, "Prophets and Fools: The Rhetoric of Hopi In-

dian Eschatology," *European Review of Native American Studies* 1 (1987), p. 36.

10. Frederick J. Dockstader, *The Kachina and the White Man: The Influences of White Culture on the Hopi Kachina Cult* (Albuquerque: University of New Mexico Press, 1985).

11. Loftin, *Religion and Hopi Life*, p. 115.

12. Dan Budnik, personal communication, March 18, 1992.

13. The term *Taiowa* is used by Frank Waters, *Book of the Hopi*, and Robert Boissiere, *Meditations with the Hopi* (Santa Fe: Bear and Company, 1986). Loftin, probably the better authority, speaks of *a'ni himu* in *Religion and Hopi Life*. The difference in terminology may also reflect different myths on the three mesas, and/or the non-written character of the language, and/or deliberate confusions to keep knowledge of the ultimate secret from outsiders.

14. Boissiere, *Meditations with the Hopi*, p. 31; used with permission. Compare Waters, *Book of the Hopi*, pp. 3–6; and Harold Courlander, *The Fourth World of the Hopis* (New York: Crown Publishers, 1971), pp. 17–18.

15. Boissiere, *Meditations with the Hopi*, p. 33.

16. Ibid., pp. 33–34. Compare Waters, *Book of the Hopi*, pp. 12–14; and Courlander, *The Fourth World of the Hopis*, pp. 18–19.

17. Boissiere, *Meditations with the Hopi*, pp. 35–37; and Waters, *Book of the Hopi*, pp. 17–20.

18. James, *Pages from Hopi History*, pp. 2–8; a photograph of the *sipapu* is given on p. 7.

19. Loftin, *Religion and Hopi Life*, p. 58.

20. James, *Pages from Hopi History*, pp. 2–8; Boissiere, *Meditations with the Hopi*, p. 41; and Courlander, *The Fourth World of the Hopis*, pp. 19–26.

21. Boissiere, *Meditations with the Hopi*, p. 42; used with permission.

22. Waters, *Book of the Hopi*, pp. 20–22; and Boissiere, *Meditations with the Hopi*, pp. 41–43.

23. Armin Geertz, "A Reed Pierced the Sky," *Numen* 32 (1984), p. 220.

24. Waters, *Book of the Hopi*, p. 31.

25. Adams, "Synthesis of Hopi Prehistory and History."

26. Harry C. James notes that there were under four thousand Hopi in 1968; see James, *Pages from Hopi History*, p. 16. A decade later E. Charles Adams said there were a total of 7,000 Hopi, with five to six thousand on the reservation; Adams, "Synthesis of Hopi Prehistory and History." I was told by several informants that there were some ten thousand Hopi, but that figure seems high. Most of the villages were tiny, though quite a few settlements are strung out along the three mesas and one can see in the distance many individual homes and trailers in the farther reaches of the reservation.

27. James, *Pages from Hopi History*, p. xii.

28. Note Adams, *The Origins and Development of the Pueblo Katsina Cult.*

29. Talayesva, *Sun Chief: The Autobiography of a Hopi Indian*, p. 363.

30. Tom Tarbet, personal communication, May 20, 1992.

31. Loftin, *Religion and Hopi Life*, p. 7.

32. Ibid., p. xxi.

33. This entrance to the underworld is located at the bottom of the canyon of the Little Colorado River above its juncture with the Colorado River. A visit to the site is of some significance for the Hopi. See James, *Pages from Hopi History*, p. 7, for a good picture.

34. Louis Albert Hieb, *The Hopi Ritual Clown: Life as It Should Not Be* (Ph.D. diss., Princeton University, 1972), p. 146.

35. Ibid., pp. 172–83.

36. Loftin, *Religion and Hopi Life*, pp. 11–12.

37. Ekkehart Malotki and Michael Lomatuway'ma, *Stories of Maasaw: A Hopi God*, vol. 10 of American Tribal Religion series, ed. Karl W. Luchert (Lincoln: University of Nebraska Press, 1987), pp. 3–12.

38. Ibid., pp. 65–71.

39. Mischa Titiev, *The Hopi Indians of Old Oraibi: Change and Continuity* (Ann Arbor: University of Michigan Press, 1972), pp. 309–10. Note also Titiev, *Old Oraibi: A Study of the Hopi Indians of Third Mesa* (Albuquerque: University of New Mexico Press, 1991 [1942]).

40. Geertz, "A Reed Pierced the Sky," p. 224.

41. Mischa Titiev, *The Hopi Indians of Old Oraibi*, pp. 99–100, 153, 158, 214–15, 293, 299, 303, 309–10.

42. With the help of astute archivists, Martin Duberman in the 1970s uncovered some remarkable affidavits taken from the Hopi between 1914 and 1921 in New Mexico and Arizona. The affidavits had lain uncatalogued and unnoticed for half a century in the National Anthropological Archives of the Smithsonian Institute. Duberman first published the material, along with critical commentary from two well-known authorities in Hopi studies, as Martin B. Duberman, Fred Eggan, and Richard Klemmer, "Documents on Hopi Indian Sexuality: Imperialism, Culture, and Resistance," *Radical History Review* 20 (Spring/Summer 1979), pp. 99–130; he later republished the most interesting and controversial documents in his more readily accessible *About Time: Exploring the Gay Past* (New York: A SeaHorse Book, Gay Presses of New York, 1986), pp. 97–106. The debate among Duberman and Eggan and Klemmer over the meaning of the documents was continued from issue 20 of *Radical History Review* to "Hopi Indians Redux," *Radical History Review* 24 (1980), pp. 178–87.

43. Loftin, *Religion and Hopi Life*, p. 115.

44. In Revelation 1:13–16, the Son of Man appears in a garment down to his feet and wrapped in a golden girdle, his head and hair white like wool or snow, his eyes flames of fire; in his right hand he holds seven stars, "and out of his mouth went a sharp two-edged sword: and his countenance *was* as the sun shineth in its strength."

45. Loftin, *Religion and Hopi Life*, pp. 34–35.

11. THE AGE OF AQUARIUS

1. Christopher Lasch, *The Culture of Narcissism: American Life in an Age of Diminishing Expectations* (New York: W. W. Norton, 1979), pp. 245, 247.

2. James R. Lewis, "Approaches to the Study of the New Age Movement," in *Perspectives on the New Age*, ed. James R. Lewis and J. Gordon Melton (Albany: State University of New York Press, 1992), p. 4.

3. The exceptions may be palm readings and faith healings, signs for which are on many streets in black neighborhoods in New York

City. The largest New Age bookstore in New York City is Wiesner's on 23rd St. and Lexington Ave., which has a section on African American spirituality. Note also the New York Open Center on 83 Spring St. in Manhattan, whose most recent (1992) catalogue is a cornucopia of workshops, courses, and lectures on New Age, which in no way excludes minorities but also includes nothing specifically designed for them. This whole question of minority involvement (or lack of involvement) in New Age is a subject worthy of deeper exploration.

4. Witches, however, include a Horned God, often black, in their pantheon. Starhawk argues he is the god of sexuality, and existed long before Christianity (or Judaism, for that matter). "He is gentle, tender, and comforting, but He is also the Hunter. He is the Dying God—but his sexuality is a deep, holy, connecting power. He is the power of feeling, and the image of what men could be if they were liberated from the constraints of patriarchal culture." It was only the medieval Christian church, Starhawk argues, that turned this god into the devil. See Starhawk, *The Spiral Dance: A Rebirth of the Ancient Religion of the Great Goddess* (San Francisco: Harper and Row, 1979), pp. 107–21 (quote is on p. 108).

5. Note Deborah Sontag's description of the New Age Convention in New York City in October 1992 that drew 21,000 people to midtown Manhattan: "Resonance and Rigidity in the New Age," *New York Times*, October 5, 1992.

6. See Papus, *Reincarnation: Physical, Astral and Spiritual Evolution*, trans. Marguerite Vallior (n.p.: Roger A. Kessinger, 1991), p. 13. Compare its New Age adaptation in Gari Gold, *The New Age: A to Z* (Albuquerque: ZIVAH, 1991), pp. 13–15.

7. See, for example, Betty Eadie, *Embraced by the Light* (Placerville, Calif.: Gold Leaf Press, 1992).

8. Erik Erikson, *Gandhi's Truth: On the Origins of Militant Nonviolence* (New York: W. W. Norton, 1969), p. 39.

9. Michael Grosso, *The Final Choice: Playing the Survival Game* (Walpole, N.H.: Stillpoint Publishing, 1985), p. 325.

10. Marianne Williamson, *A Return to Love: Reflections on the Principles of A Course in Miracles* (New York: HarperCollins, 1992). Williamson has also produced more than fifty tapes of her

lectures on subjects ranging from "AIDS/Radical Healing" to "Forgiving When It's Difficult/Illusions of Loss." The tapes are distributed by Bodhi Tree.

11. Clarissa Pinkola Estes, *Women Who Run with the Wolves* (New York: Ballantine Books, 1992).

12. Brochure for Sandy Gilbert's "Wholeness Meditation," 137 South Main St., Pennington, N.J., n.d.

13. Lewis, "Approaches," pp. xi, 5.

14. William G. McLoughlin, *Revival, Awakenings, and Reform: An Essay on Religion and Social Change in America, 1607–1977* (Chicago: University of Chicago Press, 1978), pp. 179–216.

15. J. Gordon Melton, *New Age Encyclopedia*, quoted in Lewis and Melton, *Perspectives*, p. 7.

16. Ruth Montgomery, *Strangers Among Us* (New York: Fawcett Crest, 1979), pp. 31–35.

17. Ibid., pp. 30, 38, 52, 64, 191–205, 220–21; compare Ruth Montgomery, *The World Before* (New York: Fawcett Crest, 1976).

18. Budd Hopkins, *Intruders* (New York: Random House, 1987), p. 12.

19. David Solomon, "Prophecy Update: Are We Living in the End of the Times?" *Fellowship Life & Lifestyles* 18 (1992), p. 3. Ted Daniels, editor of *Millennium News* (a publication of The Millennium Watch Institute, P.O. Box 34021, Philadelphia, PA 19101-4021) and an indefatigable researcher, graciously shared with me his background notes on New Age apocalypticism from the depths of his hard drive. For material from this research I will refer to "Daniels, Notes."

20. Nada-Yolanda, Note to Nova/Angelika, "No Hiding Place," *Main* 117, no. 7 (1988), pp. 10–15. Daniels, Notes.

21. Ted Daniels, personal communication, April 3, 1992.

22. Ashtar Command, "11:11 Doorway," *Connecting Link*, n.d.; "Spiritual Counterfeits Project," *SCP Newsletter* 10 (1991); and Swami Nostradamus Virato, "11:11 Doorway to the Cosmos: Interview," *New Frontier* 12 (1991). Daniels, Notes.

23. "Spiritual Counterfeits Project," *SCP Newsletter* 10 (1991). Daniels, Notes.

24. Catherine Albanese, *Nature Religion in America: From the*

Algonkian Indians to the New Age (Chicago: University of Chicago Press, 1990), pp. 156ff.

25. Ibid., pp. 160–61.

26. Sun Bear, *Black Dawn, Bright Day* (New York: Simon and Schuster, 1992), esp. pp. 27–49.

27. Ibid., p. 52.

28. Ibid., p. 92.

29. Ibid., p. 32.

30. Compare Otto's calculation, in chapter 2 of this book, that half the world's population will be destroyed in the events described in Revelation.

31. Sun Bear, *Black Dawn, Bright Day*, p. 37.

32. Ibid., p. 57.

33. Ibid.

34. Ibid., p. 148.

35. Ibid., pp. 149–57, 159ff, 197.

36. Ibid., p. 60.

37. Grosso, *The Final Choice*, p. 218. Compare Grosso's discussion of shamans, who he says are individuals who traditionally link the tribe with the "Mind at Large" (Aldous Huxley's phrase, which Grosso adopts) and become adept at "mapping and mobilizing the helping powers. . . . Shamans are individuals who, for different reasons, are susceptible to the creative forces of the deep psyche" (p. 210).

38. For a good discussion of the role of the astral realm in reincarnation, see Papus, *Reincarnation*, pp. 11–19, 60–69.

39. Grosso, *The Final Choice*, p. 301.

40. Ibid.

41. Ibid., p. 303.

42. Ibid., p. 310.

43. Ibid., p. 311.

44. Ibid., p. 312.

45. Ibid., p. 314.

46. John Mack, personal communication, October 9, 1992.

47. Budd Hopkins, *Intruders* (New York: Random House, 1987), pp. 59–60.

48. Compare Sigmund Freud's paper "The Aetiology of Hysteria" with his reasons for changing his mind in his letter to his friend Wilhelm Fliess; Sigmund Freud, "The Aetiology of Hysteria" (1896), in *The Standard Edition of the Psychological Works of Sigmund Freud*, ed. James Strachey et al., 23 vols. (London: Hogarth Press, 1955–1962), vol. 3, pp. 187–221; and Sigmund Freud, letter of September 21, 1897, in *The Complete Letters of Sigmund Freud to Wilhelm Fliess, 1887–1904*, trans. and ed. Jeffrey Moussaieff Masson (Cambridge, Mass.: Harvard University Press, 1985), pp. 264–66. The furthest most psychoanalysts will go in criticizing Freud on this point is from Heinz Kohut: "Freud, for example, often used the example of the hysterical patients whose seduction fantasies he originally believed. We have come now to realize that the hysterical patients were right, in a way. They didn't describe real seductions, it is true; Freud had to recognize he had been misled in his credulity. But he went much too far in saying the parents had nothing to do with their children's hysteria, that only fantasy is relevant." See Heinz Kohut, *Self Psychology and the Humanities: Reflections on a New Psychoanalytic Approach*, ed. Charles B. Strozier (New York: Norton, 1985), p. 230. In much of the recent literature on Freud from outside the psychoanalytic community, the change in Freud's thinking about child abuse has been sharply criticized (and most now feel Freud had it right the first time). Note Jeffrey M. Masson, *The Assault on Truth: Freud's Suppression of the Seduction Theory* (New York: Farrar, Straus and Giroux, 1983); and Frank J. Sulloway, *Freud, Biologist of the Mind* (New York: Basic Books, 1979). A recent view that is also critical of Freud but takes account of the political and cultural context of Freud's struggles is Judith Lewis Herman, *Trauma and Recovery* (New York: Basic Books, 1992).

49. The relative psychological normality of abductees, except in the area of their remembered trauma, is a point stressed by John Mack in his work, and Mack, as a psychiatrist, is well positioned to make such an assessment. I have had the opportunity to hear two of Mack's presentations on his work in the fall of 1991 and again in the fall of 1992, and have talked with him more informally.

50. John Mack at an informal presentation on his research at the Wellfleet Psychohistory Meetings in the home of Robert Jay Lifton, October 30, 1992.

51. As reported in *The Manila Bulletin*, May 18, 1992. Daniels, Notes.

52. Virginia Essene, "New Cells, New Bodies, New Life," *New Millennium* 3 (1992), pp. 1–3. Daniels, Notes.

53. Leonard Orr and Sondra Ray comment about deep breathing during just such weekends: "Hyperventilation is the Breath of Life attempting dramatically to free itself from a lifetime of unconscious neglect." Leonard Orr and Sondra Ray, *Rebirthing in the New Age* (Berkeley: Celestial Arts, 1977), p. 174.

54. Swami Nostradamus Virato, "11:11 Doorway to the Cosmos: Interview," *New Frontier* 12 (1991). Daniels, Notes.

55. Ibid., pp. 5–6.

56. J. Gordon Melton, "New Thought and New Age," in Lewis and Melton, *Perspectives*, p. 19.

57. Paul Shockley, "Cosmic Awareness Communications," *Revelations of Awareness: The New Age Cosmic Newsletter* 4 (1992). Daniels, Notes.

58. William H. Kautz and Melanie Branon, *Channeling: The Intuitive Connection* (San Francisco: Harper and Row, 1987), pp. 153–54.

59. Nada-Yolanda, *Mark-Age News from the Desk of Nada-Yolanda* 6 (1992). Daniels, Notes.

60. *A Course in Miracles*, 2d ed. (Glen Ellen, Calif.: Foundation for Inner Peace, 1992), pp. vii–viii.

61. Ibid., p. 664.

62. Douglas Grant, "Who Is a Prophet? I Am. Through I Am Self, We Are Modern-Day Prophets," *Main* 117, no. 7 (1988), pp. 2–9. Daniels, Notes.

63. Lucis Trust, "Transformation and the New Environmental Awareness," *Triangles Bulletin* 100, no. 6 (1992). Daniels, Notes.

64. *Prout: A New Voice for All Living Beings*, undated pamphlet from a group based in Los Altos, California. Daniels, Notes.

65. Human Ecology Party, "A Global Political Party Dedicated to 'Health and Freedom for All,'" pamphlet, 1992. Daniels, Notes.

66. Noree Liang Pope, "Letters from Spirit," *The Messenger* 12 (1992), pp. 17–21. Daniels, Notes.

67. Starhawk, *Spiral Dance*, p. 27.

68. Ibid., p. 207.

69. Ibid., pp. 206–8. American Buddhist women have also made this point. Note Sandy Boucher, *Turning the Wheel: American Women Creating the New Buddhism* (San Francisco: Harper and Row, 1988).

70. Xaviere Gauthier, "Why Witches," in *New French Feminisms*, ed. Elaine Marks and Isabelle de Courtivron (New York: Schocken Books, 1981), p. 199.

71. Starhawk, *Spiral Dance*, p. 209.

72. Ibid., p. 10.

73. Ibid., pp. 91–92.

74. Ibid., p. 10.

75. Ibid., pp. 10–11.

76. It is this healing dimension of New Age and its intimate links to feminism and other ideologies of empowerment that make it likely that the New Age will endure and perhaps cohere as a religion. Note, however, the opposite view in Melton, "New Thought and New Age," p. 16.

77. See "Bill's Story," in *Alcoholics Anonymous* (New York: AA World Services, 1976 [1939]), pp. 1–16. This book is affectionately referred to in AA circles as "the Big Book."

78. Marc Galanter, *Cults: Faith, Healing, and Coercion* (New York: Oxford University Press, 1989), p. 177.

79. Ibid., p. 178.

80. Ibid.

81. Galanter points out that many AA members have been drawn to feminist concerns in recent years, but the constraint against involvement of AA in anything but alcoholism has prevented the growth of formal alliances. Ibid., p. 183.

82. The AA message is divided into twelve steps of individual recovery and twelve traditions that describe the history and organization and purposes of AA itself. The two are intimately connected, and much of "working the program" in meetings consists of learning the steps and traditions and how they relate.

83. Galanter, *Cults*, pp. 176–90.

84. *AA Grapevine*, April 1992, p. 32.

85. *Alcoholics Anonymous*, p. 14.

86. "Bill's Story," *Alcoholics Anonymous*, p. 8.

87. Martha Morrison, *White Rabbit* (New York: Berkley Books, 1989), pp. 217, 248.

88. Catherine L. Albanese, "Religion and the American Experience: A Century After," *Church History* 57 (1988), pp. 337–51.

CONCLUSION

1. Robert Jay Lifton, *The Broken Connection: On Death and the Continuity of Life* (New York: Basic Books, 1979), p. 351.

2. A. J. Weigert makes this point, though it was very much in the air throughout the 1980s; A. J. Weigert, "Christian Eschatological Identities and the Nuclear Context," *Journal for the Scientific Study of Religion* 27 (1988), pp. 175–91. Note Lifton, *The Broken Connection*, p. 340; Michael Barkun, "Nuclear War and Millenarian Symbols: Premillennialists Confront the Bomb," paper delivered at the annual meeting of the Society for the Scientific Study of Religion, 1985; Ronnie Dugger, "Does Reagan Expect a Nuclear Armageddon?" *Washington Post*, April 8, 1984; A. G. Mojtabai, *Blessed Assurance: At Home with the Bomb in Amarillo, Texas* (Boston: Houghton Mifflin, 1986); and even Jerry Falwell, *Nuclear War and the Second Coming of Jesus Christ* (Lynchburg, Va.: Old Time Gospel Hour, Inc., 1983).

3. Gabriel Marcel, *The Mystery of Being*, 2 vols. (Chicago: Regnery, 1960), vol. 2, chap. 4.

4. Diana Trilling, *Mrs. Harris: The Death of the Scarsdale Diet Doctor* (New York: Penguin Books, 1981), p. 9.

5. Erik Erikson, *Gandhi's Truth: On the Origins of Militant Nonviolence* (New York: W. W. Norton, 1969), p. 431.

6. See Robert Jay Lifton, *The Nazi Doctors: Medical Killing and the Psychology of Genocide* (New York: Basic Books, 1986), which is as much a study of surviving physicians who carried out genocide as it is an historical interpretation of the Holocaust. Note also the book Lifton did with Eric Markussen, *The Genocidal Mentality:*

Nazi Holocaust and Nuclear Threat (New York: Basic Books, 1990).

7. James Davison Hunter, *American Evangelicalism: Conservative Religion and the Quandary of Modernity* (New Brunswick, N.J.: Rutgers University Press, 1983); and ibid., *Evangelicalism: The Coming Generation* (Chicago: University of Chicago Press, 1987).

8. Robert Jay Lifton, personal communication, May 12, 1992.

9. Matthew C. Moen, *The Christian Right and Congress* (Tuscaloosa: University of Alabama Press, 1989), p. 169.

10. The Christian Coalition, headed by Ralph Reed, is the political organization of Pat Robertson. Since 1988 it has been targeting local elections instead of focusing all its efforts on the presidency. In the November 1992 elections, according to People for the American Way (which monitored the elections), the Coalition seems to have won 40 percent of some 500 selected and representative elections. The fiercest battleground was in California, but the Coalition also scored successes in Iowa, Kansas, Florida, Texas, and Oregon. People for the American Way estimates there are thousands of "stealth" candidates throughout the country whose affiliations cannot be determined. See "Christian Conservatives Counting Hundreds of Gains in Local Votes," *New York Times*, November 21, 1992.

11. Al Ross of Planned Parenthood and a close student of the Christian Coalition was much less sanguine, in a presentation at the conference on the New Religious Political Right, University of Uppsala, Sweden, December 7, 1992. He argued that Robertson is out to create a "theocratic fascist state" and has allied himself with old and new Nazis, not to mention leaders of the KKK. Many Coalition leaders as well want the death penalty for abortion. Needless to say, I feel Ross misses the forest for the trees, though I respect his point that many local elections are up for grabs (at least for a while) since it is often the case that only 10 percent of the registered voters actually bother with most local races. Note also the Institute for First Amendment Rights, Great Barrington, Mass.

ACKNOWLEDGMENTS

The journey of this book has been an intensely personal one and changed me in ways that I never would have predicted. Many friends came along with me.

I have no adequate way to thank Robert Jay Lifton for his role in this book. The idea of studying fundamentalists at all first emerged in conversation with him. He guided me in my interview style; read and commented on early drafts of papers and chapters; provided endless support when it seemed the writing would never end; and then read the final manuscript through and made enormously helpful suggestions. I have also learned much from our dialogue in a course on the self we have been co-teaching for six years at the CUNY Graduate Center.

I draw heavily in these pages on the excellent work of researchers who assisted me: Ayla Kohn, Laura Simich, and Willie Tolliver

ACKNOWLEDGMENTS worked in three of the churches I describe and conducted some of the interviews I use in this book (I wrote with Ayla Kohn, "The Paradoxical Image of Jews in the Minds of Christian Fundamentalists," *Journal of Social Distress and the Homeless* 1 [1991]; with Laura Simich, "Christian Fundamentalism and Nuclear Threat," *Journal of the International Society for Political Psychology* 12 [1991]). Michael Perlman provided much insight over the years analyzing interviews, and read the final manuscript with care. Peggy Boyer researched fundamentalism at the beginning of my project. The late Archie Singham, whom I loved dearly, nourished me and everyone in his world. Pam Miller and Nick Humphrey were part of the research group that analyzed these interviews (and many others in a larger study). Michael Flynn read the manuscript in many drafts as it emerged and helped me understand what I was writing. And Dana Fenton helped me put together the notes to the text. This team of researchers was all part of a project funded by the MacArthur Foundation, whose support I gratefully acknowledge.

Others as well helped shape this book by careful reading and critical comments. My brother, Robert M. Strozier, first spotted the structural flaw (and other problems) that led to a re-write of the manuscript. Diane and Geoffrey Ward read several versions of my work over the years, and Diane's contacts with Dan Budnik proved crucial for my Hopi chapter. Paul Boyer and Michael Barkun both visited the Center on Violence and Human Survival at different times, and I found our conversations helpful and stimulating. As Boyer generously noted in his book, *When Time Shall Be No More*, our work overlaps in quite fascinating ways. I have also learned much over the years about the apocalyptic and contemporary politics and culture from conversations with Richard Falk. Grace Mojtabai was helpful in a conversation at the very beginning of my work (and of course I mined her book, *Blessed Assurance*, closely). I also had good conversations about my work and fundamentalism in general with Karen McCarthy Brown, Randall Balmer (and his *Mine Eyes Have Seen the Glory*), and Philip Greven (and his *Spare the Child*). Catherine Keller of Drew University heard much of this book in our extended conversations on the apocalyptic, and she read it all carefully in many drafts. Her learned disquisitions seeped into my mind in ways that my occasional footnotes to her work could only begin to acknowledge. As someone who really knows the Bible and theology, she also saved me much embarrassment. Esther Menaker read the final manuscript, even on her vacation, and made some helpful comments. For a couple of years I was a consultant to The Fundamentalism Project at the University of Chicago run by Martin Marty, whose comments and work I found helpful. I had interesting conversations with the members of the Christian group headed by Nancy Ammerman, especially with Susan Harding and David Stoll. In the larger meetings, I learned much from Sam Heilman, my colleague in City University, and profited much from the graduate course we co-taught on "Jewish and Christian Fundamentalism."

Roger Williamson provided me an unusually helpful forum to talk about my ideas at the "Life and Peace Institute" in Uppsala, Sweden, for three years running, albeit always in the deepest, darkest of Swedish winters. Perhaps one should talk about the end of the world in a place where the sun never shines except to illuminate the horizon briefly between late morning coffee break and early afternoon tea. Roger also provided many useful bibliographic suggestions, saved me from serious errors, and improved the overall manuscript with his careful reading. He also introduced me to many Swedish friends whose research interest coincided with my own, especially Owe Gustafsson and Sigbert Axelson of Uppsala University.

Peter Parrish first steered me toward the apocalyptic aspects of the Civil War many years ago, and Donald Capps gave me good advice about the sermons after Lincoln's death. Harold Holzer sponsored a presentation on Lincoln and the American apocalyptic at the Lincoln Group of New York, and read and commented on part of what is chapter 8. I also presented an earlier version of that paper at a Lincoln conference organized by William Pedersen at the State University of Louisiana in Shreveport in the fall of 1992. Other Lincoln scholars helped as well: Cullom Davis, Mark Johnson, and Tom Schwartz.

Many (perhaps too many) groups bore up listening to me on fundamentalism over the years. I am particularly grateful to colleagues at my own Center on Violence and Human Survival at John Jay Col-

ACKNOWLEDGMENTS

lege for tolerating more presentations of my work than I can remember. Harvey Cox, Daniel Ellsberg, and Rabbi Marshall Meyer (who also later read and commented on chapter 9) all made helpful comments on a preliminary presentation of my research. My friends gathered at the Open Center in New York City in the early summer of 1993 to listen to and encourage me at a time when my spirits were flagging. I thank the students in my courses over the years who gave more than they knew as I rambled on.

I was lucky to get the ideal editor for this book in Lauren Bryant. She knew exactly how to mix the stick and the carrot in the early stages, and then read what I wrote with intelligence and perception, including drafts of chapters and two versions of the final manuscript. She filled nearly every page of text with marginal comments and crossed out all my best lines in ways that vastly improved the final version.

My agent, Charlotte Sheedy, turned my offbeat idea of studying fundamentalists into a publishing enterprise that ended up as pages between the covers of an actual book. Her unflagging confidence in me is warmly appreciated.

My first-born, Michael, taught me more about fundamentalism than he may realize, and engaged me in many valuable conversations about the themes in this book. My middle son, Matthew, read early drafts of the manuscript, participated in several seminars in which I presented material, and joined me in an invaluable dialogue about endism over the years. It encouraged me that he got it all from the start. Christopher, my youngest boy with whom friends say I am fused at the hip and to whom this book is dedicated, lived through the writing of it as no one else in our cozy apartment. In time he, too, will read it and learn then what I was doing all those early mornings at the computer.

Last but not least I thank my wife, Cathy, who has lived with fundamentalists in our marriage almost as long as we have been together. She tolerated my absences at churches on Sundays and far too many Bible study meetings during the week, not to mention my endless conversation on the topic for a good seven years. She bore up well, however, and provided encouragement at dark moments. In this kind of work on the end of the world, off-center support was often the most helpful. Once, at a crucial juncture in my writing, I described the dilemma and said that I was in a high state of anxiety. "Eat," she said, and laughed. I gained a little weight and solved the problem.

Index

Abiding Light Pentecostal Church, 7–8, 10; Bible study at, 7, 19, 93, 94; declining membership of, 7, 100, 161, 166; early years of, 43–44, 99–100, 161; outreach programs at, 8, 203–4; participant-observer experience at, 19–20, 21; prayer sessions at, 7–8, 102; racial and ethnic diversity at, 7, 93; Reverend Dean as pastor of, 49; social activism at, 146

Abolitionists. *See* Antislavery movement

Abortion, 73, 115, 141, 147, 149

Abraham, biblical story of, 198–200, 206

Acts, book of, 113

Adam and Eve, 31, 60

African Americans, 2, 89, 118, 142, 259n10; Baptist, 9; Episcopalian, 10; and New Age movement, 224, 285–86n3; Pentecostal, 7, 11, 93, 102, 128–29, 136–37; and relations with Jews, 154–55, 196; and social activism, 10, 137, 139, 146; social problems faced by, 128, 134, 135, 137, 138, 139; and urban riots, 154–55

AIDS, 29, 31, 128, 135, 147, 152, 158, 182

Albanese, Catherine, 247